IMAGINING RC

Scenes from the Life of Robert 'Reschid' Stanley
1828–1911

By Christina Longden

Photograph taken from The Crescent, April 1907 and captioned
'A Distinguished British Mussulman'

61 190 058

IMAGINING ROBERT

Photographic credits: Tameside Local Studies Archives, Liverpool Record Office (Liverpool Libraries), Abdullah Quilliam Society and British Library, The Sphere, Brian Longden, Christina Longden, Arakan Creative Media, Manchester Libraries, Information and Archives, © US Copyright from G. Robinson David Urquhart; some chapters in the life of a Victorian knight-errant of justice and liberty (Boston & New York: Houghton Mifflin Co., 1920).
Illustration credits: Tameside Local Studies Archives, Liverpool Record Office (Liverpool Libraries), Brian Longden, Christina Longden, Abdullah Quilliam Society.

Robert Reschid Stanley's family website and information can be found at:
www.robertreschidstanley.wordpress.com
Email: rreschid@yahoo.com

ISBN 978-0-9928792-5-9

Cover design: hand-drawn art and design by Flora Rustamova. Islamic calligraphy art (Arabic) on back cover by Razwan Ul-Haq. It says 'Robert Reschid Stanley'.

CONTENTS

For Mum

*The woman who taught me that fiction can be even
more powerful than the facts*

PRAISE FOR 'HIS OWN MAN' AND 'IMAGINING ROBERT'

'Rooted in the past, deeply personal and shaping our present … a necessary and timely read in the debate about identity and belonging.'
BARONESS SAYEEDA WARSI

'*A*n essential read for anyone interested in challenging preconceived ideas of Muslim and working-class community life. Chris Longden must be congratulated for writing these books; which Robert Reschid Stanley would have been deeply proud of.'
DR SHAMIM MIAH, *Senior Lecturer, University of Huddersfield.*

'History matters.
It matters because we are who we are and what we are. Not only because of our own personal history - but also because of our familial, local, regional, national and international histories.
History matters because it teaches us that life is not about 'me' and 'I'. It is about 'we' and 'us'.
History matters because it belongs to everyone and not to one person.
History matters because it brings to the fore continuity and links the past, the present and the future in a vital chain.
History matters because it brings together the local and the global and, through so doing, it calls out to us of the need to understand, respect and embrace those who may appear to be different to us: for through knowing our histories we recognise the commonality of the peoples of the world.
History matters because it is not only about the past, it is about making the present and shaping the future in a more inclusive, caring and appreciative way.
These books by Christina Longden matter because they embrace all those vital concepts of history. Important and pioneering works, they highlight the need not for tolerance of each other's beliefs but of acceptance: an acceptance that can only arise through the understanding of the importance of our shared histories.

Herein lies the power of Christina Longden's research, writing and passion: the celebration of that which we have in common – our humanity.'
PROFESSOR CARL CHINN, *MBE, Ph.D.*

ACKNOWLEDGEMENTS

One of the things that I most love about my family and friends is that they will quite happily encourage my eccentricities and my desire to do things a bit differently. My great x3 grandfather, Robert 'Reschid' Stanley, was in many ways a conformist, but he was also happy to break the mould and try out a new approach to things. He certainly held no truck with anyone who told him anything along the lines of, 'You can't do that! Know thy place!'

This is what *'Imagining Robert'* represents for me. It is a rather different approach to telling a true story and it certainly would not have happened if it wasn't for my immediate family; Ian, Ruby and Gregory - because each one of them had to suffer early drafts and endure embarrassing voice recordings of the scripts. My big brother, Steven, sister-in-law Rozina and nephews Eesaa and Yaaseen also never failed to feed my fire for writing these books. Not forgetting too, my auntie, Gay Oliver, and my uncle, David Stanley. Other champions who believe in the power of 'faction' (as I like to call this book's genre) include the world's best vicar-activist, Ian Stubbs, the Rustamovas, Razwan Ul-Haq, Shamim Miah, Yahya Birt, Jamie Gilham, Steve Miller, Stuart Vallantine, Claude Nealy and Conor Ibrahim of Arakan Creative Media (who came up with the idea of having Robert's great x2 grandson star as the man himself in our film trailer).

But, of course, my parents deserve a special mention; first of all, my dad, Brian Longden, who made the initial discovery about Robert's conversion to Islam, who carried out inordinate amounts of research into his ancestor's life and who is a stickler for 'the facts'. But of equal importance is my mum, Yvonne Longden. She made it her mission in life to educate and subvert her children through the subtle influence of a damned good story. It is not an understatement to say that my parents are the unsung heroes of this book.

Thanks, as always, to Tameside's Local Archives department for their ceaseless enthusiasm for both of my books about Robert, to the

Liverpool Public Records Office and to Manchester Libraries, Information and Archives. Afzal Khan MP, Baroness Sayeeda Warsi, Professor Carl Chinn and Chris Gribble of the National Centre for Writing have also encouraged my rather unconventional approach to writing. Mohammed Amin MBE, Rima Hadid, Muhammad Umar and Sofia Zaynab also deserve a special thank you for their ongoing kindness and belief in this work.

Of course, a huge cheer and abundant gratitude should go to Flora Rustamova for the wonderful cover design and to Razwan Ul-Haq for his astounding Islamic calligraphy. Finally, thanks to fantastic editor Graham Brown, who has clearly earned his title of 'Honorary Stanley'.

INTRODUCTION

This book has been inspired by its companion publication: *His Own Man – A Victorian Hidden Muslim – The Life and Times of Robert 'Reschid' Stanley*. *His Own Man* is a historical biography which recounts the extensive research of Robert's life and his journey towards Islam.

Imagining Robert, however, takes a different approach. It accepts that not everyone likes to read non-fiction and so instead it reflects on Robert's life using 15 scenes - vignettes - that blend fact with fiction.

The 15 scenes reflect the same facts as the non-fiction book. Robert was born into the Victorian working class at a time when those of the lower classes did not record personal views and feelings. So, no personal diaries, letters or notes can be found from his life or from those of his close relatives. Everything that our family has discovered about Robert Stanley comes from birth, marriage and death certificates and census statistics. My own research has had to rely heavily on independent sources gleaned from Victorian newspapers and from records kept on his public life and work.

Even though there is a lack of information about Robert's personal life, he lived through some amazingly turbulent and truly fascinating times. Born into the historical context of Peterloo, he began work at the age of ten and witnessed the Plug Riots, Chartist murders, Lancashire Cotton Famine, the Bread Riots and the anti-Catholic Murphy Riots across Manchester. He was raised within the Christian Israelite sect and was a family friend of Prophet John Wroe, the man who attempted to build a new Jerusalem in Ashton-under-Lyne and who fell from grace during the seven virgins scandal.

A fair-minded magistrate, Robert set up a protection association in order to help factory workers who were being bribed by their cotton master employers for their votes. He was called to Parliament in 1869 to give his expert opinion on widening the franchise and whether the secret ballot should be introduced. He caused some consternation amongst the well-heeled men of

Lancashire when he was elected as mayor of Stalybridge, one of the country's first working-class mayors.

After running a pub in Ashton-under-Lyne for nearly two decades, Robert moved to Manchester where he had already been spending much of his time in the city's Corn Exchange, overseeing his tea-trading business. This exposed him to merchants from across the world and to interactions with Manchester's Jewish and Muslim communities, as well as with well-known public figures such as the Pankhursts. Over the course of his life, Robert had become fascinated with the Ottoman Empire and even wrote to the caliph himself, offering him advice and support. Finally, at the age of 69, Robert became a close friend of Britain's 'Sheikh of Islam', the famous convert Abdullah Quilliam. He decided to become a Muslim himself, eventually being appointed vice-chairman of the country's first mosque in Liverpool.

Robert's fez

Robert's last days were spent in Stalybridge. His family took the decision to bury him in a Christian graveyard. For nearly 100 years his conversion to Islam was kept a closely-guarded family secret until his own great x3 grandson and my brother – a Muslim convert himself – was shown a copy of a fading old magazine. This was *The Crescent*, Britain's first Muslim publication, and our family soon began to put two and two together. Not long after receiving this copy of *The Crescent*, an elderly relative handed us an item that he had kept for many years he had never really understood why Robert Stanley had owned a fez. Finally, after my grandmother died, we discovered a jewelled tie pin set with a star and crescent which had been passed on to her from her own grandfather, Bob Stanley – one of Robert's sons. This pin, we believe, was a membership pin of the Liverpool Muslim Institute.

I faced much frustration when carrying out the research for both books about Robert. It irritated me greatly that the simple fact of Robert being working-class meant that enormous amounts of information were missing. However, conjecture and guestimates can prove to be far more fulfilling for a writer when it comes to creative interpretation. We can ponder why someone like Robert Stanley - a 69-year-old working-class, conservative, former mayor, magistrate and upstanding pillar of the community - decided to convert to Islam in 1898. Was he a traitor? Brainwashed? Delusional? Bitter and disappointed? Or was he an attention-seeker, attempting to gain some notoriety by nailing his colours to the mast of Islam?

Imagining Robert contains some of the most exciting stories from his life and encourages us to examine his possible motives and the consequences of his actions. It also aims to inject some humanity into the character of Robert. If we can imagine and understand why a deeply traditional Victorian man turned to Islam, then we can perhaps apply similar empathy to any of our friends and neighbours who choose a different lifestyle or beliefs to those which we ourselves follow.

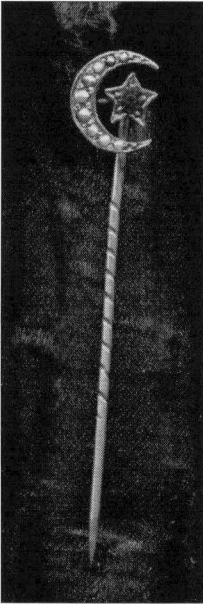

Robert's tie pin

These scenes from Robert's life have been written using a script format, dispensing with the need for unnecessary detail and allowing the reader to get straight to the heart of the action. For those who wish to find out more about a particular episode in Robert's life they can of course pick up *His Own Man* and find out much more.

Whilst the reader will (hopefully) enjoy reading the scenes themselves, the medium of live performance can bring additional colour and warmth to the story of such an unusual man. Using live performance also means that we can bring to the forefront of the narrative those characters that are too often overlooked during this period in history. Women, of course, always linger in the shadows of history and none more so than those from the working class. *Imagining Robert* has tried to correct some of this gross imbalance.

Through learning the facts of Robert's life, and by being entertained through imaginative interpretation, it is hoped that we can – collectively - bring about a greater depth of understanding of other peoples' choices, cultures and beliefs. Some of our greatest British patriots have been ordinary men and women, individuals who did not have access to the internet, to books or even to a formal education but who were ferociously intelligent, who fought for justice and who were brave enough to stand up against uncritical nationalism and to the attitude of 'my country, right or wrong'.

So, let us learn from OUR collective histories as we set forth with this particular attempt at *Imagining Robert*.

AUTHOR'S NOTES

Each of the 15 scenes contained in *Imagining Robert* are preceded with some basic historical context: nationally, internationally and from Robert's own life in Stalybridge, Ashton-under-Lyne, Liverpool and Manchester. Nearly all the content included in the scenes is based on fact. Footnotes add a few more ingredients to the narrative but for those who want to find out more detail about a particular time – or theme – in Robert's life, they may wish to read *His Own Man*. There are certain words that appear in this book – such as 'Mussulman', 'Muhammedan' and 'Moslem' which are more archaic adjectives or spellings used to describe those who follow Islam. These have been kept in the dialogue in order to reflect historical accuracy. *His Own Man* includes a full glossary, detailed bibliography and appendices.

NOTES FOR PRODUCTION

For the purposes of performance, it is suggested that the context could be narrated to the audience or contained within a written programme. I have also included footnotes; this is not the usual approach, perhaps, but they may be of help to casts and production teams.

The scenes have been written in such a way that they run consecutively within a chronological historical context. However, they could not possibly be performed concurrently, unless an audience was willing and able to sit through a production that lasted for seven to eight hours! Instead, the production team can adopt a 'pick and mix' approach as to which vignettes are performed, depending on the make-up of the audience, their backgrounds, interests and motivations. Two scenes are monologues and the rest are short scenes, using between two and five actors.

I hope that the different elements of *Imagining Robert* can be used in whatever way is deemed to be the most appropriate, the most enlightening and the most entertaining for an audience.

CHARACTERS: *From all scenes/ monologues*
ROBERT STANLEY (*various ages*)
EMMA STANLEY (*various ages*)
UNCLE JOHN STANLEY
WILLIAM STANLEY (*Robert's father*)
SARAH STANLEY (*John's wife*)
PROPHET JOHN WROE (*Christian Israelite founder*)
JACK STANLEY (*Robert's older brother*)
BETTY STANLEY (*Jack's new wife*)
THOMAS MEREDITH (*Emma's father*)
WILL STANLEY (Robert's son)
ALICE STANLEY (Robert's daughter
THOMAS STANLEY (Robert's son)
MARY-JANE STANLEY (Robert's daughter)
COUNCILLOR SHAW
BLETCHLEY
SHEIKH ABDULLAH QUILLIAM
MARY LYON (Quilliam's second wife through a polygamous marriage)
GEORGE STANLEY (Robert's grandson)
EMMELINE PANKHURST (Leader of the suffragette movement)
(VARIOUS OFF-STAGE VOICES)

Characters per scene:

1.   **Brothers – and Babes – in Arms:** WILLIAM AND UNCLE JOHN STANLEY
2.   **Escaping Sanctuary:** PROPHET JOHN WROE, JOHN STANLEY, SARAH STANLEY
3.   **A Gift Horse:** WILLIAM, ANN, JACK AND ROBERT STANLEY
4.   **Meeting a Visionary:** PROPHET JOHN WROE, UNCLE JOHN STANLEY, ROBERT STANLEY
5.   **An Arresting Reverend:** JACK, BETTY AND ROBERT STANLEY
6.   **A Wedding to Please All:** EMMA MEREDITH, ROBERT STANLEY, TOM MEREDITH, UNCLE JOHN STANLEY

7. **Bread Riot:** EMMA, WILL, ANNIE, ROBERT AND THOMAS STANLEY, V/O OF BILLY THE BRUISER, PLUS MALE AND FEMALE RIOTERS

8. **From Magistrate to Mayor:** EMMA, MARY-JANE, SARAH AND ROBERT STANLEY, COUNCILLOR SHAW.

9. **The Mayor for TEA:** ROBERT STANLEY, MR BLETCHLEY

10. **Foreign Matters in the Pub**: EMMA, MARY-JANE, SARAH AND ROBERT STANLEY

11. **The Famous Mr Quilliam:** ABDULLAH QUILLIAM, ROBERT STANLEY

12. **Peas in his Pockets:** EMMA STANLEY (Monologue)

13. **The Mayor and the Showgirl:** ABDULLAH QUILLIAM, GEORGE AND ROBERT STANLEY, MARY LYONS

14. **Mrs Pankhurst has her Cake:** ROBERT STANLEY, EMMELINE PANKHURST

15. **Gunpowder Tea and Plot:** MARY-JANE STANLEY (Monologue)

1. BROTHERS - AND BABES - IN ARMS

CONTEXT:

Robert Stanley's parents were William Stanley of Dukinfield, a hatter, and Ann, who was originally from Gloucestershire. Robert's eldest sibling was born to the couple in 1808. However, the only information that is available on the beginning of William and Ann's relationship is census data for the following decades. This indicates that William would have been 20 and Ann would have been 12 or possibly 13 years old when she gave birth to their first baby in Dukinfield. At this time in England it was impossible for a couple to marry below the age of 21 without obtaining their parents' permission.

Leech's Mills, Stalybridge, built 1806

We know that they went on to have nine children altogether, the other eight being born in Cardiff where the couple seem to have relocated. William's older brother, John Stanley, went on to become one of the richest industrialists in Ashton and was a leading member of the Southcottian Christian sect which later morphed into the millennialist Christian Israelite group.

This scene provides the reader with an imaginative construct of what may have occurred at the time.

ASHTON-UNDER-LYNE, SUMMER 1808

DUSK, AND AN EERIE EVENING LIGHT FILLS THE
CORNER OF A COBBLED YARD WHERE TWO YOUNG
MEN ARE STANDING. IT IS THE COURTYARD OF A HUGE
IRONWORKS ON OLDHAM ROAD, CHARLESTOWN,
ASHTON-UNDER-LYNE. THE WORKS ARE IN DARKNESS
ALTHOUGH A ROOM ABOVE HAS LIT CANDLES AT ITS
WINDOWS. WE HEAR HEBREW HYMNS BEING SUNG;
THIS IS A MEETING ROOM OF THE SOUTHCOTTIANS.
WILLIAM STANLEY, AGED 19, IS HANDSOME. HE WEARS
A RED JERKIN AND A WHITE SHIRT, TOPPED OFF WITH
A BROAD-BRIMMED BEAVER HAT. HE HAS A KNAPSACK
SLUNG OVER ONE SHOULDER AND A FLAGON OF ALE
IN ONE HAND. THE OTHER MAN, HIS BROTHER, IS **JOHN
STANLEY,** AGED 21. JOHN HAS JUST BEGUN A CAREER
IN IRON AND HAS A MORE SOBER AIR. HE IS DRESSED IN
A DUN-COLOURED JACKET, ALSO WITH A BEAVER HAT.
WE GLIMPSE A FINE POCKET WATCH WITHIN HIS
WAISTCOAT. JOHN FREQUENTLY WIPES HIS BROW AND
CONSTANTLY GLANCES TOWARDS THE SOUTHCOTTIAN
MEETING ROOMS ABOVE THEM.

JOHN: You understand why this must happen, William? We
cannot afford to continue with … this state of affairs.
WILLIAM: You mean *you* cannot *afford* to continue with this *state of
affairs*.
JOHN: I beg your pardon?
WILLIAM: I mean *you*, brother John. Your ambitions. You've just
bought a stake in these ironworks here (*nods towards the buildings*) and
you're terrified that some of us, the more scurrilous members of the
Stanley family, will get in your way … (*laughs hollowly*)
JOHN: (*Intake of breath*) I've worked my way up, William. I began as
a cordwainer, then a mechanic and now I'm managing half of these
ironworks. But … you fail to see that some of us are more
concerned with life in the hereafter, as opposed to living for the
pleasures of the flesh.
WILLIAM: Well *I've* done nowt to be ashamed of. You're wrong to
judge me.

JOHN: I do not judge you, William.

WILLIAM: No. Judgement is to be made by our townsfolk. Well, those who come to purchase your machinery. It's *their* judgement that you're most worried about, their purse-strings that matter.

JOHN: No. Judgement comes from above.

WILLIAM: D'you think I'm a simpleton? And never mind the good gents of Ashton. You're even more fretful about what the old hag of Exeter would say if she'd heard that you were related to a sinner such as I.

JOHN: You should not speak of Mother Joanna in such a fashion![1]

WILLIAM: She's no mother to me! And she's no *prophetess* either. I was never convinced by her visions – *(growing louder)* by her rantings ...

JOHN: Hush! *(Turns to check that there is no-one nearby)* Keep your voice down. George will be leading on the prayers in a minute and then we'll ...

WILLIAM: Ha! George Turner! He's another one with crazed ideas. They'll lock him up with the madmen one of these days, what with his visions of angels and devils and ...[2]

JOHN: George is a good man – a great man – and I'd caution you to mind your tongue when speaking of those far closer to the Lord than you'll ever be.

WILLIAM: Oh, enough. Even if I needed to repent, I wouldn't seek benediction from a woman who's never known the joy of being with child, like your Mother Joanna. 'Mother' – ha! *She'll* never be with child unless there's a man blind enough to ...

JOHN: *(Sharply)* William!

WILLIAM: No matter what the circumstances, this child has been conceived in love and in ...

JOHN: *(Hissed)* For pity's sake, you fool! Enough with your poetic meanderings! Ann is a child herself - about to birth a child!

WILLIAM: Ann is no child!

JOHN: The law says she is. She's just short of thirteen years old.

WILLIAM: There's no law in England that states such a thing.

---

[1] Joanna Southcott was leader of the Southcottians, a Christian millenarianist sect. She gained thousands of followers across the country, made prophecies, received visions and eventually claimed to fall pregnant with the Messiah. See *His Own Man*.

[2] George Turner, an Ashton man, was in the running to take over the Southcottians after Joanna's death. He was, however, committed to a mental hospital and on release continued to engage in some unusual religious practises. See *His Own Man*.

JOHN: The shame of it ...! Our father may have furnished us both with the gift of education, but you've squandered your learning ... used your station in life to take advantage of a mere child!

WILLIAM: (*Menacingly*) Like I said, Ann is no child. And I've seen the way that you look at her. I've seen you - I know that look in another man's eyes ...

JOHN: You disgust me! Whatever filth scrolls through your own mind, don't imagine it to be in the minds of others!

WILLIAM: You have no idea about how the fairer sex are – what the differences are between a child and a woman ...

JOHN: Her Aunt Maggie states that she is a child. Our parents object to any marriage between you both because she is a child. Therefore, she is *a child* – and certainly is one, in the eyes of God.

WILLIAM: Ha! Ann's Aunt Maggie! Maggie only brought her up here from Cardiff to live with her because she could not bear children of her own.

JOHN: Maggie is a good woman. A godly woman.

WILLIAM: She wanted to mould Ann into her spoiled little poppet - a little dressed-up dolly. To marry her off to some rich gent as soon as she could.

JOHN: Well, *that* will never happen now, thanks to you.

WILLIAM: Ha! I'm betting that you wanted her for yourself!

JOHN: I shall ignore that. (*He turns his back for a few seconds, trying to calm down*) So you believe that Ann is a woman? And not a mere girl?

WILLIAM: Every female is different in terms of ... of development. Laws and legalisms are all very well for parochial business but when it comes down to the greater laws of humanity and individualism then ...

JOHN: For someone who was born with a frightening amount of natural intelligence you can be astonishingly naïve.

WILLIAM: (*Lowering his voice and leaning towards JOHN*) I caution you, John. By God, you and your religious friends ... you're all a bunch of hypocrites!

JOHN: None of us claim to be perfect. But I ... I managed to control my own carnal desires before I married Sarah, which...

WILLIAM: Well, no wonder you've been so damned jealous, if your own younger brother managed to get his end away long before you ever did!

JOHN: (*Hisses*) Hold your tongue!

WILLIAM: Hypocrisy, I say!

JOHN: How easy to spout such words, when you have no…

WILLIAM: What about your Bible tales? Joseph of Nazareth – 'an old man' - took the young girl, Mary? And then there's Abraham and his much younger Sarah? And in Leviticus, girls as young as five are married …

JOHN: Stop! Your words repel me. You talk of five-year-olds!

WILLIAM: I do *not* talk of five-year-olds. I talk of *your* religion – how your church picks and chooses which words from your Bible that you prefer to use that day.

JOHN: We do no such thing!

WILLIAM: In order to control … those who possess more feeble minds.

JOHN: Ah, (*Holding his hand up*) a good education was wasted on you; you were meant to provide Ann with a spark of learning and yet you …

WILLIAM: And who was it that told Aunt Maggie that *I* would be the best person to teach her Ann to read and to write? 'Twas *you*, brother John!

JOHN: (*Shakes his head*) I foolishly thought better of your morality.

WILLIAM: Ha! You only wanted to impress Aunt Maggie with your benevolence! To bring her into the fold of Mother Joanna. Well, you got your wish there. I can hear her now, (*nods upwards*) screeching her heart out.

JOHN: Well, at least I prefer to spend time around godly women, unlike you.

WILLIAM: Oh aye?

JOHN: Yes – you! A man who prefers to squander what money our father has already given him on ale and on sluts!

WILLIAM: (*Snarls*) You've always hated my ability to catch the eye of the fairest lasses!

JOHN: Poppycock!

WILLIAM: Yes – and you were forced to hitch yourself to the likes of Sarah. Was it her parents' money that attracted you to that pious heifer?

JOHN can no longer control himself, seizes WILLIAM by the lapels. He is shaking with rage. Both of their hats are knocked to the floor in the struggle.

JOHN: Don't you ever …
WILLIAM: Go on! Swing for me!
JOHN: *(Swallows air and blinks, moving away a few steps. He stoops to pick up his hat, dusts it and replaces it on his head)* Enough. That is enough.

WILLIAM bends down to pick up his hat. He has dropped his flagon of ale in the struggle and checks to see that it has not broken. It hasn't. He takes a swig from it and wipes his mouth as he holds his hat under one arm.

JOHN: William, I don't understand … you yourself used to come to our meetings. What hardened your heart so much to the Lord?
WILLIAM: *(Shakes his head reproachfully)* No. I only went because you'd managed to con our mother into attending. I soon saw through it all.
JOHN: You think yourself cleverer than those who have received revelation. Mother Joanna's prophecies have manifested themselves time and again, she …
WILLIAM: *(Hisses)* Lunacy! This talk of a Shiloh – of the Messiah being born to an old crone! Joanna Southcott is 58 years of age … it's impossible!
JOHN: A miracle is a miracle.
WILLIAM: Even Ann, a young lass, can see it - all of this - for what it is! Trickery and illusions!
JOHN: *(Quietly)* Ah well, perhaps the same manner of illusion that you once convinced me of.
WILLIAM: How so?
JOHN: I mean, that *you* could be trusted to tutor a 12-year-old and not have caused *her* to be with child.
WILLIAM: *(Turns to go, swiping him away)* Oh! You can stick your virgins and your miraculous births …
JOHN: *(Grabs him, forces him to turn back)* William, your soul is in mortal peril. And it is only for our own dear mother's sake that I am doing this.

JOHN reaches into his pocket and shows him a smallish parcel, bound with brown string. WILLIAM does not take it

WILLIAM: What is this?

JOHN: On the understanding that you do not come back to anywhere near Manchester - until …

WILLIAM: Till?

JOHN: Until Ann is of an age that will meet with the full approval of our parents. And of society in general.

WILLIAM: You have no need to …

JOHN: Stay away from the girl. And … give yourself time; to consider your own standing in the world – your reputation and … *(He continues to hold the parcel out to WILLIAM)*

WILLIAM: You mean the reputation of the Stanleys?

JOHN: Why not? Have respect for our family name.

WILLIAM: And what does that name mean, exactly?

JOHN: That we're decent people. And we do things in a … a just fashion.

WILLIAM: *(Looks at the parcel)* What's inside?

JOHN: One hundred pounds. Take it and make good with it. But I caution you – do not even dare to dream of returning as the prodigal son.

WILLIAM: And … what else is in here?

JOHN: A Bible. I imagine that you would have neglected to pack your own.

WILLIAM: *(Considers all of this. Then purposefully places his hat on his head and taps it down)* I have my hat, brother. And I have my hatting trade. I carry both wherever I go. I don't need to be obliged to you. I am a man of my own devices and means.

JOHN: Perhaps. But you are at the mercy of the fashions of society. From what I hear on the trading floor in Manchester there will soon be a down-turn in the demand for hats made of beaver fur.

WILLIAM: Not likely.

JOHN: People prefer the tall, silk top hats.

WILLIAM: Untrue.

JOHN: Yes. And the beavers are dying out. Too many vain men causing their deaths.

WILLIAM: Poor little beavers. And anyway, who'd wear a prissy silk hat in the north of England?

JOHN: Well, your skills and your ability to make a living will soon be redundant. Unless you heed what I say.

WILLIAM: So, it's prophecies about hat-wearing next, brother! Damn it! Go on and give me that parcel of yours!

JOHN hands him the parcel. WILLIAM takes it, gauging the weight of it.

WILLIAM: So... (*He is silent for a few seconds*) Whatever is in here, I do not owe you?

JOHN: No. It is a gift. And as well ... I have made plans for where you might next be best bound.

WILLIAM: Have you now?

JOHN: Yes. Liverpool.

WILLIAM: Liverpool?

JOHN: It is the obvious course. There is a ship docked there now. The name of *Elisa*. Just this morning, I sent a message to the captain of the vessel to say that my younger brother needs employment and that he can turn his hand to most jobs on board.

WILLIAM: You wish me to improve my moral aptitude and you send me off to become a sailor!

JOHN: This captain goes by the name of Captain Nebuchadnezzar Lees; he is a cousin of the Lees family of Ashton. A godly and upright man and ...

WILLIAM: What? Cousin of Henry and Samuel Lees ... the Widow Lees and your other Southcottian crazies?

JOHN: The Lees' are powerfully connected. But more importantly, they are a truly righteous superior breed. Captain Lees would hardly be the sort to employ a rough crew of fellows.

WILLIAM: But this is *sailing*, brother ... you have no idea what goes on in ... (*he thinks better of it*) Very well then. I will take the ... the gift. And I will ... head towards Liverpool.

JOHN: (*Looks upwards towards the window. The singing stops and we hear the mumblings of a prayer*) Good, then.

WILLIAM: Aye. I'll go there alright. But not for you.

JOHN: Of course not.

WILLIAM: For the continued affections of our parents.

JOHN: And for the child – when it is older and needs a father to provide a steady hand, a steady income.

WILLIAM: So. *(He rubs his chin and gazes at JOHN.)*

JOHN: The coach leaves Henry Square at half past nine. Keep the notes well hidden.

WILLIAM: I am not green.

JOHN: I must go. Sarah will be wondering …

WILLIAM: Good old Sarah. Good old John.

JOHN: Perhaps it is too much to expect a thank-you. Or even a handshake.

WILLIAM: Yes. *(Turns to leave.)*

JOHN: Yes. It is too much.

WILLIAM walks off into the darkness. We hear a loud 'Amen' coming from the Southcottian rooms.

---ENDS---

2. ESCAPING SANCTUARY

CONTEXT:

William and Ann Stanley left Dukinfield to live in Cardiff, where they brought up nine surviving children. They struggled desperately for money. Meanwhile in Ashton, William's older brother, John Stanley,

The Sanctuary, Ashton

grew extremely rich. He became a close friend of Prophet John Wroe, who established the Christian Israelites, a millennialist sect which he had developed out of the Southcottian followers. The Christian Israelites followed an Abrahamic tradition, with Wroe's many new rules alongside his famous visions and prophecies. Wroe decided to build a 'New Jerusalem' in Ashton, and four gatehouses for this holy city were constructed at each corner of the town. John Stanley paid for the construction of a sumptuous 'Sanctuary' for the congregation and was one of the Number Four – the most important leaders alongside Wroe. We know little of Sarah Stanley, John's wife, other than the fact that she had previously been a follower of another rival leader, George Turner, and that Wroe railed against her in his diaries, seemingly for spreading gossip.

In 1831, Wroe was accused by the press of appointing seven virgins to "wait upon, nourish and comfort him and be as wives unto him, except that he should not carnally know them". Two of the women accused him of sexual impropriety, saying that he had attempted to sire the Shiloh through them. Wroe denied all charges, explaining that the women were just servants and that one of them was pursuing a vendetta against him. He was not prosecuted, only subjected to a church hearing which cleared him of sexual wrongdoing. Wanting to take justice into their own hands, the people of Ashton vented their anger at Wroe, rioting and vandalising the church and attacking Wroe and the other Christian Israelites on two separate occasions. John Stanley came to the rescue both times, ushering Wroe and his followers through a secret tunnel under Ashton's Park Parade road that led to his house.

This extract imagines the scene in John Stanley's house after the second riot at the Sanctuary.

ASHTON-UNDER-LYNE, OCTOBER 1831

THE RECEPTION ROOM OF NUMBER NINE PARK PARADE, ASHTON-UNDER-LYNE. THE ROOM IS DOMINATED BY A GRAND FIREPLACE CONTAINING THE EMBERS OF A FIRE. ALTHOUGH THIS IS OBVIOUSLY A GENTLEMAN'S HOUSE, IT IS NOT RICHLY FURNISHED - THE CHAIRS AND SIDE-TABLES ARE OF PLAIN MAHOGANY WITH NO EMBELLISHMENT. THERE ARE NO PAINTINGS ON THE WALLS, LENDING THE PLACE A RATHER GLOOMY FEEL. THE ONE REDEEMING FEATURE IS A BEAUTIFUL VIEW FROM THE LARGE WINDOWS ACROSS THE RIVER TAME AND THE VALLEY MEADOWS. THE OWNER, **JOHN STANLEY,** AGED 45, IS CLEAN-SHAVEN AND WEARING THE TRADITIONAL DUN COLOURS REQUIRED OF CHRISTIAN ISRAELITE MEN. HE IS IN SHIRT AND TROUSERS ONLY HOWEVER, LACKING BOTH A JACKET AND A HAT. **PROPHET JOHN WROE** ('YAAKOV'), AGED 49, IS BY THE WINDOW, CROUCHING DOWN SO THAT HE CANNOT BE SEEN BY ANYONE OUTSIDE. HE IS A SMALL MAN WITH A HUMP ON ONE SHOULDER. HIS BEARD IS LONG AND GREY AND HIS HAIR IS TIED INTO A RAGGED PONYTAIL; HE, TOO, IS HATLESS. HIS CLOTHES ARE TORN AND HE IS ONLY WEARING ONE SHOE. HIS FACE HAS CUTS AND FRESHLY BLOOMING BRUISES.

JOHN: I think it has quietened down now, Prophet. I think the crowds must have moved away from the Sanctuary. I hear less shouting.

WROE: It seems - yes ... somewhat quieter.

JOHN: My goodness, but I'm perspiring like a navvy. We must see to these cuts on your head promptly.

WROE: *(Touches his neck)* My neck, too.

JOHN: I must find a handkerchief. *(Starts opening drawers on the dresser)* I'm sure Sarah keeps some spare ones in here, for occasions such as these ...

WROE: For occasions such as these! *(Begins semi-hysterical laughter)* Ha-ha-ha!

JOHN: Prophet ... please, sit. Catch your breath. *(Gestures to a chair)*

WROE: So ... does Sarah anticipate 'occasions such as these' where ... where some threescore Christian Israelites are half beaten to death and chased down a secret tunnel to her home at Number Nine Park Parade?[3] *(Continues to laugh)*

JOHN: Well, unfortunately, this is now the second occasion that the people of Ashton have rioted outside of the Sanctuary and tried to kill you.

WROE: A cesspit of sinners, this place!

JOHN: And Swire and Corrie and myself did advise you to stay in Bradford for a much longer period of time.

WROE: *(Waves his hand)* Pah! Did Christ balk when he entered the gates of Jerusalem on a donkey? No! Not even when he knew that the hour had cometh and that the people of Jerusalem would turn against him!

JOHN: With all due respect, Yaakov, Christ never faced an angry mob of braying Ashton hooligans.

WROE: *(Half-laughs)* True enough.

JOHN: Vicious vandals who have now wrecked our Sanctuary twice in their desire to attack you for what they believe you to have done!

WROE: It's despicable. I've never met with such blind ignorance and thuggery. You Lancashire folk possess minds like a closed trap.

---

[3] In his own accounts, Wroe claimed that John Stanley saved his life on two occasions thanks to the existence of secret tunnels. During the late 1960s, when Park Parade was being developed into a dual carriageway, builders discovered these bricked up tunnels.

JOHN: (*Somewhat offended, he slams one of the dresser doors shut*) Well, let us not forget that your fellow Yorkshiremen have now made similar allegations in relation to your behaviour over the border.[4]

WROE: None of these slanders have any substance! You know this as well as I do. But… Perhaps it is time to abandon the New Jerusalem. To leave Ashton.

JOHN: That would be a tragedy, Yaakov. No … No. Everything would have been peaceable again here if it wasn't for these new accusations about that serving girl in Bradford.

WROE: (*Throws up his hands*) John – you know as well as I do that for those who are virtuous and godly and who hold a public position Satan prepares his attacks in the swiftest form - that of malicious rumour.

JOHN: Hmm. Yes - Proverbs 18, Verse 8: *'Gossip is so tasty…'*

WROE: (*Completes for him*)*'… we all love to swallow it.'* And have you noticed, John, that it is always the women who love the sweet taste of rumour the most? Beware of Eve and the honeyed tongue!

JOHN: That's true enough …

WROE: Yes – the tittle-tattle! Your own family fell victim to this. I heard myself from such rumourmongers that your younger brother, William, had been the talk of the town not so long ago.

JOHN: What did you hear?

WROE: That he caused a twelve-year-old girl to be with child. And that he was forced to flee from here.

JOHN: (*Containing anger, he yanks another door open*) I shall not attempt to defend my brother. William shall answer for any of his sins on Judgement Day. But I shall say this for him – he stood by the girl and they are still together, many more children later.

WROE: Oh, shush! Did you hear more shouting?

JOHN: No. I think that was Sarah shouting at one of the maids. But let us close the curtains so those outside cannot see your presence.

WROE: Yes.

JOHN: The folds on the curtains are rather complex, I'm afraid; Sarah is very particular about how they are arranged.

---

[4] Wroe was from Bradford, West Yorkshire. An allegation had also been made that he had caused a 14-year-old serving girl to become pregnant. See *His Own Man* for more details and for more information in relation to 'the truth' behind the Seven Virgins scandal.

JOHN stops what he is doing with the dresser drawers and both men look at the rather grand curtains. They seem rather intimidated by them. Neither moves.

JOHN: I … I am tortured by thoughts of the damage that those horrible people were inflicting on our Sanctuary just now. Last time the repairs of the pews took so long. The cost!

WROE: John, surely your concerns should lie not with the material interior and decorations of the Sanctuary but with the more spiritual …

JOHN: Oh no, I didn't mean to…

WROE: (*Holding his hand up to stop him*) Whilst I acknowledge the vast sums that you donated from your own personal wealth, I must point out the mortal errors of obsessing over items which are of earthly, perishable material.

JOHN: I … (*Gives up*) I apologise. My anxiety over all of this is perhaps wrongfully directed.

WROE: Very well. And in the meantime, let us close the curtains.

JOHN: Yes. Well… We must see to your cuts, too. I can't find the hankies. (*He slams the last dresser drawer shut*) We must … Sarah! Sarah!

JOHN calls out as he walks to the door and yanks it open. **SARAH STANLEY,** *aged 43, practically falls into the room. She has been listening at the keyhole and tries to muster some dignity. A tall and sturdily built woman, she towers above WROE and rarely smiles. She wears a white linen dress and shawl, a blue bonnet and blue shoes – the colours that must be worn by Christian Israelite women.*

SARAH: Well … well! I am clumsy today. All of these terrible happenings must have upset my bearing.

JOHN: Sarah! What were you …? Did you need us for something?

SARAH: Oh, yes … I was just coming to say that … that – yes, that the women and the children who fled through the tunnels with us have all gone home now. Fearful that they will be attacked, of course, but…

WROE: I shall pray for their safety.

SARAH: Most helpful, I'm sure. Now, can I offer you, Prophet, some form of sustenance after your shock? Some bread? Cheese? There's a fine Cheddar in the pantry and Alice can bring you …

JOHN: *(Cutting her off)* Medical attention might be more helpful to the Prophet at this particular moment rather than a lump of cheese.

WROE: And we must hide from view. We must close the curtains.

SARAH looks from one man to the other. They both look at the curtains and then at SARAH. Having shrugged off any embarrassment, she now returns to her natural state of dissatisfaction.

SARAH: Oh. So, *we* must close the curtains, must *we*? *(She goes to the curtains, yanking them together rather viciously)*

JOHN: We didn't want to upset you; they have very elaborate folds and…

SARAH: Well, that was hardly too difficult, now, was it?

WROE: *(To John)* How do my wounds fare?

JOHN: None too deep. But they will require cleaning, promptly. Sarah?

SARAH: Of course, Prophet; if Christian Israelites were permitted to keep mirrors in their houses you would be able to see your injuries for yourself.

WROE: Sarah! The Lord directs us never to possess an image of a living thing.[5] Even our own reflections – and especially our own reflections!

SARAH: But surely mirrors were never specifically mentioned in the Word.

WROE: Perhaps not, but the …

SARAH: *(Cutting him off)* It is a trial sometimes, you know, for a lady to have to do without a mirror. The servants complain, too, that they never know if their hair is tied up all skewwhiff, or if their faces are covered in flour or in coal dust.

WROE: Sarah …

SARAH: Mind you, in some respects it can be quite useful; I was always able to discern when our previous cook had been helping herself to the food. She had crumbs all over her whiskers.

---

[5] Wroe set out a number of rules for the Christian Israelites to follow, one of them included keeping no images of a living thing, similar to some Jewish and Muslim practises.

JOHN: *(To Wroe)* A very whiskery woman. Not nice to look at when you were eating. Made you feel queasy.

WROE: Ah. The Lord prescribes the wearing of beards for the men but not for the women! *(Chuckles to himself)*

SARAH: Although the Lord seems to have one rule for the men with money *(nods at her clean-shaven husband)* and another for those without…

JOHN: Well, we would have considerably less money, Sarah, if I turned up on the trading floor of the Corn Exchange sporting a set of whiskers. You know as well as I do that beards are frowned upon by the upper classes of Manchester.

WROE: Your husband pays the beardless tax to our Church for the right not to wear the beard. This way, he can raise sufficient income to support his family and to support the family of our church, as well. You know this.[6]

JOHN: Anyway, Sarah; please stop challenging the Prophet like this. Fetch some rose water so that he may clean his wounds.

WROE: Yes. And a glass of port wine. Or perhaps even some whisky may do better than rose water. The Bible teaches us that such substances can provide healing power.

SARAH: But the Christian Israelite rule lies against the consumption of alcohol, Prophet.

WROE: Well … well. As with all things, there are exceptions for medicinal reasons.

JOHN: Really? Hmm. Be that as it may, unfortunately we don't keep any in the house.

SARAH: If your energy is flagging, Prophet, I can furnish you with some cheese pie. Our new cook has taken to baking us a handsome one every Sabbath.

JOHN: Admirable cook, that one.

SARAH: Despite her own 'challenges'. She came to work for us only last month and was all set on baking a Sabbath pork pie. But when I told her that, no, we're Christian Israelites and expressly

---

[6] Locals referred to the Christian Israelites as 'the Beardies'. The richest Christian Israelite men who needed to trade on the floor of the Manchester Exchanges were permitted not to follow the 'beard' rule, providing that they paid a tax to the church. After the Seven Virgins scandal and people began to leave the church, the Manchester Guardian joked that the people in Ashton who were the happiest about this were the local barbers.

forbidden to eat the meat of any animal that chews the cud,[7] she was all ready to leave us as she felt that her skills …

JOHN: (*Cutting her off again*) Thank you, Sarah. Promptly does it.

SARAH narrows her eyes and walks stiffly to the door.

WROE: A slice of cheese pie would be welcome, though, Sarah. And whisky, too, if you could possibly send out for some …

SARAH: I'm not sure that smelling of alcohol will help your case, given that some of your enemies have accused you of …

JOHN: (*Raising his voice and his hand to dismiss her*) Thank you, Sarah!

SARAH closes the door behind her. Not quietly.

WROE: I see that Sarah does not change from one month to the next. (*He shuffles to a chair to sit and examines his bare foot*)

JOHN: No, Sarah will never change, I am afraid. There is always prayer, of course, but…

WROE: Unfortunately, the nature of a woman is to challenge the authority of the man. Witness the story of Adam and Eve; the unfortunate outcome of Adam's inability to stand his ground led to sin and damnation for mankind.

JOHN: Yes … of course. Yes.

WROE: I give you my every sympathy, John. Mrs Wroe, herself, has been known on several occasions to act in a headstrong manner. Ruled by female whims and excessive emotional impulses.

JOHN: Indeed.

WROE: … you see, she *will* still listen to the idle gossip that we were just talking about.

JOHN: Ah.

WROE: Yes! She seems unable to keep mentioning … that servant girl.

JOHN: Hum. Which one?

---

[7] Christian Israelites had the same dietary requirements as Jews – i.e. kosher only. John Stanley's shop sold such food. Years later, Robert Stanley would have found a halal diet to be practically the same to that enjoyed by his Uncle's family and friends. See *His Own Man* for more on the other rules required to be observed by the Christian Israelites.

WROE: *(Swipes his hand in the air)* Which one?! Why, the one who stole the jam! The one that all the newspapers said I employed as a 'virgin' to see to my every 'need'.

JOHN: Oh, her. Entirely to blame for both riots in our Sanctuary, she is.

WROE: Yes! Mrs Wroe cannot find it in herself to see that the accusations against me were simply because I demoted the girl for her stealing. And that the foolish chit wanted her revenge on me!

JOHN: Ridiculous. Our church hearing found no truth in the allegations against you.

WROE: Of course it didn't!

JOHN: Well. Women can be a suspicious lot. Watching your every move.

WROE: And your own wife, John, has been afflicted with … listening to gossip and then pushing the issue with the person concerned. But I have said all of this to you before about Sarah Stanley![8]

JOHN: Yes, you have. On several occasions.

WROE: I have contemplated it and prayed against it and spoken with you about it enough times and yet … Sarah Stanley remains unchanged.

JOHN: *(Forlorn)* It is true. But it is the … not so much the gossip or the answering back that depresses me, it is the … the sarcasm. Unbearable.

WROE: Ah. The sarcasm. The prerogative of a peevish and embittered female.

JOHN nods sadly and walks to the fire, takes the poker and – unconsciously – whacks it into his other hand.

JOHN: Of course, our church cannot permit divorce.

WROE: *(Instantly dismissive)* Out of the question! The marriage laws are sacred. No matter how terrible a burden it is, to suffer a wife of dark moods and bad tempers … we are bound to her for life.

---

[8] In his personal journal, 'Divine Communications', in September 1821, Wroe wrote *'How often has the Lord ordered John Stanley to cease wrestling with his wife; let him give her up, for she is not for the kingdom on earth, for she adulterates the Lord's word, for she is a wolf among the Lord's sheep''*. Wroe believed her to be stirring up trouble in the church. 'Give her up' is a strange phrase to use, however, as Christian Israelites were not permitted to divorce. This difference of opinion between Wroe and Sarah will have been caused by the fact that her husband had just parted with nearly half a million pounds (in today's prices) in order to build the Sanctuary for Wroe.

JOHN: Yes … out of the question. Although … I must say that I have often wondered at our namesakes and their practises.

WROE: How so?

JOHN: Well, of course, the Israelites themselves took more than one wife. For example, if the first wife was troublesome - or not the one that a man originally wanted…

WROE: As in the case of Jacob and Leah, you mean.

JOHN: Yes – exactly. The poor fellow was blighted with Leah. When he had been instantly attracted to the far comelier – and probably far more pliable – Rachel. *(He starts to poke the fire)*

WROE: And so … if a man was permitted to take another wife…

JOHN: Well, there are plenty of societies in the world where more than one wife is permitted. The Muhammedans, for example. They state that having a harem is one way to curb a man's inclinations to wander outside of the marital home and to prevent one woman from trying to dominate a man.

WROE: Hmm. Yes. The Muhammedans. Claim to be direct descendants of Ishmael. Claim to follow the same Jehovah as us. And they do honour the Judaic tradition more than Christians do. But, of course, they're very misled.

JOHN: No doubt.

WROE: But, think on it this way, John. If a man took another wife, it simply would be bringing another set of challenges into the home. The extra set of in-laws, for example.

JOHN: Goodness, yes. I hadn't thought of that. Urgh. (He *picks up a log and throws it onto the fire*)

WROE: So, perhaps we are best not to think of the early Abrahamic practises - with regards to more than one wife, at any rate - as something we could easily adopt.

JOHN: True enough. *(Somewhat sadly)* Society would never permit it. They're negative enough about the beards of the Christian Israelites. *(He throws another log onto the fire)*

WROE: I have also found, John, that leaders such as yourself often seem to have been dealt a wife of a … a difficult nature, shall we say. It is as though "these things are sent to test us." A trial. To make us stronger in the way of the Lord.

JOHN: A trial. Yes.

Both men are quiet for a moment. Then there is the sound of a horse neighing from the stables outside, jolting them out of their shared melancholy.

WROE: But look! How easily we have managed to distract ourselves from the hideous events of this morning! Talk of cheese pie and gossip and…

JOHN: We're as bad as the women!

WROE: I wouldn't go so far as to say that. But … yes. Perhaps we should conclude by drawing from the words of the Law, rather than the Lord, that the man in the married state must 'do his time,' and that if he is patient, joy will be his reward.

JOHN: Well, then, whom is this Joy and where can I meet her? *(Both men burst out laughing, just as SARAH enters the room again)*

SARAH: It's nice to see that someone can find mirth in this situation.

JOHN: Well, we were only …

SARAH: Here's the rose water. And, Prophet, I've brought you a pair of John's shoes. I'm sure that they will be far too big for you. You have uncommonly small feet for a man. *(She drops them at his feet)*

WROE: *(Offended, stiffly.)* Thank you, Sarah.

SARAH: Would you like me to see to your cuts?

WROE: No. John - just point at where they are. I shall tend to them myself. Goodness knows, I do not need any more allegations of a woman coming within ten paces of me.

JOHN moves closer to WROE and points out where the cuts are. WROE applies the water with some lint cloth. SARAH stands back, observing. She is twisting her hands and obviously has something to say.

SARAH: Have you had any thoughts, Prophet, about where-to next?

WROE: *(Stops applying the water)* What do you mean?

SARAH: Only that … Wouldn't it be wise for you to return to Bradford for a little while? Mrs Wroe and the children seem to prefer your house over there and …

WROE: *(Coldly)* You think that some people would like to see the back of me?

44

SARAH: Well. Not us, not us of course. We would be like … like sheep without a shepherd. But there are others contesting for leadership that will surely not rest until they are satisfied.

WROE: Satisfied with having me killed by the good folk of Ashton, you mean?

JOHN: That would never happen.

SARAH: Well, I for one am not so sure of it! You saw the way that they took a-hold of him, John; one of Walker's men was all set to throw him right through a window!

JOHN: Well, there were raised emotions, of course. But all of that was entirely due to the mischief-making of just a handful of men, those who have never been content with the appointment of our Prophet as successor to Mother Joanna.

SARAH: Well, I know that, and you know that, but the people of Ashton are a dim and backward lot of brutes. With long memories. The last time they attacked the Prophet, they fashioned an effigy after him. And he replaced the evil Black Knight effigy on horseback during the annual parade!

WROE: Really? I replaced the famous Black Knight effigy? Goodness. I never knew that.

SARAH: Yes! It was a frighteningly good image of you, too …

JOHN: Some of the lower classes always need to raise up a villain to hate. If not you, Prophet, it would be …

SARAH: … Because they used an old dishcloth for your beard. It looked just like yours. And then they paraded you through the streets of Ashton and booed you and threw rotten eggs at you.

JOHN: They were shouting very unspeakable things about the people of Bradford and Yorkshire. *(To himself)* Some of the chants were quite amusing, actually…

SARAH: The thing is, Prophet, these common people – they're saying … that we're happy to have a monster as a leader.

JOHN: Sarah …

SARAH: … who preys upon vulnerable young serving girls!

WROE: Do they, indeed?

SARAH: Yes! And it does not matter how much you speak of God's word - if someone hears that a woman has been encroached upon by an older man … his reputation is in tatters! Even if it is an untruth.

JOHN: Sarah! I think that you have said quite enough.

SARAH: I was only …

JOHN: I suggest that you go and see to the children,

SARAH: I shall do that then! They are most upset after seeing grown men fighting with each other, in a church of all places, and then the poor mites were dragged, terrified, through a dark and slimy tunnel!

JOHN: Sarah …

SARAH: And our dear Annie said to me, "What about the financial burden, Mama? The pecuniary impact of the vandalism to our beloved Sanctuary yet again! Will our father use up even more of our inheritance on the fixtures and the fittings?"

JOHN: Sarah, Annie is a rather dull-witted and backward twelve-year-old girl at the best of times. I hardly imagine her capable of constructing such an eloquent sentence.

SARAH: *(Huffs)* Well … well! I am glad that you have at least noticed the age of your children!

WROE has decided to take a stand. He straightens himself and points one finger at SARAH and one at JOHN.

WROE: Enough! Sarah, you have said your piece and you can fetch me a tumbler of whisky! John, send a servant out to tell any families that wish to join me that I will meet them at the Mossley Road gatehouse once this day is over.

JOHN: *(Bowing his head)* Indeed. When?

WROE: Whilst the morning is still dark. We shall leave for Huddersfield at five o'clock.

JOHN: *(Turns to his wife)* Sarah, go to the stable boy and instruct him to convey that exact message. I do not trust a female servant to be engaged with such a mission.

WROE: And say that whomsoever from the congregation wishes to traverse beyond Huddersfield with me we can find them some temporary lodgings in Bradford.

JOHN: Prophet, the thing is though, I cannot – of course – join you myself. My commitments to the…

WROE: Yes, yes. It is fine. Your business needs you at its helm. Your endeavours sustain the work of our Church.

SARAH: And I shall not be leaving Ashton. Certainly not for a place such as Bradford!

WROE: *(Icily)* No one would expect you to, Sarah.

JOHN: *(Depressingly)* And you're needed here too, Sarah.

WROE: Now, John. I need you to assist with us taking the printing press over to Bradford. It is so very valuable to our mission. These vandals of Ashton would smash it to pieces if left here.

JOHN: Of course.

WROE: If you can spare us a cart and the use of your black horses.

SARAH: Oh – but we only keep the black horses for Sunday best...

JOHN: *(Cutting her off)* Of course. Sarah, instruct the boy to get the horses ready as soon as he has conveyed the message.

WROE: And we could cover the printing press with cloths and sit the younger children on top of it.

JOHN: Yes.

WROE: Excellent. But John – I do not intend to creep from Ashton so meekly. Tell your boy to inform the people that we require all woodwind and trumpets to be at the ready. We shall sing glories to the Lord as we travail across Marsden Moor!

JOHN: Indeed. Sarah? The stable boy.

WROE: And further! *(Wagging his finger in the air)*. I prophesise that in a few weeks' time, those who have caused all of this consternation will be struck down by a most violent thunderbolt!

JOHN: *(Sharply)* Sarah! The boy!

SARAH: *(As sharply back)* The boy! *(She turns to go)*

WROE: And, Sarah? The whisky.

JOHN: Yaakov – as I said, we don't keep anything like that in...

SARAH: *(Tossing her head)* Poppycock, John! Of course there is whisky in the house! I shall fetch it. Promptly.

SARAH flounces out the room and slams the door shut behind her. Then she opens it again and hisses back at them.

SARAH: And *I* shall prophesise now! I intend to take the very first sup of that whisky myself! *(She slams the door shut)*

---ENDS---

3. A GIFT HORSE

CONTEXT:
By 1831 Robert Stanley was three years old and living with his parents, William and Ann, in Cardiff. He was the seventh of ten surviving children. The couple were struggling to feed their family, because the beaver hats that William was skilled in making had recently fallen out of fashion. Up in Ashton-under-Lyne, however, John Stanley continued to make vast amounts of money as a leading industrialist and continued to stay loyal to his friend, Christian Israelite Prophet John Wroe, following the 'Seven Virgins' accusations and the riots in their Sanctuary. Over time, at least four of William's and Ann's sons moved back home to the Ashton area in order to gain employment, thanks to the generosity of their Uncle John.

This scene pictures how William and Ann may have felt on hearing the news from 'back home' and considers how the plans may have developed to send their boys – including a very young Robert – back up north.

CARDIFF, OCTOBER 1831

A TINY KITCHEN IN A CARDIFF TERRACE. ON AN OPEN RANGE A COPPER KETTLE HAS JUST FINISHED SINGING AS A WOMAN – **ANN STANLEY,** AGED 34 – LIFTS IT AND BEGINS TO BREW THE TEA IN A TEAPOT. SHE IS SMALL BUT STURDY AND WEARS AN APRON AND A CAP. WE CAN SEE DARK BLONDE CURLS PEEKING THROUGH AND A SMATTERING OF FRECKLES. HER SON **JACK STANLEY,** AGED 14, IS SIMILAR TO HIS MOTHER IN LOOKS. WASHING IS DRAPED ON A CLOTHES HORSE AND ON A PULLEY ABOVE THE FIREPLACE. JACK IS DOING HIS BEST TO TRY AND FOLD VARIOUS PIECES OF IT WHILST MERRILY WHISTLING AWAY. A BABY LAYS ASLEEP IN A PLAIN WOODEN CRIB IN THE CORNER OF THE ROOM AND A LITTLE BOY – **ROBERT STANLEY,** AGED 3 – CROUCHES NEXT TO IT, PLAYING WITH SOME WOODEN BLOCKS THAT HAVE THE LETTERS OF THE

ALPHABET SCRATCHED UPON THEM. **WILLIAM STANLEY,** AGED 43, IS SITTING AT THE KITCHEN TABLE AND HAS PLACED HIS BEAVER HAT ON THE TABLE IN FRONT OF HIM. ON TOP OF IT HE HAS PERCHED A LETTER OF MANY PAGES AND IS READING ALOUD FROM IT. FROM OUTSIDE WE HEAR CHILDREN'S VOICES.

WILLIAM: *(To ANN)* Just sit down for a minute and listen, woman!

ANN: William - I've got a hundred and one things to do before I go and visit Auntie Maggie. Jack — will you hurry up and fold that washing for me, I'm in the middle of brewing the tea …

WILLIAM: *(Brusquely)* Leave the tea alone and sit down.

ANN: *(Ignoring him)* I can pour the tea perfectly well whilst I stand up. And whilst listening.

WILLIAM: Will you give over whistling that tune, Jack! Or learn a new tune. I'm sick of *Gypsy Rover*.

ANN: Wipe your hands before you touch those sheets, Jack.

WILLIAM: Now, Ann, listen up; things never change with our John!

ANN: Oh, yes? *(She stirs the tea leaves)*

WILLIAM: As always, my dear brother gives no real details about what's really going on in Ashton. Just a load of drivel.

ANN: He's never been much to the point.

WILLIAM: No. Loves the sound of his own voice. Two pages where he witters on about the price of coffee versus tea. Another two where he describes the health benefits of taking sarsaparilla. And one on the sad story of Mr Bates - how he's lost a leg.

JACK: That was careless of him.

WILLIAM: *(Ignoring him)* And then — finally - just a few lines on the … the what-not in the temple.

ANN: *(Correcting him)*. The scandal. The Sanctuary getting wrecked. Again.

WILLIAM: He says, *"You may have heard some outrageous newspaper reports regarding our friend and Prophet, John Wroe. The Prophet was most grievously accused of immoralities, but we have been brought much comfort when the accusations were discharged at our church hearing."*

ANN: Well, that doesn't sound like the way the newspapers put it! They all made him sound quite guilty.

WILLIAM: Aye. But don't interrupt. *"…Sadly, though, certain Ashton ruffians used the episode as an opportunity to engage in acts of violence – twice – rioting both inside and outside of the Sanctuary. Most recently on the holy day of Easter Sunday itself, where the Sanctuary was most grievously vandalised, and the beautiful mahogany pews were ripped up and used as weapons. The stained-glass windows above the entrance door were smashed too, and the bronze, silver and even some of the gold fittings were stolen. It pains me less that I provided the monetary outlay for the entire Sanctuary; no, the true pain comes from the fact that the temple of the Lord was defiled in such a way by these gross marauders."*

ANN: *'Gross marauders.'* Honestly. Your John!

WILLIAM: *'Pains me less!'* He paid nine thousand and five hundred pounds for that place to be built.

JACK: Blimey!

WILLIAM: Imagine the good he could have done with that sort of money! That could have fed, what, a thousand families for a year! When the likes of us can barely feed our own children.

JACK: I think you've got your sums wrong there, Dad. Most families have six or seven mouths to feed. Well, let's say an average of seven per family, so you'd have to have a bit more than…

WILLIAM: Well, no one asked your opinion, Mr Clever Clogs.

ANN: *(Beaming at JACK)* He's such a way with his sums. You could go into a job where you do the accounts for businessmen! You could help your father if he…

WILLIAM: I don't need the help. I do quite nicely adding my own amounts up for my business, thank you very much.

ANN: *(Sarcastically)* Not a great deal for you to add up at the moment, though, is there?

WILLIAM: Well, that's hardly my fault! This government!

ANN: Well, whatever. At least your John gives to a church, rather than take from it. Unlike that Reverend Chetwode in Ashton. He makes a pretty packet out of St Michael's. He's only ever preached there about three times, from what I've heard.[9]

WILLIAM: Ha, well, *his* father's the Earl of Stamford. So, he expects to be able to feed off the poor like a parasite.

---

[9] One of the reasons the Christian Israelites were able to flourish in Ashton was because of the neglect of its parish church and the greed of its priests. See *His Own Man* for more information.

JACK: So … they allowed it to happen twice? Two riots in one church?

WILLIAM: Aye. Just a few months apart.

ANN: They say it's about the … scandal. But if you ask me, it's all being whipped up into more than it is by those other fellas wanting to be leader of the Southcottians instead of Wroe.

JACK: So, did this Prophet Wroe 'invent' the Christian Israelites?

WILLIAM: Oh, aye. They were all claiming to have had visions, to see signs and miracles, so that the poor deluded Southcottians would think that they were the chosen successor after their Mother Joanna died. But Wroe won the day.

ANN: I always think it's a shame that they didn't get another woman-leader after their Mother Joanna died. It was nice to hear of a woman in charge for once.

WILLIAM and JACK stop what they're doing and stare at each other. WILLIAM rolls his eyes. JACK grins. ANN is too busy pouring the tea to notice.

WILLIAM: Oh, aye, that's exactly what the world needs. Yet more women claiming to have birthed a supernatural infant.

ANN: *(Sets her mouth)* Well, it's what I think.

WILLIAM: *(Taking his cup of tea from her and swigging it)* Wroe was plain stupid, returning to Ashton just a few weeks after they'd already had a go at trampling him to death. Probably wants those feeble-minded rich women in Ashton – like that widow Lees – who're throwing their coins into his coffers, to think that he's some kind of a martyr.

ANN: There's not that many women, William. The Lees and the Swires and the Corries and … well … your John and his sons... Most of the names that we hear are keeping Wroe going are … men.

WILLIAM: Apart from his virgins! They're keeping him going, alright!

Father and son burst out laughing. Robert looks up from his play.

ROBERT: What's 'hissvirgins'?

ANN: Never you mind, Robert.

WILLIAM: The richer they are, the less brains they have. Wroe was a canny one alright, cosying up to the richest folk in town the minute he set foot in Ashton.

JACK: Oh, Dad – do you think Uncle John's hoping that this prophet will get him a virgin of his own, 'to nourish and comfort him'?[10] *(Starts giggling)*

ANN: Jack!

JACK: It's what the newspapers said he wanted the seven virgins to do!

WILLIAM: Well, if your Aunt Sarah has any say in the matter, he won't be getting one. Everyone knows who wears the trousers in *that* house. Right po-faced old heifer, is Sarah.

ANN: You're too harsh, William.

WILLIAM: And you're far too quick to forgive. If it wasn't for brother John, I wouldn't have been stuck on the other side of the world whilst you were bringing up a baby on your own.

ANN: Hush, William! *(Glances at the children.)* Anyway, I wasn't on my own. Auntie Maggie helped.

WILLIAM: And that's probably why our Will's turned out to be such an odd bod. Anyway, it's time our kids knew what sort of a man their uncle is. Has he ever sent us so much as even a penny? Has he buggery.

JACK: I thought I was Uncle John's namesake? Why would you name me after someone who was so stingy?

ROBERT: *(Looking up from his blocks)* What's a 'naymeshake?'

ANN: Never you mind, big ears.

ROBERT: Ha-ha – Big ears Jack! Big ears Jack!

JACK goes to cuff ROBERT, who jumps away in time and squeals.

ANN: Now! That's enough, Jack – he's only a nipper!

JACK: I'll nip him alright! I'm sick of him laughing at my ears.

WILLIAM: Oh, grow up. Men will tease you for a lot worse than your ears when you get a job and you're in the outside world rather than folding washing with women all day.

---

[10] The Seven Virgins scandal was interpreted by Jane Rogers in her book 'Mr Wroe's Virgins' which was adapted into a BBC TV series in the 1990s. See *His Own Man* (plus appendices) for more on the truth behind the allegations against John Wroe.

JACK: I'd rather have that, anytime. Anything would be better than being stuck in this house (*kicks out at ROBERT, who dodges again*) and having these babies all over the place.

ANN: I'd prefer it if you found a job, too. Instead of you loping about with a face like a smacked arse.

WILLIAM: Ann, that's not very ladylike language.

ANN: Well. He gets my goat, he does. Taking his temper out on us just because he's mooning over some silly serving wench from the Dog and Partridge.

JACK: I'm not mooning over no one! I'm happy, I am! You've just told me off for whistling!

WILLIAM: Well, you should take my advice. Get a job. It's not natural for a boy of 14 years to be spending so much time in the company of women and babies.

JACK: I've tried and tried - there's no work to be had round these parts!

WILLIAM: Well, try harder. I can't support you anymore. Things are that bad for me now that I'm going to have to let our Will go…

ANN: (*Has been warming her hands on the teapot but suddenly drops it on the table – then checks it hasn't broken*). Oh, John! No! He can't lose his job! They've a baby on the way!

WILLIAM: Can't be helped. I just can't shift the beaver hats. They're all after the silk hats these days. I can't suddenly begin a brand-new trade at my age.

ANN: Well, your John did say that to you years ago, didn't he? Said that you'd best learn how to…

WILLIAM: Blast it, woman! (*Picks the letter up and screws it into a ball*) Do you take joy from rubbing my nose in it?

ROBERT: Daddy, don't shout!

ANN: Hush!

ANN goes over to the crib to check, but the baby sleeps on.

ROBERT: I think that baby is deaf. He always sleeps through it, when everyone's shouting here.

JACK: Deaf or maybe just stupid – like you, Robert.

ROBERT sticks his tongue out at his brother. WILLIAM finishes his tea and bangs the cup back on the table. Robert looks up from his lap.

ROBERT: Daddy, can you tell me what's a naymeshake is?

ANN: *(Answering for WILLIAM)* It's 'namesake', poppet. You can give your child the same name as the person that you admire.

JACK: So … you must have admired Uncle John, then, once upon a time?

ANN: Well, it was your dad's idea to name you 'John'. It was in the hope that his brother would send us a bob or two every now and then.

WILLIAM: Don't give me that look, Ann! Enterprising, it was, Ann. Trying to play brother John at his own game.

ANN: *(Under her breath)* Another failed business venture.

ROBERT: But he's our 'Jack'. Not John!

WILLIAM: No, Robert. That's a nickname. Like … sometimes we call you 'Bobby', don't we? 'Bobby' – or 'Bob' - is a nickname for 'Robert'. And a nickname for 'John' is 'Jack'.

ROBERT: Why?

WILLIAM: Well, it just is. 'Jack' has always been short for 'John'.

ROBERT: That's silly.

WILLIAM: It's not silly at all. It's just the way that it is.

ROBERT: I'm hungry, Mam.

ANN: *(Sharply)* You'll have to wait until supper, Robert. There's nothing in the cupboards.

ROBERT: But I'm very, very, very, very, very, very, very, very hungry!

WILLIAM: Give him some tea, Ann. It'll take the edge off.

ANN pours ROBERT a cup of lukewarm tea. He sips it gratefully.

JACK: Can I read the rest of that letter, Dad?

WILLIAM: *(Grudgingly)* If you must.

ANN: It lifts my spirits to see how good you are with your reading these days, Jack. No thanks to your father, mind.

WILLIAM: Oh, don't start again.

JACK picks up the balled-up letter and straightens it. There is silence for a half minute whilst ANN finishes folding the linen and WILLIAM closes his eyes. ROBERT is singing 'A, B, C' to himself.

WILLIAM: Robert, button it, will you? I'm getting a headache what with that and *Gypsy Rover*.

JACK: *(Looks up from letter)* It doesn't sound like Uncle John's trying to lord it over us in the way that he writes.

WILLIAM: Oh, he's full of the polite manners, is John. He never possessed any brotherly affections towards me.

JACK: Well, you can't choose your relatives. *(Looks pointedly at ROBERT)*

WILLIAM: He always said I was your grandfather's favourite. Load of codswallop. See, your Uncle John claimed that I had brought the Stanley name into disrepute. Never did nowt of the kind. We just…

ANN: *(Trying to phrase it carefully)* We … just decided that we wanted to be together – to be wed.[11] And some people…

WILLIAM: Thought we were doing wrong.

JACK: Why? What's wrong about that?

WILLIAM: Well, it's not like Cardiff, where we come from up north. In Cardiff anyone can marry anyone.

ANN: Usually their sisters.

WILLIAM: *(Ignores her)* Yes, in Dukinfield, in Ashton, they're … cold. Cold fish. Heartless.

ANN: Well, I wouldn't say that. Aunt Maggie's a Dukinfield girl and you could never find anyone with a bigger heart. That's why she moved back down here, to look after us.

WILLIAM: *(Under his breath)* To bleed us dry, more like.

ANN: *(Doesn't hear him)* No, I wouldn't put it quite like that. They're more … judgemental people, perhaps. Sterner than the Welsh.

WILLIAM: Definitely

ANN: But those towns up north have been going through all sorts in the last 20 years. Families being broken apart, being shoved into those terrible factories. You can sympathise with those Luddites going 'round smashing up the power looms. People are angry up there. Unforgiving.

---

[11] Census data for later years indicates that Ann was either 12 or 13 when she gave birth to their first child (in Dukinfield, before her move to Cardiff). There is no evidence that the couple were ever married despite having at least ten children together.

55

WILLIAM: So, you're saying that our John was unforgiving with us because he was worried about the Luddites? Women's logic that is, Jack...

Father and son eye each other and grin.

WILLIAM: No. John treated us the way he did because of religion. The more religious they are, the bigger hypocrites they are. (*Gestures at the letter*) Like your Prophet Wroe and his dalliances with his seven virgins...

ANN: None of that's been proven.

JACK: So, Dad, was it because Grandma and Grandad didn't approve of you getting married?

ANN: It wasn't that simple ...

WILLIAM: Your grandparents were under ... a certain amount of pressure. They thought your mother too young. That I should have taken a bride of my own age.

JACK: (*Looks at his mother*) What IS your age exactly, Mam?

ANN: Well, I'm not too sure anymore. Having you lot has aged me. Not to mention losing five babies. And having another on the way. (*Puts her hand on her belly.*)

WILLIAM: Y'see, Jack, there aren't any rules of age when it comes to...

ANN: ... Love.

JACK looks at his mother, expecting to see the sarcasm in her face, but he doesn't find it. His father rises from the table and kisses his wife's neck – both parents are smiling soppily at each other for once.

JACK: Hmmm. Well. That's put me off my dinner. I feel proper queasy now.

ROBERT: I'll have his! I'm so very, very hungry still!

JACK: Shurrup, you! (*Reaches over and tries to swipe Robert*)

WILLIAM: (*Kisses Ann again and then sits down*) Well, your mother's right, Jack. Having babies has addled her noggin'. She's not even sure of her own children's dates of birth, are you?

ANN: (*Laughs*) Of course I am! Don't forget that I can read and write. It was unusual for a young girl to learn that sort of thing when

56

I was a lass. And it's more than your own sisters can do, isn't it, Will?

WILLIAM: True. And that's how we met, Jack, see - I was teaching your mother to read and write. My sisters were too busy helping round the house and getting married off.

ANN: Your Aunt Maggie asked your Dad to show me how to learn to read and write. A proper man of letters, I thought he was.

WILLIAM: *(Grimly)* Hmm. And how far the mighty have fallen. Look at me. *(Bangs the top of the hat)*. Flogging beaver hats that no one wants, on a freezing, soggy-wet Welsh market morning.

ANN: Oh, piddle. We might be having hard times at the moment, but… everyone admires you. Thanks to your stances over things like fighting the unfair taxes.

WILLIAM: *(Bangs the table with his fist)* Tried to tax me ten times the amount I was due, they did! Just because I'm an Englishman. But I fought 'em – and I won it in court!

JACK: *(Eyes to the ceiling)* I know. You've told us a thousand times. So, Dad – you went off a-travelling, whilst Mam had our Will up in Dukinfield?

WILLIAM: Yes. I needed to prove I was worthy of her love and all of that. And to make a bob or two. And after I sailed the world and killed a hundred lions and tigers in Africa, I…

JACK: Well, that's a tall story, Dad, because everyone knows you don't get tigers in Africa.

WILLIAM: I think you'll find that you do.

JACK: I think you'll find that they're an Indian species only.

WILLIAM: Well, a she-lion anyway. Lionesses are very similar to tigers. It's easy to confuse them. They don't have a mane, you see. And sometimes the sunlight fades their stripes, so you can't see them.

JACK: Sheesh.

WILLIAM: Yes, after all my adventures and travels on the high seas, I came home to your mother and to our Will. And we moved down to Cardiff where you lot were all born.

JACK: So why is there an eight-year gap between me and our Will?

ROBERT: *(Pipes up)* Will said to me that Jack was a horrid baby. And that a bad fairy left him on the doorstep.

JACK: (*To ROBERT*) Shut thi' gob, boyo - go and play in the fire grate!

ANN: Well, it's just that two of my babies died before you. And then, of course, after you … we lost our George and Thomas and … Matilda died, too.

JACK: Oh. I didn't know that.

ROBERT: That's sad. How old were those babies?

ANN: Let me see… Well, two of them were so little that they weren't ready to be born at all. And baby Matilda was just three days old. And George, he was six, and Thomas, he was five. Poor little mites.

ROBERT: (*Alarmed*) Will I die too?

JACK: Maybe, if you carry on with…

ANN: (*Cutting him off*) No, lamb. You won't. They were always quite sickly children. You're a very strong little lad. Now run off and play with Ann-Lexcey outside.

ROBERT: I wish I had brothers to play with. Sisters are girls. And they pinch you.

WILLIAM: Cheer up, lad. You're nearly as big as her and soon you'll be able to box her ears. Now, do as your mother says.

ROBERT: I want to stay here and read my letters. (*Looks at his alphabet blocks which he has lined up in a row to spell 'Godislove'*)

JACK: (*Referring to ROBERT*) Soft in the head. (*He commences with reading the letter*) Blimey! Now, look! (*His voice suddenly becomes an adolescent high-pitched wobble*).

ANN: (*Leaves the washing and comes over*) What?

JACK: See! Dad, did you not read the 'P.S' at the bottom?

WILLIAM: No. I got fed up of all the talk of the town and the God-business before I got to that bit.

JACK: Well, you should have done. It says, *"Sarah and I were discussing the fact that we might be able to help you out, in relation to the prospects for your eldest two. We have gathered that times are extremely difficult for all in Wales at the moment. I am currently looking into branching out into the mining industry and am aware that there is a need for colliers in these parts. If this is of interest to William junior, I should easily be able to find him an opening and assist with accommodation for him and his wife. There also happens to be an opening for an assistant bookkeeper at my ironworks. Our parents have mentioned that your John excels at figures, so if he is interested in* *an apprenticeship I can help in that regard. If you can respond to this letter forthwith, I can then supply further details. I must, however, remind you that such jobs are very much in demand here, so a speedy response is essential. Yours, with fraternal regards, John."*

ANN: Goodness me!

WILLIAM: *(Has snatched the letter back off JACK)* "A speedy response is essential," just listen to him! We might be struggling at the moment, but what does he think I…

ANN: *(Goes to William and gently puts her hands on his shoulders)* Well now, William, this is one of your favourite sayings; 'Don't look a gift horse in the mouth'.

WILLIAM: Huh. Doesn't apply to our John.

ANN: *(Grabs the letter back off him)* Oh yes it does. And I'm going to be the first one to say this; Jack – you're going. Go and find our Will. Tell him that the two of them need to prepare to go to Ashton, too.

JACK: Ashton! But it's such a long way off! And the last time we went to see Grandma I was sick all down the side of the Manchester stagecoach!

ANN: Jack - you keep telling me you're practically a grown man now. So *be* a man – and start planning. You father and I are going to write back straight away to your Uncle John and say yes.

WILLIAM: Are we now?

ANN: *(Sits at the table)* Yes, we are. Fetch the paper, William. And … Jack. Don't look like such a mardarse. There's lots of pretty girls up in Ashton.

JACK: *(Brightening)* Are there?

WILLIAM: *(Pulls his face)* Well… maybe … better than here, at any rate.

JACK pulls his overcoat on and deliberately kicks ROBERT'S blocks out of line as he does this. ROBERT shakes his fist at his brother, who ignores him.

JACK: Alright. Well, maybe I'm game them. I'll go find our Will.

ROBERT: Can't I go up there to Ashton? There's never anything to eat here.

ANN and WILLIAM look at each other and then at Robert. The baby starts to cry.

ROBERT: Can't I go?

ANN picks the baby up from the crib and puts is to her breast. JACK leaves the house and outside, we hear a little girl's voice shouting 'Where yer going, our Jack?'.

ROBERT: Uncle John might have lots of food. Can't I go?
WILLIAM: Maybe one day, son. Maybe one day.

---ENDS---

4. MEETING A VISIONARY

CONTEXT:

Robert Stanley came to live in Ashton in 1838 at the age of ten. He

Prophet Wroe

was apprenticed to his wealthy uncle, John Stanley, in one of John's many businesses: Th'Owd Joanna's shop.[12] As a result of the violence following the debacle of the 'Seven Virgins' scandal in 1831, Wroe stayed away from Ashton, keeping a much lower profile for a few years.

By 1839, Robert was living in Ashton with his older brother, Jack (who had also come north to find work through their Uncle John Stanley), and Wroe had begun to make more public appearances in Ashton, preaching at the Christian Israelites' Sanctuary.

Although we have no evidence that the young Robert knew Wroe, the timeline and the friendships between John Stanley and Prophet Wroe strongly indicate that they would have met and spent time together. Ten years later, Robert himself got married in the Christian Israelites' Sanctuary.

This scene imagines the first meeting between Prophet Wroe and a very young Robert Stanley.

ASHTON-UNDER-LYNE, JANUARY 6TH 1839

MID-MORNING OUTSIDE THE STABLES AT JOHN STANLEY'S HOUSE ON PARK PARADE, ASHTON-UNDER-

---

[12] The real name of John Stanley's shop was the 'Christian Israelites' Shop' – but locals always called it Th'Owd Joanna's after Joanna Southcott's Christian group, the precursors of the Christian Israelites. John Stanley sold general produce and also food suitable for the Christian Israelites' diet i.e. kosher meat.

LYNE. **PROPHET JOHN WROE,** AGED 57, AND **JOHN STANLEY,** AGED 53, ARE DISCUSSING THE PREVIOUS NIGHT'S HURRICANE. GLASS, SLATES AND BRICK ARE STREWN ACROSS THE YARD, WITH BUCKETS, BRUSHES, HAY AND BARRELS ALL HAPHAZARDLY LYING ABOUT. WROE STILL LOOKS EVERY INCH THE PROPHET – HIS BEARD IS NOW WHITE AND SHAGGIER THAN EVER. HIS BROAD-BRIMMED HAT IS FIXED FIRMLY ONTO HIS HEAD AND HE HOLDS A THICK WOODEN STAFF. JOHN HAS AGED CONSIDERABLY SINCE THE 1831 DEBACLE. HIS HAIR IS ENTIRELY GREY, ALTHOUGH HE IS STILL CLEAN-SHAVEN AND IMMACULATELY DRESSED, WEARING HIS USUAL SILK HAT AND CARRYING A RIDING CROP.

JOHN: Well, I certainly shan't be attempting to ride one of my horses this morning. Last night's storm has put them all on edge.
WROE: Your fine black horses are far too grand for me. I prefer a lowly donkey, as our Lord did.
JOHN: You have a point, Yaakov, but … my business would no doubt suffer if I turned up to the trading floors in Manchester perched atop a donkey.
WROE: Ha! But you are not called to endure the sort of deprivations as those of us gifted with prophecy are. Your calling is to provide for our Church through financial support and sustenance.
JOHN: Indeed. But … now, look at all of this! It was a true hurricane! (*Gestures to the yard*) Did you ever see such a mess?
WROE: Certainly. And worse. Outside our own Sanctuary, a few years ago.
JOHN: (*Inclines his head*) Although last time the disorder was entirely due to destruction by Ashton hooligans as opposed to that of nature.
WROE: But John Stanley, do you not recall that I predicted this? That when the Lord moved me to return to Ashton that there would be great disturbance in nature?[13]

---

[13] Wroe made hundreds of predictions, including this one and others that related to John Stanley's wealth. He recorded them in his own journal, 'Divine Communications'. The most important members of the congregation (i.e. John Stanley and his second wife, Mary) were chosen to sign to attest to their validity. See *His Own Man*.

JOHN: Of course! Your vision… How remarkable.

WROE: (*Shrugging*) Less remarkable to one who's entire life has been spent receiving words from beyond this earthly realm.

JOHN: At least your journey over here from Huddersfield this morning left you unmolested. These people of Ashton can be unforgiving and violent brutes.

WROE. I was entirely unharmed. All was peaceable in comparison with a few years ago.

JOHN: Perhaps their attentions are now directed towards the factory and mill owners. The people complain more than ever that the masters barely keep them alive with the amounts that they are paid.

WROE: Hmm. In Bradford I have never seen such hatred towards the wealthy men of the towns. Violence on the horizon, no doubt.

JOHN: Yes, you can hang a few Luddites, but there will always be certain elements …

WROE: It will all be a result of these trade associations. They whip men up on a daily basis. Even the womenfolk! They clamour for strikes and all manner of pointless agitations. Are you not concerned for yourself, as a factory owner?

JOHN: Less so than you may think. As you know, I have always paid a decent wage. And I operate in iron and coal; it is the cotton masters of Ashton, that the people reserve most hatred for.

WROE: True, true.

JOHN: And of course, at the heart of it all, they see me as John Stanley. Just the humble grocer; proprietor of their local Christian Israelite-run shop, giving them their everyday necessities at low prices and treating every customer with respect.

WROE: Ha! John Stanley – the humble grocer! That will be the day.

JOHN: (*Smiling*) I have been sensible as to where I invest my wealth.

WROE: Indeed, you have.

JOHN: But there was no prouder moment for me than when I built the Sanctuary. And you, of course, prophesised more wealth and worldly successes for me.

WROE: But more important, are the rewards that you will receive in heaven.

JOHN: Ah, paradise. How different it will be, in comparison to the life of gloom, dirt, smog and the ignorance and drunkenness of the Ashton people.

WROE: I hear that the women of this town, grow shriller and more rancorous with every passing day, rolling about the town drunk, neglecting their responsibilities.

JOHN: (*Shaking his head violently*) It is frightful! Have you observed, too, that the womenfolk here are becoming even more slatternly in their dress? In the styling of their hair?

WROE: I have. And I do not envy you, being surrounded by such temptresses.

JOHN: In fact, I was recently approached by one of those harpies – one of those 'ladies of the night'.

WROE: Yes?

JOHN: I was walking back from the gun shop last week and there - in broad daylight - this flea-ridden creature offered to show me her knee in return for a ha'penny.

WROE: Her knee!

JOHN: Yes! The Jezebel! And then she told me, "Tha's a rich gent an' they allus will 'ave a grope, as sure as eggs is eggs."

WROE: Now ... that's the difference between an Ashton and a Bradford harlot!

JOHN: Pardon?

WROE: Yes, in Bradford the price would be double that – and you'd be invited to view the other knee for an extra penny.

JOHN: (*Stroking his chin*) Hmmm. I see, Prophet, that your attempts at one-upmanship in relation to Yorkshire versus Lancashire profiteering has not diminished.

WROE: (*Laughs heartily*) My, but you're perhaps correct in that observation. But ... where in Ashton, exactly, did this floozy accost you?

JOHN: It was Crab Street. I had no idea that the place had such a reputation. But thankfully a constable happened to walk by and was able to rescue me from the hideous wench. Carted her off to the police station.

WROE: 'Crab Street'?

JOHN: Apparently it is Ashton's centre for all manner of vice and prostitution. I had no idea of what occurs only several hundred yards from our Sanctuary!

WROE: *(Begins to laugh again)* Ga-hah! Oh, these Lancashire folks! Naming the place 'Crab Street'!

JOHN: I'm sorry, I don't follow…

WROE: You know, 'Crab Street'? [14]

WROE stares at JOHN, trying to fathom out John's true level of innocence.

WROE: Never mind, never mind. But yes. How much further into the pit of sin and inequity can the females fall? Even in this place that we always called the New Jerusalem!

JOHN: Indeed. And have you heard that many of the women are gibbering for their 'right to vote'? Surely the last hours must be at hand!

WROE: Ah, yes. The cry for the Charter is excessively strong in these parts. Although, the womenfolk are deluded if they think that their men will give them the vote.

JOHN: I have heard much the same myself from the lips of trade unionists.

WROE: They'd become milksops.

JOHN: Even the most radical of the trade association members realises that if women ever received the vote, they would soon expect an equal wage to men.

WROE: They'd be wanting to wear trousers next!

JOHN: They would neglect their domestic duties. They would spend all their time in the mills, earning good money, so that they could buy new petticoats and drink gin.

WROE: But speaking of our womenfolk, how goes your Sarah?

JOHN: *(Shakes his head)* It does not get any easier, Prophet. Once again, I have had to have strong words with her.

WROE: Challenging your authority again?

JOHN: Sadly, yes. She wanted to buy a red frock! When she knows full well that Christian Israelite women can only wear white or blue or yellow and …

---

[14] This is true. I discovered it after reading many editions of the Ashton Reporter from the 1870s. Crab Street was notorious as the place where Ashton's prostitutes touted for their business.

He stops speaking as ROBERT STANLEY, aged 10, enters. He is dressed neatly, but plainly. He does not appear to be a poor child, but his clothes are somewhat worn and dusty. He is whistling a tune and carrying a bucket.

JOHN: Ah now, here is our most faithful little friend of the Sanctuary. Robert - come and meet our Prophet.

ROBERT: I needed to …

JOHN: *(Frowning)* But why are you carrying a pail? It is still the Sabbath and we should not be working.

ROBERT: I know, I'm sorry. But I were needing to feed the horses. They're awful hungry and jittery after the storm.

JOHN: "Was," Robert, not "were". And it should be "awfully" hungry.

WROE: Ah, John – the boy is still young. He will learn his grammatical semantics at some point! So. How do you know Mr John Stanley, young Robert?

ROBERT: Well – he's my uncle! He brought me here to live in Ashton.

WROE: Ah.

ROBERT: But I've been wondering, Prophet, why don't I hear anyone at the Sanctuary talk much about building the walls around our 'New Jerusalem' anymore?

JOHN: Robert! Remember that children should be seen and not heard!

WROE: No, no - don't be harsh. Let the little children come to me, as Christ said. That's a good question, Robert.

ROBERT: *(Uncertainly)* Thank you.

WROE: But, let me question you first. Now. Do you know your scriptures?

ROBERT: Mostly. I think.

WROE: And how is your reading? And your writing?

ROBERT: Good. Even though I didn't have no schooling in Cardiff.

JOHN: "Any" schooling.

WROE: *(Ignoring him)* Go on.

ROBERT: Yes, er… I always played with my alphabet blocks. And I learned properly with my mam. She taught me through using my dad's newspaper.

WROE: Your father didn't help?

ROBERT: Well … he were – was – always very busy trying to sell his hats.

JOHN: (*Mostly to himself*) William's always been a fine one for escaping any form of responsibility, or any opportunity for self-improvement.

JOHN: And you attend classes here, don't you?

ROBERT: Yes. After I've finished work in the shop, I go to Mr Furness's school[15] on Oldham Street.

JOHN: Good, good.

ROBERT: And Uncle John pays for me to attend the Hebrew school here in Ashton. Although I sometimes wish I could go to the Hebrew school in Mottram.

WROE: Why's that?

ROBERT: Because the people in Mottram are always getting into scraps with the people of Glossop over the strikes[16]. And that'd be a spectacle to see!

JOHN: He talks too much.

WROE: Not at all, John! It is something of a spectacle to enjoy, witnessing the Catholics getting walloped – although I perhaps shouldn't really say that. But, Robert. Tell me, are you liking learning Hebrew?

ROBERT: I do. But not as much as working in the shop.

WROE: Ah. Your uncle's shop?

ROBERT: Yes. It's very enlightening for me, being in the shop. I learn an awful lot. About people and money and trading. But …

WROE: But?

ROBERT: But I think I should feel more enlightened if I could work in the Christian Israelites' printing press.

WROE: Well, being in print is a fine vocation.

---

[15] By 1839, a dozen private academies and day schools existed in Ashton. By 1844, working hours had been restricted for children, and those who still worked were required to attend schools. Francis Furness taught from Oldham Street, the street that Robert lived on.

[16] Hebrew schools existed in both Ashton and Mottram. There was huge animosity between the people of Glossop and its surrounding towns. This was because more paternalism existed between factory master and employee in Glossop, leading to accusations of strike-breaking.

ROBERT: If I could work in printing, I could help with telling people about the plans to build a New Jerusalem. So, don't you want to build it here anymore?

WROE: Ah, you're a persistent little one, aren't you?

JOHN: I do apologise, Yaakov …

WROE: No need. He has every right to ask. But you see, the problem is, Robert, the people of Ashton clearly do not want the New Jerusalem to be built here.

ROBERT: That's a sorry state of affairs.

WROE: *(Chuckles)* True, true. But I have prayed long and hard on this matter. And it has been revealed to me that, like Christ, a prophet can sometimes only shake the dust off his feet in one town and move onto another.

ROBERT: *"And Jesus said unto them, A prophet is not without honour, but in his own country, and among his own kin, and in his own house."* That's Mark 6, Verse 4, that is.

JOHN: He's right.

ROBERT: But I'd like to help with everything. To try and build the New Jerusalem here.

WROE: That's an admirable thought.

ROBRET: See, I can write letters in both Hebrew and English. And I'm always writing letters of protest to important people. If I could learn how to operate a printing press, I could help make the magazines for all of the Christian Israelites in England – and you wouldn't need to pay me.

WROE: *(Places his hand on ROBERT'S head)* You are a very tender-hearted boy.

JOHN: Aspirations are all very well, Robert, but it helps to keep one's feet firmly on the ground. I think you're better off in shop employment.

WROE: Not necessarily, John Stanley. Now, tell me Robert; letters, you say? To whom do you write letters?

ROBERT: Oh, to anyone that I have something to say to, really. I've written to the Queen. Nice letters to her. I like the Queen.

WROE: Well, well.

ROBERT: And to the Prime Minister.

WROE: Indeed?

ROBERT: And to the Archbishop of Canterbury, when I heard how much money Reverend Chetwode was taking from St Michael's here in Ashton.[17] How he does nothing to help the poor folk.

JOHN: *(Tetchily)* I think that this letter writing needs to stop, Robert. The letter to the Archbishop was the last straw.

WROE: Oh?

JOHN: Yes. Reverend Chetwode was very upset when he heard that someone from Ashton had complained about him to the head of the Church of England. He threatened never to return to a town of such ingratitude.

WROE: But this is quite the thing to hear, John Stanley! At the age of ten years old - to be taking such interest in advising his elders!

ROBERT: I don't think I'm advising them. I just try to … point out things.

WROE: As did a very young Jesus in Jersualem's Temple when he stayed behind to teach the priests!

JOHN: *(To himself)* I wonder if folk thought him a bit precocious too …

WROE: Well, we must bring you on with your learning, so far as we can. So, tell me, Robert; do you live here with your Uncle John now?

ROBERT: No – I live on Oldham Street with my brother, Jack, and his wife, Betty. Our Jack was sent up to Ashton from Cardiff before I was, for work.

JOHN: Things have not been easy for my brother. Too big a family. And beaver hats have fallen out of fashion.

WROE: So, you offered to help?

JOHN: Yes. To gain employment for his two oldest sons. And now Robert.

ROBERT: We're all very grateful. We live in two rooms over Uncle John's iron works.

WROE: And do you enjoy living there?

ROBERT: *(Carefully)* It's not as nice as Uncle John's house, of course. But our Jack said he wouldn't have me live anywhere else, as it was a matter of pride.

WROE: Ah.

---

[17] Ashton's parish church horribly neglected its local people, whilst its parish priest prospered considerably and lived in Buckinghamshire. See *His Own Man* (although there is no evidence that a young Robert ever wrote a letter of complaint to the Archbishop!)

JOHN: (*Rolling his eyes*) Jack's just like his father.

ROBERT: Yes. So, I have to share a room with Jack and Betty. I sleep on a mattress in their room. But sometimes, if Jack says to Betty "I'm feeling like a bit of 'ow's yer father'" and if she smiles instead of cuffing him, – which she does do every now and then…

JOHN: Very much like his father.

ROBERT: … Yes, on those days I have to sleep under the kitchen table, with the coats on top of me, to keep me warm.

WROE: Tsk, tsk. That won't do at all!

JOHN: I wasn't aware of that. That is … most unhygienic for the child.

ROBERT: There are mice in our house, too. I don't mind the mice, actually. It's the rats that I hate. I keep a knife with me and if they get too near, I try and stab them.

WROE: John – you must do something about this. What manner of employment is your nephew Jack engaged in?

JOHN: We attempted to bed him into the grocery trade, as we are doing with young Robert here. But he had a surly way with him around customers. Again, like …

WROE: … his father.

JOHN: Yes, I'm sorry to say. And he was a trifle too free with some of the young ladies who attend the shop. Remarkably like his …

WROE: (*Cutting him off*) So, tell me, Robert; does your brother like you to go to Sanctuary?

ROBERT: No. (*Shakes his head firmly*) He says father would be angry, too, if he knew. Because, Jack says, the Christian Israelites chased our parents out of this town for not having an approved-of marriage. Although I'm not sure what that means…

WROE: I see. So why do you attend?

ROBERT: I like the music. I like to sing. And I'm in the wind band. And it's splendid to look at, is our Sanctuary! Like Solomon's Temple. And it's warmer than our house.

WROE: A real Sanctuary for you then.

ROBERT: Yes … and also because on Sunday mornings Jack and Betty just stay in bed all day, because they've been at The Spread Eagle for most of the night. So, they never hear me leave. Or come back again.

WROE: This really will not do! Not do at all. John – what do you propose to do about this?

JOHN: I'll think on. I'll have a word with Jack.

WROE: Good. And now, Robert, we must think further about you becoming more officially involved with our church. Are you aware that your uncle here still retains the important duty of carrying out the prescribed ritual that weds a man to our church?

ROBERT: You mean the knife thing? I know that he has very sharp knives.

WROE: Yes, knives are certainly involved.

ROBERT: Because I wondered whether I could perhaps borrow one, so that I can stab a big fat rat right between the eyes when they come sniffing me in my sleep.

JOHN: Most certainly not, Robert. My knives are kept for the spiritual act of performing the holy rite of circumcision on our menfolk.[18]

WROE: John, have you not discussed with Robert that this is a most important ceremony to be undertaken if he wishes to continue to attend Sanctuary?

ROBERT: (*Shoving the bucket in front of his crotch*) I'm not having my knackers chopped off!

JOHN: (*Horrified*) Robert! Control yourself! Where on earth did you learn that sort of language?!

ROBERT: (*Gabbling*) Our Jack! He said … he said that you'd have my knackers off if I carried on going to the Sanctuary! But I tell you, I'm not having it!

JOHN: That's not what happens at all, Robert; circumcision is nothing to do with your knac – I mean to say …

WROE: … That the most ancient and holy ceremony of circumcision involves simply removing a piece of the end of a man's…

JOHN: Appendage.

WROE: Quite. You know what we mean by that, Robert?

ROBERT: I think so. The drainage end of the pipe? Not the knackers.

---

[18] All Christian Israelite men – as with Jews and Muslims – were circumcised. John Stanley and Henry Lees carried out this holy rite. There was some disquiet after an infant died following a circumcision by Henry Lees, but in court he was not found not guilty. *See His Own Man.*

JOHN: Erm…

ROBERT: It still sounds awful brutal to me. Just so that you can carry on going to church. And didn't that baby die of it?

JOHN: No, well … sadly, the child died, and the newspapers seized on the tale and neglected to give the full truth. The child had been a sickly one. His death was nothing whatsoever to do with the holy rite.

WROE: Most certainly!

ROBERT: It still sounds … very horrible to me.

WROE: (*Claps him on the back*) But we've all undergone it. And if you think about what the fragile female body has to bear - the simple act of childbirth, for example, can bring excruciating pain and anguish and often death for a woman.

ROBERT: They're always dying of that, the women. Left, right and centre!

WROE: Precisely. So, surely a little snip of an unfeeling smidgen of your body is something that a real man can face up to.

JOHN: And we have laudanum, of course.

WROE: Yes, yes. Although, when I insisted on the rite being performed on me, it took place with no laudanum whatsoever, in the river Medlock in front of a crowd of hundreds.

ROBERT: Were women there when you had it done? Did they watch it?

WROE: Oh yes – we informed them beforehand and those who were the most liable to faint…

ROBERT: To faint?!

WROE: I mean – those females who are delicate-minded and who drop down at the hint of a mere nosebleed, they averted their faces in their bonnets.

ROBERT: Oh. But I wouldn't want ladies to watch me, if I had it done.

JOHN: There would be no women present at your ceremony, Robert.

ROBERT: But … (*his bucket is remaining firmly in front of his crotch*) I still don't understand why the Lord would want me to have my knack – I mean, my smidgen bit cut off.

JOHN: (*Rallies himself*) It is an ancient and holy ritual. The act of circumcision is what separates the Lord's chosen people from the Gentiles.

WROE: The Lord revealed himself to me that we should follow the very same practises that the Jews have done for thousands of years.

JOHN: And Christ himself was a Jew, so he would also have undergone the holy operation. So, would you argue with the basics of the Abrahamic faiths, Robert?

ROBERT: No...

WROE: Speaking of the Abrahamic faiths, Robert, were you aware that beside the Jews there are others who say that they follow Abraham's religion?

ROBERT: No.

WROE: Yes. They call themselves "Islam-followers" Or "Muhammedans". Sometimes "Mussulmen". And their menfolk also practise circumcision, you see?

ROBERT: I've never heard of those sorts of people.

WROE: They are eastern peoples. But I have met them in London and talked with them. They are a very clever breed.

JOHN: And as our empire grows and our cotton trade increases, I am encountering them more and more in Manchester, in the trading halls.

WROE: Indeed?

JOHN: Yes – it's looking as though we might well be swamped by them soon!

WROE: But they bring good money into the country.

JOHN: They certainly know a thing or two about business. They wear flowing robes, Robert, as they come from a hot climate. Many that I have met are from the land of the Turks. Others are from further east.

WROE: And like us Christian Israelites, they also refuse to eat pig meat and all other manner of food deemed to be unholy to God. Some of them also have more than one wife.

JOHN: Perish the thought. But my, they are colourful sorts. The men wear beards and sometimes an earring. And they enjoy swords and other such weaponry. I have seen some of them keep pet monkeys.

WROE: They are, in the main, a very peaceable and prosperous manner of person. They bring much interest and colour to the streets of Manchester.

ROBERT: I should like to see their swords. And especially any monkeys. And read more about them. I should like to have more books to read.

WROE: Such keenness to learn! But master the scriptures thoroughly first. And your Hebrew.

JOHN: Yes. *(Putting a hand on ROBERT'S shoulder)* One thing at a time. We shall talk further about you undertaking the rite, yes?

ROBERT: *(Somewhat reluctantly)* I suppose so.

WROE: Good. That is settled. Now. Are you joining us for lunch, Robert?

ROBERT: I should see to clearing up the yard after the storm.

JOHN: It is the Sabbath, Robert. It can be left for tomorrow. Come along, lad. I believe that Sarah has organised for us to enjoy a cheese pie.

ROBERT: I'm not particularly fond of cheese. But today I'd be glad of that. Betty cooks beef sausages for us of a Sunday.

WROE: Good boy. Precisely the sort of thing our Christian Israelites rules prohibit.

ROBERT: It's not that so much, Prophet.

WROE: Oh?

ROBERT: No. *(Looks down at the bucket, still in front of his crotch)*. I couldn't stomach even looking at a sausage, after what we've just been talking about.

---ENDS---

5. AN ARRESTING REVEREND

CONTEXT

In 1839, Britain was suffering from yet another economic downturn. The worst affected were the poor in northern England's cotton towns who worked in highly dangerous conditions, faced insecure employment and received paltry wages. The newly formed trade unions in Ashton and Stalybridge tried to use strike action against the factory owners in their call for 'a fair day's wage for a fair day's work'. This new 'popular radicalism' merged with the demands from the Chartists – those who wanted voting reform and the enfranchisement of the working classes. Long before Robert Stanley came to live in Ashton at the age of ten, the Reverend Joseph Rayner Stephens from Dukinfield had achieved national notoriety for his fiery rhetoric against the hated Poor Laws and the appalling conditions faced by working people. In November 1838, Stephens was arrested for sedition – in relation to words spoken by him at a Chartist meeting - where he was accused of inciting violence amongst the working classes. The Chartist groups were increasingly demonstrating acts of aggression, as they practised military manoeuvres with pikes and home-made weapons. Local people were horrified at Stephen's arrest and outraged when their hero was sent to prison for a year a few months later.

Joseph Rayner Stephens

At the time of Stephens's sentencing in August 1839, Robert was living with his older brother Jack and Jack's wife Betty, just around the corner from Robert's place of work at Uncle John's Christian Israelite shop on Stamford Street. The two brothers would have been acutely aware of the miserable plight of the poor in the area and of the anger directed towards the cruel factory owners. But they would also have felt a sense of obligation towards their rich industrialist uncle - John Stanley – who had taken them under his wing and provided jobs for them both.

ASHTON-UNDER-LYNE, 16ᵗʰ AUGUST 1839

A DAMP SUMMER'S MORNING IN A SPARSELY FURNISHED ROOM ABOVE JOHN STANLEY'S IRON WORKS IN ASHTON. THIS IS JACK AND BETTY STANLEY'S HOUSE. **JACK STANLEY**, AGED 21, IS A GOOD-LOOKING YOUNG MAN AND IS NOW UNCLE JOHN STANLEY'S BOOKKEEPER. HE IS WEARING A CHEAPLY MADE – BUT RESPECTABLE ENOUGH – WOOLLEN SUIT. WHILST WAITING FOR HIS BREAKFAST, HE READS FROM A CRUMPLED NEWSPAPER. **BETTY STANLEY**, AGED 21, WEARS A DRAB, GREY MILL-WORKER'S DRESS, BUT CRACKLES WITH ENERGY. SHE IS STIRRING A POT OF PORRIDGE ON THE STOVE, IN BETWEEN MAKING THE TEA.

JACK: Betty, have you moved my knife? I put it on the mantlepiece last night.
BETTY: Oh, you were that exhausted you probably … Oh, hello Master Sleepyhead!

A bleary-eyed boy enters the room. ***ROBERT STANLEY****, aged 11, is of average height, dark-haired and serious looking. He is smoothing his clothes out, although they barely need it. He is rather meticulous about his776 appearance.*

ROBERT: Morning. Ooh, I'm starving.
BETTY: You always are, growing lads like you. Did you get any sleep last night? I hardly got a wink. All of that yelling!
JACK: Ey-oop – why're you mixing those oats with water, Betty?
BETTY: Ran out of milk.
JACK: Urgh. I hate porridge made with water. Robert, have you been guzzlin' the milk again?
ROBERT: No more than usual.
JACK: That'll be a 'yes', then. Well, you'll be having cement porridge for breakfast. Serves you right.

ROBERT: Dad used to say it 'sticks to yer ribs' when you make it without milk.

JACK: Aye, well, I'd hoped those days were over, when I lived with a family that didn't have enough pennies to buy enough milk for porridge.

BETTY: Oh, stop moaning. You can wait until Mr Shuttleworth delivers tomorrow. I'm sure you survived worse when you were in Cardiff.

JACK: That reminds me, Robert; have you emptied out the slops?

ROBERT: Oh, sorry. I forgot.

BETTY: No, don't worry about that, Robert, I can…

JACK: *(Flapping his hand at her)*. No, let him do it. A child needs to learn responsibilities in life.

ROBERT leaves the room and calls over his shoulder to his brother.

ROBERT: *(Off-stage)* I'm eleven! I've got a job! I'm not a child!

BETTY: *(Stirring pan of porridge on the stove)* Don't you think that the poor lad has earned enough responsibilities in life? He's left his parents and all of his friends; he works all of the hours God sends. And now he's being forced to chuck out your slops!

JACK: *Our* slops.

BETTY: No – yours! I can make it through the night without having to go and do a tinkle, because I…

JACK: Don't drink beer, dear.

BETTY: Exactly.

JACK: Anyway, Robert always got the slops job in Cardiff. Don't think he minds it.

ROBERT enters the room again.

JACK: Done already? You must have run with it. Hope you didn't spill it all over yourself.

ROBERT: No, there wasn't any slops in it after all.

JACK: Oh, aye, I forgot. Went to the privy in the middle of the night instead, when I went outside to see what was what.

ROBERT: It was all very foolish. Grown-ups behaving like that. It was ridiculous. Men brawling outside the window about poor Reverend Stephens going to prison. I barely slept. (*Yawns*)

JACK: (*Mimicking ROBERT*) 'All very foolish'! 'Ridiculous'!

BETTY: I know. I heard you huffing and puffing all night. (*To JACK*) And it doesn't help that he's still sleeping on the coats in the corner of the room.

JACK: Could be worse. He could be on the streets like plenty of other kids 'round here.

BETTY: No - you've got to sort out getting him a proper mattress off your Uncle John. It's not fair.

JACK: John's got enough on his plate without fussing about Robert and a mattress. Aunt Sarah's having one of her episodes again.

BETTY: I know. Mrs Barnsley told me.

JACK: Who the 'eck's Mrs Barnsley?

BETTY: She's their cook, Jack. Or was. Sarah's gone and sacked her. Claimed she was trying to poison her or something. You never listen to 'owt that I say.

JACK: Well, you say that much, I can't keep track of it all.

BETTY: So, they've only a housemaid now after Sarah gave Mrs Barnsley her marching orders. It can't be easy for them.

JACK: (*Clutches his chest*) Oh, my heart bleeds for them.

BETTY: (*Ignoring him*) It must be tricky for your Uncle John when she's not so well.

JACK: Not so well! She's gone loopy! Ever since her Hannah ran off with our Strongi'th'arm! The woman's not much more than an imbecile these days!

BETTY: Aye, but it's a terrible thing … your daughter running off and marrying her cousin. Without your permission.

JACK: We've always married cousins in our family. I can't see why it bothered her so much. Anyway, it was a year ago, all of that. They're back here living down the road. John's accepted it.

BETTY: I think it's the shame of their baby being born so soon …

JACK: More likely that Uncle John thought Strongi'th'arm wasn't good enough - what with him being a common bookkeeper.

BETTY: It's queer thinking to me, that the son of your own brother isn't good enough for your daughter! (*Takes the newspaper from him*) I'll have that now you've done with it. Need some kindling.

JACK: Forgotten where he's come from, has John Stanley. He was a cordwainer himself - and a joiner - before becoming Mr Iron and Mr Coal and making his fortune from that.

ROBERT: *(With a mouthful of porridge)* Uncle John must have a poor memory, because he's always telling me what jobs he used to have. To work his way up. He tells me time and again.

JACK: Huh. Lords it over us all. Thinks none of us are good enough.

BETTY: Well, maybe you should be grateful, Jack. If your cousins hadn't run off together then you'd still be an apprentice bookkeeper. You did end up with Strongi'th'arm's job, after all.[19]

JACK: I'm sure that my natural talents would have caused John to notice me.

BETTY: Big head. But as well as that, if you hadn't been moved into Strongi'th'arm's job you'd never have met me on the factory floor!

JACK: Well now, that means that Strongi'th'arm's ruined my life too!

BETTY: Cheeky swine! *(Raps him over the head with the newspaper)*

ROBERT: Actually, I think Aunt Sarah is getting a bit better now.

BETTY: Aye?

ROBERT: Because she doesn't say that Hannah's baby is 'the spawn of the devil' anymore.

JACK: Then she's still a moron. It's a pig-ugly bairn, that one.

ROBERT: She usually seems quite … calm … for someone a bit …

BETTY: *(Completing his sentence for him).* 'Feeble-minded.'

ROBERT: Yes. I go 'round there and chat to her quite a bit.

BETTY: Do you? What do you chat about?

ROBERT: Usually just about things we've seen in the encyclopaedias.

JACK: In the what?

ROBERT: Aunt Sarah's encyclopaedias. She has a very fine set. She lets me go there and read them after I've finished work.

---

[19] Robert's much older cousin, John Strongi'th'arm (yes, this is a real name!) eloped with his other cousin, Hannah - daughter of Uncle John and Sarah Stanley. During this period it was not particularly contentious for cousins to marry, but given that the couple had to elope, it indicates that there was more than a whiff of scandal or disapproval. Either way, they soon returned to Ashton and John Stanley put Strongi'th'arm in charge of several of his businesses.

JACK: Well, that'll be half the problem! John's let her have her own set of encyclopaedias – women don't need any dafter notions than they're already born with.

BETTY: *(Ignoring him)* Does she have much to say for herself, Robert?

ROBERT: Not much ... Sometimes she sings.

BETTY: *(Has set the kindling in place and begins sweeping the fireplace)* What does she sing?

ROBERT: Hymns mostly.

BETTY: That's nice.

ROBERT: Yes, but she changes the words.

JACK: How d'yer mean?

ROBERT: She sort of uses the tune of a hymn to the words of the encyclopaedia.

BETTY: In what way?

ROBERT: Well ... instead of singing, 'Come, ye disconsolate, where'er ye languish, come to the mercy seat, fervently kneel' she'll sing - to the same tune - 'Our feathered friends of the Serengeti are over 850 known species and they exist on a diet mainly of insects'.

BETTY: That's ... unusual.

ROBERT: She's got over 50 hymns, well, 'songs' like that now... She's memorised half of the encyclopaedias, I think.

BETTY: *(Empties the shovel into the fireplace)* Well, she's probably had the time, being shut up in that house on her own all day.

ROBERT: She's very clever for doing that. Fitting the words to the tunes is quite a challenge.

JACK: I bet John loves being serenaded like that of an evening. What a lark!

BETTY: The poor woman.

JACK: 'Poor woman?' She's had a very nice life compared to most, thank you very much.

BETTY: A gilded cage more like.

JACK: What d'yer mean?

BETTY: Marrying your Uncle John so young - him being so involved with the Christian Israelite thing. Having to watch John shove her children's inheritance in building that stupid Sanctuary church. And then all of that rioting that happened because of their prophet. Enough to send anyone round the bend.

JACK: He was a mucky old devil. That Wroe.

BETTY: *(Takes her coat off a peg and picks cotton fluff off it)* It's right damp out there this morning. You'd never have thought it was August.

JACK: Still can't believe he comes over here from Wakefield to preach. Dirty old devil.[20]

BETTY: None of that was ever proven …

JACK: No smoke without fire. Bunch of idiots, the lot of 'em.

BETTY: I'm sick of people being cruel about the Christian Israelites. Their way isn't my cup of tea, but people should be a bit more open minded towards them.

JACK: Open-minded! A load of odd bods, that lot, what with their beards and their weird food.

BETTY: They do no-one any harm. And they're always helping the poor. Just because they choose not to cavort around the Spread Eagle or wherever…

JACK: Another reason I can't be doing with them. They don't drink booze! Think they're a cut above everyone else …

BETTY: People are just jealous of them all because they're just happy in their own ways.

JACK: Lunatics are always happy, dribbling away in their corners.

BETTY: And they're kind business people too. Your Uncle John pays a good wage and his shops always charge fair prices.

ROBERT: *(Interrupting)* What *did* happen with Prophet Wroe? No-one's ever explained it properly to me.

BETTY: Well…

ROBERT: Whenever I've met him, he's always been awfully kind to me. And Uncle John won't have a bad word said about him.

JACK: Well, Uncle John was probably involved in it all himself. Probably hoping for a nice virgin or two under his own roof …

BETTY: Jack!

ROBERT: Aunt Sarah doesn't like the prophet very much.

BETTY: Hmm. I heard they never really got on.

ROBERT: Is it because the prophet took our cousins' inheritance? To build the Sanctuary and his own houses?

BETTY: *(Hands Robert his coat)* Here, you'd best wear it, the sky's looking a bit…

---

[20] Jack is referring to the Seven Virgins scandal. See previous scenes for more, as well as *His Own Man*.

ROBERT: (*To himself*) Yes, I think it's because of the inheritance.

BETTY: Well, some grown-ups just don't see eye-to-eye. Personalities. That sort of thing.[21]

JACK: Rubbish, woman. No 'probablys' about it! Our Uncle John went and spent nine thousand five hundred pounds on that ruddy Sanctuary![22] Money that should have come to his own kids! Not to mention the rest of his family.

BETTY: Ah. (*Wags her finger at him*) Were you hoping for a bit of it for yourself?

JACK: Well, you'd have done nicely out of it too! But no. He goes and squanders it on pews and organs and hymn books and silver fittings and what-not.

BETTY: People can spend their money on whatever's important to them. You spend enough of ours on beer, after all.

JACK: At least I don't waste it on a bunch of delusional nutters who think that Jesus Christ is all ready and waiting to pop up in some Ashton backstreet.

ROBERT: Aunt Sarah doesn't go to Sanctuary anymore. But I still enjoy going there myself.

JACK: Well, you're as barmy as that lot, then.

BETTY: Robert can worship wherever he likes. You're not the Pope, Jack.

JACK: Not the Pope! That's a good one, woman.

ROBERT: I once said John Wroe's name to her … to Aunt Sarah … and she turned 'round and started biting the back of her armchair. Bit a proper hole in it, she did. So, I've not said it since.

BETTY: No. Best not to, then.

ROBERT: I wonder if she heard all of the commotion last night, over Reverend Stephens being sent to prison?

BETTY: Well, if she didn't, Robert, you're best not raising the issue. It could set her off again.

ROBERT: No … I'd not want to do that.

BETTY: And Jack, I'm still not happy you took Robert with you last night to watch it all. We're meant to be looking after him.

JACK: I didn't take him.

ROBERT: No, I followed him.

---

[21] Wroe lambasted Sarah Stanley in his personal diaries. See the 'Escaping Sanctuary' scene and *His Own Man*.
[22] Half a million pounds in today's prices.

BETTY: That was naughty of you, Robert!

ROBERT: Sorry. I just wanted to see …

JACK: You're not sorry. You shouldn't apologise if you're not really sorry.

ROBERT: I am! I mean – I don't want to be a cause for inconvenience for you, Betty. But I *am* eleven now and …

BETTY: (*Ruffling his hair*) Ah, listen to him with his 'cause for inconvenience', bless him … but – oi! What on earth!

BETTY suddenly yanks ROBERT'S head down hard, examining it.

ROBERT: Yooowww! Ooow – nooo. Betty! I'm going to be late if you start doing that…

BETTY: I *told* you not to play with the McGregors; they're always crawling with lice … they're proper ragamuffins, they …

ROBERT: I don't play with them! It'll be from when I was down in the dirt and fighting with that Seamus McGregor again. He was calling me 'Taffy-Boyo' and I lost my temper …

BETTY: Ooh … it's going to be a terror and a half to get this lot out. You can't go to work with a head like this! Your Uncle John will have you out on your ear!

JACK: I hope you kicked his arse, Robert!

ROBERT: (*Looking from BETTY to JACK*) Who? Uncle John?

JACK: Ha – no! Seamus McGregor. Bloody gypsies. Bloody Irish.

BETTY ignores him and fetches a comb; she starts sectioning ROBERT'S hair and removing the nits, wiping them onto a handkerchief placed on the table.

BETTY: Irish and gypsies aren't the same thing, Jack. Anyway, Robert – the next time someone picks a fight with you, fetch a policeman.

ROBERT: Well, there's certainly a lot more policemen here, compared to Cardiff.

JACK: Place is crawling with them now. Government thinks this is the most dangerous town in the country.

ROBERT: There were lots of the bobbies there last night. I was worried some of the Chartists would stab them with their pikes.

BETTY: You should never have gone outside…

ROBERT: Look, Betty, I'm going to be late…

JACK: Anyway, 'fetch a policeman'! That's a fine way to tell a kid to defend himself! Give Seamus McGregor a good battering, I say!

ROBERT: I'd rather not batter anyone. I'm trying the tactic of just crossing over the other side of the street when I see him.

BETTY: Good boy.

JACK: I'll batter him for you. I'd happily kick an Irish black and blue.

BETTY: Oh, hush up, going on about the Irish. Right … that's ten nits and counting - no crawlers yet, thank God.

JACK: I'll go on about the Irish if I want to. They come over here and nick all of our jobs.

BETTY: Says a Welshman who moved up here for work.

JACK: That's different. Our family were from up here to begin with.

BETTY: Well, they hardly nick *your* job! They're mostly navvies and labourers!

JACK: There'll be more of 'em over here before you know it. Mark my words.[23]

BETTY threatens to flick her collection of nits at JACK. He grimaces and shuts up.

BETTY: (*To ROBERT*) Stop moving your head, I can't get these things.

ROBERT: I don't want to be late!

BETTY: We got up early and the town clock hasn't even struck quarter-past yet. You'll be fine.

JACK stands and stretches, reaching for his coat.

BETTY: Now you've shifted your bum, you can sort us our butties out.

JACK: Making dinners is women's work.

---

[23] Eight years later the Great Hunger ('Irish Potato Famine') began and both Ashton and Stalybridge experienced a massive influx of Irish immigration. Nearly 50 per cent of Stalybridge's population were Irish by 1869, when the anti-Catholic Murphy Riots took place in the area.

BETTY: Well, if you prefer, you can take your brother's nits out instead.

JACK: Oh, alright. What do I do?

BETTY: *(Exasperated)* 'What do I do?' You just slice some bread there and put it in our pockets.

JACK: Cheese?

BETTY: Run out.

JACK: Robert!

ROBERT: Sorry.

BETTY: Just bread is fine.

JACK: It's not a bloody butty if there's nowt in it!

BETTY: Oh… just pretend. That's what I'll be doing.

JACK: *(Slicing bread)* You have to ask yourself; if we can barely feed ourselves with three wages and only three people … how the hell can the Irish feed their families? Breed like rabbits they do.

BETTY: Says you, coming from a family of ten.

ROBERT: I like having so many brothers and sisters. I write to them all of the time. They're not very good at writing back to me, though.

BETTY: I'm sure you do miss them, chickie. It's hard when you come from a big family and you have to leave … *(To JACK, who is stuffing slices of bread into his coat)* Not straight in your pockets! Honestly!

JACK: What then?

BETTY: You wrap them in newspaper first.

JACK: What's the point?

BETTY: Think of the crumbs! It'll be me having to clean out your pockets again. Bad enough that; I have to wash your … Robert! Will you stop moving your head about?!

ROBERT: *(Dreamily)* Yes, I'd like to have an enormous family one day.

BETTY: Well. You'd best get your wife's permission for that.

ROBERT: Why?

BETTY: Well. Not every woman wants to have as many children as … as your own mother did.

ROBERT: I don't see why not. And anyway, the Bible says, 'Go forth and multiply'.

JACK: Huh. (*He has now wrapped the bread and stuffs it into each of their pockets*) Well, the Bible obviously doesn't count for the fact that some of us have to put up with our little brother sleeping on the floor next to them every night.

BETTY: Jack …

JACK: Fat chance I'd have to go forth and multiply.

BETTY: Robert doesn't need to hear that sort of thing.

JACK: Robert doesn't get to hear any sort of thing. That's half the problem!

BETTY: Oh - will you just shut your gob for a bit! Robert's a lot more … religiously minded than you are. And he doesn't need …

ROBERT: Actually, even though I'm not a Methodist, I think that Reverend Stephens is my favourite. He was famous even when I was in Wales.

BETTY: True. He's a good 'un. Proper man of the people.

JACK: Rayner Stephens has never been my favourite. But, still. Giving him eighteen months. Bit harsh. No wonder they were trying to riot last night.

ROBERT: I like what he writes. He makes sense. Although perhaps he could do with using fewer words.

BETTY: When have you been reading what Reverend Stephens says?

ROBERT: (*Airily*) Oh, I read the newspapers, you know. And I heard him speaking to the workers, out in George Square, one dinnertime. And I met him once.

JACK: You met him?

ROBERT: In the shop. Hurry up, Betty. He wanted some brown boot polish. I told him that I agreed with him on many things. Although not all.

BETTY: Blimey, that was a bit forward of you, Robert.

ROBERT: That's what Uncle John said. Uncle had come into the shop to check on Mr Magnus again – what with him … and the misappropriation of flour. Possibly.

JACK: (*Proudly*) I was the first to spot that, when I was going through John's books. Definitely on the fiddle, that one.

BETTY: Maybe. But you don't repeat what your brother just said, Robert. Until …

ROBERT: I won't. Innocent until proven guilty. But yes, Uncle overheard me talking to the reverend and said, 'Robert - I don't think that you should be so forward with our customers.'

BETTY: So, what did you do?

ROBERT: I said that I was sorry.

BETTY: Good.

ROBERT: But the reverend just laughed and said I was a very fine boy. And that he was charmed to hear that I could read so well.

BETTY: That was kind.

ROBERT: He said that it was probably because I was a Welsh lad, and that the Welsh had a far healthier respect for learning and for the Lord than other nations do.

JACK: Huh. Clearly never been to the valleys, then.

ROBERT: And then Uncle John said, 'I do hope, Reverend, that you've not felt the need to pop in and check that I'm overworking any children in my businesses.'

JACK: Heh.

ROBERT: Yes. And then Uncle said, 'Because, my young employees only work from seven until three and after that they go to Mr Furness's school, for which I pay their fees.'

BETTY: What did the reverend say?

ROBERT: Oh, he said, 'Not at all, Mr Stanley; I've heard much about how well you look after your employees. I only wish that there were more masters like you in these towns.'

BETTY: Bet John liked that!

ROBERT: He seemed to smile.

JACK: More likely he had wind.

ROBERT: And then the reverend said, 'You Christian Israelites lead by example. You've had a hard press ... and despite it all you have come through and have the respect of most townsfolk.'

BETTY: Well now. If only more reverends were as generous about other churches. I might bother going myself!

ROBERT: And then the reverend asked me – seeing as though I liked reading and writing so much - would I like to write some tales of what it's like to be a working boy. For his newspaper.

BETTY: Blimey.

ROBERT: Yes. He said that Mrs Stephens makes a very fine jam roly-poly and I would be most welcome to have afternoon tea with them.

BETTY: How lovely! See, (*to JACK*) I told you that he was a good man!

JACK: *(Frowning)* Not sure about that. He was probably trying to bribe my little brother with jam roly-poly for his own political ends.

BETTY: Don't be silly.

JACK: Getting Robert to write 'tales of woe by a working boy forced to survive by eating brown boot polish,' or something.

ROBERT: I really wanted to go, too, but after he'd gone, Uncle John said that under no circumstances was I to go to the parsonage.

BETTY: Oh?

ROBERT: He said that Reverend Stephens was an insurrectionist. That sooner or later the law would catch up with him.

JACK: Well, he was right enough about that.

ROBERT: But I don't think that the reverend would have gone 'round telling men to kill others so that they can get the vote.

BETTY: And I'm with you on that one, Robert. I don't think he did.

ROBERT: Well, whatever Uncle John thinks about writing for newspapers, I'd like to do that. One day.

BETTY: You could do worse things than that in life.

ROBERT: Yes. Oh, hurry up Betty. But also, when I'm older, I'm going to see to it that everyone has to read the papers. So, they know what's really happening in the world.

BETTY: Your opinions, Robert! I think that you should go into politics with them! I'd vote for you.

ROBERT: But you can't. Females can't vote.

BETTY: True – although if it were up to the Chartists, I could.

JACK: Another good reason not to encourage the buggers.

BETTY: Jack!

JACK: Be the ruin of us all, the day they let the lasses cast their mark.

The clock strikes outside

ROBERT: Have you done? Please, Betty, I'm…

BETTY: Yes, yes – go on. I'll check you for any more tonight. At least it'll stay light until late and I'll be able to see what I'm doing.

BETTY wipes the comb on a piece of paper and throws the paper onto the fire. ROBERT *is finally liberated. He jumps up off his chair, dashes to her and kisses her.*

ROBERT: Thank you, Betty. I appreciate your attentiveness.
BETTY: (*Chuckles*) You and your words.
ROBERT: Bye. If I run, I'll make it on time.
BETTY: Yes – but if you do go and visit your Aunt Sarah after work, don't mention what happened last night. With Rayner Stephens.
JACK: Ah, Betty - she must have heard it all from her window. I bet it'll have driven her batty. Battier.
ROBERT: No, I won't mention it. She likes Reverend Stephens. That's something else she says Uncle John argues with her about. Oh, and Jack…?
JACK: What?
ROBERT: I'm sorry; I took your knife last night. I was a bit worried going to sleep after all of the marching.
JACK: Thieving little tyke!
ROBERT: It was just a temporary acquisition. And it sounded like someone was trying to kick the door down at the end of the street.

ROBERT takes the knife from his pocket and passes it to JACK.

JACK: Hmm. Well. (*Examines the knife*) Points for honesty, I suppose.
ROBERT: Yes. I'm glad I remembered. It wouldn't be a good idea to have it on me when I go to see Aunt Sarah.
BETTY: Why?
ROBERT: Well, she's getting rather morbid.
BETTY: Oh?
ROBERT: Yes, she keeps telling me that she thinks Uncle John is trying to kill her by dabbing arsenic on the pages of her encyclopaedia.
BETTY: Blimey.

ROBERT: And … John keeps all of their knives in a locked box now.

BETTY: Oh dear.

ROBERT: So, she's been asking me if I have anything sharp from home that I can bring for her.

JACK: *(Slapping his forehead)* See what I mean! Women and books! Dangerous combination!

---ENDS---

6. A WEDDING TO PLEASE ALL

CONTEXT

In October 1847, Robert Stanley and Emma Meredith were married. Uncle John Stanley's first wife, Sarah, had died in 1845 and just a few weeks later he married Mary Deane. Mary was some 28 years younger than him and they immediately started a new family together. Prophet John Wroe now based himself at a new mansion in Wakefield, but he was still on the scene in Ashton, performing marriages and sermons at the Sanctuary.

John Stanley's shop is a few buildings up, on the right hand side

Although we know nothing at all about how Robert and Emma met, we do know that Emma was working as a live-in domestic servant, that she was originally from Tewkesbury and that her father was a bricklayer.

Robert and Emma married at the Christian Israelites' Sanctuary. They may have been familiar with attending there already, or perhaps Robert felt obliged to marry at the opulent church that his uncle had personally funded. As soon as the couple were married, Robert left his job at Uncle John's Stamford Street Christian Israelite shop and they moved to Stalybridge where Robert set up his own grocer's. Given that he was only 20 and his parents had no money themselves, it seems likely that his new home and business was funded by a rather generous Uncle John.

This extract is an illustration of what it might have been like when the two families met each other and some of the experiences that the young couple might have faced.

ASHTON-UNDER-LYNE, OCTOBER 1847

THE RECEPTION ROOM OF JOHN STANLEY'S HOME, NUMBER NINE PARK PARADE, ASHTON. ALTHOUGH A VERY GRAND HOME, IT IS NOT OSTENTATIOUS IN ITS FURNISHINGS; THE CHAIRS AND SIDE-TABLES ARE OF PLAIN MAHOGANY WITH NO EMBELLISHMENT. THERE ARE NO PAINTINGS ON THE WALLS. **EMMA MEREDITH, AGED 21,** IS A SMALL WOMAN WITH LARGE, EXPRESSIVE EYES AND AUBURN CURLS. SHE IS WEARING A SUNNY, YELLOW DRESS AND HAS MADE A SPECIAL EFFORT TO LOOK PRESENTABLE TODAY. SHE HAS BEEN TRYING TO LOOK IN ONE OF THE WINDOWS IN ORDER TO SEE HER REFLECTION (MIRRORS ARE NOT ALLOWED IN A CHRISTIAN ISRAELITE HOME) AND SHE JUMPS AS ROBERT ENTERS THE ROOM. **ROBERT STANLEY, AGED 19,** IS A LANKY, DARK-HAIRED LAD. HE LOOKS PALE AND WASHED OUT AS HE SEMI-STUMBLES INTO THE ROOM, TRIPPING OVER A DOORSTOP.

EMMA: Robert! Whatever is the matter? Oh … it's not like you to be unshaven!

ROBERT: *(Slaps his face)* Oh, blimey oh riley! I forgot … I didn't get to sleep until nearly four. I've overslept. I had to run here …

EMMA: Never mind.

ROBERT: *(Rubbing his cheeks)* But they'll both be here any minute!

EMMA: Not to worry. It's not the end of the world. But why were you up so late?

ROBERT: A terrible night. A gang of vagabonds attacked us on our way back from Manchester.

EMMA: No! You and your Uncle John?

ROBERT: Yes. We spent half the night at the police station at Openshaw.

EMMA: Were you hurt?

ROBERT No. They were just a gang of idiotic youths. Hijacked the coach.

EMMA: Hijacked! How?

ROBERT: We'd finished Uncle John's business in the Corn Exchange and then he said he was going to treat me to dinner at one of the Jewish taverns. So, it was dark by the time we set off back up the Ashton Road.

EMMA: I suppose that was nice of him. The dinner.

ROBERT: I think it was more to do with him hoping to get back home *after* Mary had gone to bed with the baby. He's a bit too old for crying babies these days.

EMMA: Hmm. She's struggling a bit with her first, isn't she?

ROBERT: And it's set to get worse, what with another… *(Stops himself)*

EMMA: Ah. *(Diplomatically changes the subject)* So, these lads?

ROBERT: Eight of them. One of them dashed in front of the carriage then pretended he'd been stomped on by one of the horses. And then the others swarmed the coach. Grabbed the reigns from Mr Miller. Thumped him on the head.

EMMA: The poor fellow!

ROBERT: He was alright. Proper thick skull, Mr Miller. Been kicked by horses on the noggin that many times.

EMMA: Even so …

ROBERT: Bundled Miller in the coach with us and then they drove us down some pitch-black side street.

EMMA: It's scary down Openshaw. Even in the daytime.

ROBERT: I know. Well, then they started demanding to know who we were. Two of them had pikes – threatened to shove them right through John if he didn't cough up.

EMMA: Pikes! Like the things the Chartists keep parading about with?

ROBERT: Yes. But they didn't seem to be Chartists. Although you can never tell with that lot.

EMMA: You must have been terrified!

ROBERT: Not really. I felt bad for Uncle John, though. Dad always says that Uncle John is as meek as a lamb when it comes to a bit of fisticuffs.

EMMA: Did they rob you?

ROBERT: Unfortunately. Obviously seemed to think that they were a Manchester version of Dick Turpin.

EMMA: The rotten cowards.

ROBERT: Well, the funny thing was that we had practically no money at all between the two of us! I'd not taken any with me. And John had spent nearly all of his on the dinner and the ale.

EMMA: The ale? But your Uncle John doesn't drink!

ROBERT: Well... I think he probably does ... now. Since Mary and the baby...

EMMA: Oh.

ROBERT: So, John only had a few pennies to give them. They ended up getting more out of poor old Miller than us. The daft a'poth was travelling with half of his weekly wages on him.

EMMA: That's dreadful.

ROBERT: Anyway, their ringleader ... he seemed to think himself a bit of a revolutionary. Saying that it was toffs like John who treated the working people of Manchester like shi ... like dirt on his shoes.

EMMA: Goodness.

ROBERT: They took John's watch and his hat. Luckily, he didn't have his wedding ring on. He'd been letting the baby play with it earlier on in the day.

EMMA: That was a bit ...

ROBERT: Fortunate!

EMMA: Well, that's not what I was going to say, exactly ...

ROBERT: *(Not picking up on her meaning.)* Well, Mary had gone crackers at him over it - shouted at him - saying the baby had nearly swallowed it. So, he'd left the house, forgetting to put it back on.

EMMA: Losing your wedding ring would have been awful. I hope I never lose mine!

ROBERT: You won't.

EMMA: You ... you have bought it by now, haven't you, Robert?

ROBERT: *(Takes her hand and kisses it)* Don't you worry about that. Luckily, I'd decided not to buy it in Manchester. I didn't want to be walking around with that in my pocket on some of those streets.

EMMA: Very sensible. So, what did they do then?

ROBERT: Well. We sat there for a bit, them trying to needle us. Going on about 'you toffs'. You know what the lower classes are like. Trying to grab a bit of power whenever they can.

EMMA: How did your Uncle John deal with it?

ROBERT: Not well. Thing is, he's not used to insolence and rough treatment. Because he's always so ... good ... to his workers.

EMMA: True. Everyone likes him – despite his religious … preferences.

ROBERT: So, he's not good at confrontation. With the common man.

EMMA reaches out to him to smooth his hair down.

ROBERT: So then, the lads started saying they'd take the coach to his house and rob the place.

EMMA: What did you do?

ROBERT: I doubted if they'd have the mettle to do it. But just in case, I told them that John's house is a good forty miles away over Saddleworth Moors. I said that he's a Yorkshireman – that he lives in Huddersfield.

EMMA: What?

ROBERT: And I said that I was his nephew. That I'd come up from Cardiff. That I'd been an apprentice in a shop since I was ten years old.

EMMA: *(Laughs)* You never…

ROBERT: I did. I showed them my shoes – I was wearing the ones with hardly any soles left. Funnily enough, John had actually ticked me off for wearing them to the Corn Exchange earlier on in the day; 'giving the wrong impression to fellow traders,' he said.

EMMA: *(Pinches his cheek)* Well! They came in useful for something, then!

ROBERT: And I also went all Welsh on them *(exaggerates a Welsh accent)*. I said that I lived in Ashton with my brother and his wife and two lodgers and I slept under a kitchen table.

EMMA: That's true. Although they've finally gotten you a mattress now.

ROBERT: And that I was only in John's coach because he had promised my dad that the next time he was over in Manchester doing business, he'd let me have a ride in it.

EMMA: Ha!

ROBERT: I said that I'd worked practically every single day since I was ten years old. And then the leader gave John a shove and said he should treat me better. Should buy me some shoes.

EMMA: Really? They believed you?

ROBERT: Well, it was the truth, Emma! Sort of. Anyway. A good lie should always be built on strong foundations of the truth.

EMMA: Don't tell me things like that, Robert! I'm about to marry you!

ROBERT: So, then they all started arguing about whether they should try and take the coach over to Huddersfield. And then they started hitting each other.

EMMA: Not very professional criminals, then.

ROBERT: No. So, I interrupted them and said that if they wanted to engage in some very lucrative coach-robbing … if they got over to the Stockport Road in the next half an hour, the wealthiest gents from the Corn Exchange would be going home in the Cheshire direction.

EMMA: You never did!

ROBERT: Yes. And at that point there was some shouting in the street next to us, so they all legged it. Turned out that someone had seen what they'd done and had managed to find a bobby.

EMMA: So, you went to the police station?

ROBERT: Yes. Robbery and abduction, plus assault. And by the time the constables had taken our statements down, the clock was striking three. Mr Miller came up trumps, though.

EMMA: Yes?

ROBERT: He had a bottle of brandy stuffed under the coach seat. So, between us, we finished it off on the way home.

EMMA: John too?

ROBERT: John had the most of it … joked with Miller that he was obviously paying him too much.

EMMA: Oh, I do hope he repays Mr Miller his wages.

ROBERT: Course he will. He's fair and square like that. And then … then! He told me off for informing the gang of which road to head for if they want to rob the gents from the trading floors!

EMMA: Well, Robert. It sounds like you managed to talk your way out of a very sticky situation.

ROBERT: Well. You know …

EMMA: I'm proud of you, Robert.

She goes to kiss him. They break apart after a couple of seconds.

EMMA: But, Robert. About us getting married in the Sanctuary. Is there no way we can… delay things a bit?

ROBERT: Well …

EMMA: I mean, get married at St Michael's instead? The banns have been called, so we could get married there anytime really …

ROBERT: Oh, Emma – we've talked about this. I owe this to John. He's done … so much for me ... for us.

EMMA: I know, but … the Christian Israelites; they're just so …

ROBERT: What? I've been going there for years now and …

EMMA: Yes, but you're different. You keep an open mind. Although, I don't know how you can manage to do that, what with all of their…

ROBERT: We can ignore all of that side of things, Emma. John's paying for everything. We just need to get married there. We don't have to attend every Sunday if you don't…

*The door opens and they are interrupted, as two men enter. One is **UNCLE JOHN STANLEY**, aged 61. He is dressed like a gentleman, but today he is slightly more crumpled than usual; he is hatless, and his nearly white hair has not been waxed down. He is unshaven. Accompanying him is **TOM MEREDITH**, aged 42. TOM is EMMA's father. He is an enormous man; a brickie by trade with steely grey curls. He has done his best for this meeting and is wearing trousers and a jacket with a shirt. He is uncomfortable, though, pulling constantly at his collar. ROBERT stops talking to EMMA and bounds over to TOM, shaking his hand firmly.*

ROBERT: Good to meet you again, Mr Meredith! It was just after Christmas, wasn't it? When we last saw each other? It seems like years ago, but I see that you've already met my Uncle John.

JOHN: Yes, yes – we just met in the yard as Mr Meredith was arriving; I was showing him the horses. They're much calmer now.

TOM: *(Can't contain himself)* Now, come here you, ma love! *(He grabs EMMA in a huge bear hug and squeezes her)* Ooh, it's been forever! Too long, it has! And just look at yer! All plumped out and glowin' she…

TOM suddenly realises how this might sound to the other two men and stops himself.

TOM: Well, not too fat, I mean. Just right. For a lass – a lady, I mean.

JOHN: You, er … you never mentioned that your father was from around these parts originally, Miss Meredith. A Mossley lad, I believe.

EMMA: Yes, it's Mam … mother who's from Tewkesbury.

TOM: Aye. We settled down there in order to live with *her* mother. Well, now … the mother-in-law, I always said she'd be the death of me, and she very nearly were once, when…

EMMA: *(Cutting him off)* And how is Mam - Mother - doing now?

TOM: Well, she's 'ad better days. And to be honest, she's weepin' 'erself silly about not bein' able to travel up 'ere for the weddin' but…

EMMA: Oh, poor Mother. She shouldn't … we'll be down to Tewkesbury as soon as we can. It's only a wedding, only a formality, after all.

JOHN: Well, I'm not sure that our Prophet Wroe would agree with you on the marital ceremony being a mere formality. He takes the issue of nuptials exceptionally seriously.

TOM: I think Emma's just wantin' to protect her mother's feelins.

EMMA: Yes.

TOM: Like most women, she's very driven by feelins is my Margaret. I've had thirty years of 'er feelins.

JOHN: Ah. I know what that can be like.

The two men share a sympathetic glance. EMMA pretends not to notice

TOM: So, er … they said at the Spread Eagle last night that it's a reet – a right grand buildin'. Yer … Sanctuary church-place. So, er … will that … er … yer prophet be doin' the weddin' service, then?

JOHN: Well, he is here quite regularly, carrying out the divine ceremonies for couples.

TOM: Ah?

JOHN: But, sadly no. He's very disappointed about not being able to - personally - perform Robert's marriage. He's always had a high regard for my nephew.

EMMA: He'd be a foolish man if he didn't.

JOHN: *(Disregards her)* It's a shame, but he has an arrangement that he simply couldn't break. He's scheduled to be travelling to Hull.

TOM: Ah, well. I've 'eard people say that about him.

JOHN: I'm sorry?

TOM: He'll be in 'Hull' before y'know it. Y'kn – you know – 'Hell' – 'Hull'.

JOHN: Ah yes. *(Laughs politely)* People say the strangest things.

ROBERT: *(Helping out)* Mr Meredith, I do hope that the Spread Eagle provided adequate accommodation for you?

TOM: Perfectly nice, thank you. Music's a bit bawdy. Had a lass a-singin' and performin' last night in their Singin' Room. She were quite a treat. But nowt as – nothing as good as what our Emma is. Voice, I mean.

JOHN: Ah yes, I've heard glowing reports about Miss Meredith's singing voice.

EMMA: Robert's been joking that I should sing at my own wedding. Imagine!

ROBERT: I don't see why not. People hire professional singers and you've got the best voice in the whole of the north!

EMMA: *(To her father)* He's only saying that because you're here, Dad. Usually he tells me to stop squawking as I'm setting the cats off again.

They all laugh, apart from JOHN who perhaps is not used to engaging in extended chit chat with people from the lower classes.

TOM: I've often said to Emma's mam that 'er talents are wasted servin' in the domestic line of work an' that. She'd be far better up on th' stage. *(Notes the look of horror on JOHN's face)* Well, not th'stage, exactly …

JOHN: I should hope not!

TOM: No … although they do better'n the mill work in that stage line o' business. What they pay them singin' girls at the theatre – it's a pretty packet, so ah'm told… *(he trails off)*

JOHN: *(As if to a child)* I'm sure, Mr Meredith, that you want far better for your daughter than her appearing in public alongside a gaggle of dubious characters.

TOM: Oh, aye – course. Of course. Nowt – nothing is good enough for our Emma. That's why I'm right glad she's tekken up with our Mr Stanley here.

EMMA: 'Taken up'! You make it sound like we've decided to live over the brush and moved into a barn!

TOM: Heh – well, it were good enough for me and yer …

EMMA: *(Quickly interrupting him)* Because after all, Dad, we're going through all of the bells and whistles here … *(Corrects herself)* I mean, our wedding, it's very formal. And proper. And all down to Robert's Uncle John.

JOHN bows his head to acknowledge this, although he is still unsure at the lack of conventions that EMMA seems to be displaying.

ROBERT: Yes. We are very grateful, Uncle – the fact that you're paying for it all and –

TOM: *(Trying to loosen his collar, embarrassed)* I feel awful that I can't really 'elp out like…

JOHN: *(Shaking his head firmly)* Not at all, Mr Meredith. The tradition of a dowry or of the father of the bride paying for a ceremony and celebrations is most certainly not the requirement of the Christian Israelite church.

TOM: That's good, that's …

JOHN: The Lord commands us that those who are wealthier in the earthly realm have a duty to support those who are not.

TOM: Well, I'm very grateful of it. Mother – Margaret - too. We both are.

JOHN: In fact, if anyone should be chipping in with costs, it should be my brother, William – Robert's father.

ROBERT: *(Looks sheepish)* Well, you know what Dad's…

JOHN: I certainly do. But in his absence, it falls to me to act in loco parentis for you, Robert.

ROBERT: Yes

JOHN: And although I am aware that you've given your consent, I must ask you, formally, Mr Meredith, if… *(looking at ROBERT)* he meets with your approval?

ROBERT: *(Impishly)* Uncle John! You're talking about me as though I'm a prized cow!

EMMA: *(Even more forwardly)* Yes. That's supposed to be me in this situation!

All three men are taken aback by Emma's words. She is joking, but they aren't quite sure of this.

JOHN: Well, Mr Stanley and Miss Meredith do seem to have been going about this business in a rather more … modern way than … I prefer, myself.

ROBERT: *(Sensing his uncle's displeasure)* Uncle, I did try my best. What with me taking on the new shop in Stalybridge, we wanted to get married as soon as possible. I wrote to Mr Meredith asking for Emma's hand, but I never received a response … and…

ROBERT stops, embarrassed.

ROBERT: Oh, I didn't mean to sound discourteous, Mr Meredith.

TOM: *(Waving him away)* Oh, not at all – not at all.

ROBERT: Yes, I really didn't mean …

TOM: Thing is, we *did* get your letter but neither me nor the wife can read. Shameful it is, I know. I know.

EMMA: You shouldn't apologise for not having had an education, Dad.

TOM: Well, neither did you, love! And you've med somethin' of yerself!

EMMA: Hardly. I'm a serving girl.

TOM: Rubbish. It's what's up 'ere what matters. *(Points to his head)* *(To JOHN)* Reads and writes beautiful, she does. As good as her singin'. And wi' no proper schoolin' – education, I mean.

JOHN: Well, reading and writing will surely get a young lady further on in life than singing ever would.

TOM: *(To ROBERT)* Thing is, we asked a neighbour to read your letter for us. But he couldn't mek head nor tail of the writin'.

ROBERT: Sorry. Handwriting has never been my strong point.

JOHN: This is exactly why I tried to get you to take your script seriously when you were younger, Robert!

ROBERT: I've just never been …

JOHN: And I remember full well that, at the age of thirteen, you said to me "Uncle John, I think that a man of intelligence is judged by what pours out of his mouth and not what pours onto the page."

EMMA starts to giggle. JOHN looks at her sternly.

EMMA: I'm sorry. You just make him sound so …
JOHN: Precocious. Well – he was.
ROBERT: I may have been a bit …
TOM: Well, I agree with you, young Ro… I mean, Mr Stanley. There's folks in charge of this country what are far better at readin' n' writing' than you or I - and look at the mess *they're* mekkin'!
ROBERT: *(Robert looks slightly insulted)* Well, although my handwriting isn't the best in the world, I wouldn't say that I'm lacking in …
TOM: *(Holds his hand up)* No, a man can talk as fancy as he likes and promise everyone the moon on a stick – but it's his actions what matter.
JOHN: Hear, hear, Mr Meredith. I wish that most people who have been granted the right to vote held such sentiments. Now … we all favour the Tory party here…
TOM: Aye? I'd have thought you'd all be Liberals, bein' a factory owner n' all…
JOHN: Not at all. The Tories are the party of the working man!
ROBERT: True.
JOHN: And despite all of this *(Gestures to his home and to the stables)* I am a working man at heart. The Stanleys are from humble but hard-working origins. At first, I was a cordwainer, and after that, I was a joiner and then I trained as a mechanic and entered into iron, where…

ROBERT and EMMA are eyeing each other and trying to disguise their mirth.

JOHN: *(Notices their reaction)* Yes, I know, Robert. You've heard all of this before. I'm a terrible bore, aren't I?

ROBERT: *(Not apologetic - more affectionate)* No, Uncle. The older generation have a duty to remind young people about this sort of thing. And we should listen.

JOHN: Well, it's a good job that I'm not too easily offended.

ROBERT: Yes.

JOHN: And I've no doubt that you'll be saying the very same sort of thing to your own children, one of these days.

EMMA: Yes, when we have children, it'll be Robert forever saying to them, *"Oh, I was an apprentice in a shop at the age of ten, you don't know how lucky you are!"* He says it enough now as it is!

ROBERT: No, I'll be saying to our children, *"No one would marry your mother because she was nearly three years older than me and an old maid!"*

EMMA: Cheeky! *(She swipes him on the arm and they both laugh)*

JOHN stares oddly at them both.

ROBERT: Well, if you like, I can tell them instead how I raised you up from the floors of domestic servitude and turned you … into the Lady Mayoress of … of Stalybridge or something!

EMMA: Hah! Imagine that!

TOM: Ha! I don't think that'll ever happen. They'll not have a grocer as a mayor ever. And even if they did, you'll not get to be a mayor – not with that handwriting of yours, you won't.

ROBERT: *(Stops laughing)* Is it really that bad? *(Looks to JOHN)*

JOHN: *(Fed up with all the lack of levity now)* Hmmph, don't ask me; I just pay the bills 'round here.

EMMA: Oh, forgive our silliness, Mr Stanley. We're a pair of giddy kippers today.

ROBERT: Yes. It's all a bit exciting, getting married in a few days' time. And you helping me out so generously with my – our – new shop.

JOHN: Yes, well. It's certainly a good distraction from the horrible incident that occurred last night. I was telling your father about it just before.

TOM: Terrible, terrible.

JOHN: He agrees with me – that this sort of brutality is entirely a result of the revolutionary sentiments. Thoughts that are now infecting the lower classes across the continent.

TOM: Oh, er. Yes. Quite.

JOHN: These crazed fools, who've read the scribblings of that lunatic Marx and his friend Mr Engels![24] 'Socialism', they're calling this new philosophy! Redistribution of wealth from the rich to the poor. Insanity, isn't it, Mr Meredith?

TOM: Er, yes. 'Orrible.

JOHN: So, how do you exercise your vote, Mr Meredith?

TOM: Well, truth be told – I don't. There's only fourteen men in our village what – that – have the vote. An' I don't get one. 'Cause we rent our house.

ROBERT: The Chartists are wanting to change all of that, of course. If the Charter gets granted, a man won't have to own his own home to be able to vote.

JOHN: Well, if it ever comes to you receiving the vote, I'm sure, Mr Meredith, that you wouldn't want to vote any other way ... than for the Conservative man.

ROBERT: Uncle John, you're sounding just like one of those terrible factory owners! The sort that bribes his men if they don't vote his way!

JOHN: Heh! I do apologise, Mr Meredith. I didn't mean to intrude upon your political views.

TOM: No, no.

ROBERT: But really, society does need to do something about protecting the working man and his political views from bribery and threats.[25]

JOHN: Well, very commendable, Robert. But, Mr Meredith - I can't imagine such reforms will be in your - I mean *our* – lifetime, eh?

TOM: Probably not ...

JOHN: I had to correct myself there, see! I have a very young wife and a baby, you see. It keeps me young *(he looks anything but, at the thought of it.)*

---

[24] Friedrich Engels lived in Manchester from 1842. He visited Ashton and Stalybridge in 1844, describing 'the shocking filth and repulsive effect of Stalybridge' in his *Condition of the English Working Classes*. In 1845, his friend, Karl Marx, visited Chartists in Manchester with him. The two men then worked on *The Communist Manifesto*, published in 1848. It was written in Chetham's Library, Manchester and visitors today can sit at the very desk where Marx and Engels worked on it.

[25] Robert was called to parliament in 1869, as a witness on voting reform and the bribery of factory owners for working men's votes in Stalybridge. The committee that questioned Robert, drafted the Ballot Act of 1872 which introduced the secret ballot for the first time.

There is no time for ROBERT to reply as EMMA rescues the discussion from politics.

EMMA: I'm so glad that you got my letter in time, so that you can give me away on Sunday, Dad. What a silly phrase that is, though!
JOHN: How so?
EMMA: Well, I've not been living at home for ten years now and it's not like I really *belong* to anyone.
TOM: Well now, Missy… (*to JOHN*) With views like that, yer can see why I'm up 'ere so quick. Can't give 'er away fast enough!

The men laugh, EMMA subtly rolls her eyes again.

EMMA: But Dad, how did you manage to read my letter to you, and not the one that Robert sent?
TOM: Well, the neighbour said he could read yours because you write properly.

JOHN bursts out laughing. ROBERT folds his arms, fed up.

EMMA: Hmm. If we're to be running a grocer's business, you can't send people bills that they can't read, Robert. They'll never pay us!
ROBERT: Well, of course I …
EMMA: No. I think that I might be best being in charge of writing the bills and demands.
JOHN: It looks as though you've picked a fine business partner there, as well as a wife, Robert.
ROBERT: That hadn't really occurred to me until now…
JOHN: No, well…. you've been wasted in domestic service, Miss Stanley. Yes, she'll keep you on a steady course, Robert.
TOM: Aye, she will. She'll probably do better wi' you, Mr Robert, bein' a grocer's wife, than on that singin' career that I had in mind for her!

They all laugh politely.

JOHN: Goodness – look at the time. I must be off to the colliery offices. Again - wonderful to meet you, Mr Meredith.

TOM bows his head in acknowledgement.

JOHN: So, I'll let you three sort out all of the details of the wedding ceremony and the breakfasting feast with my wife. It's the sort of thing that my Mary is very good at. Dresses and ribbons and puddings and whatnot.

ROBERT: *(Gravely serious)* Thank you, Uncle. I really, truly cannot even begin to …

JOHN: Not at all, that's quite …

ROBERT: …to thank you for all that you've done for me over the course of my life. As soon as we're married, Emma and I plan on bringing up James - *(To TOM)* - that's my little brother in Cardiff - to be an apprentice for us.

TOM: Very nice.

ROBERT: Just as Uncle John did for me. Helping your family out is so important. I've learned that from you, Uncle, most of all.

JOHN: Splendid. I only hope that your parents will appreciate the gesture.

EMMA: *(Interrupting)* Uncle John – may I call you that?

JOHN: Of course. If I may call you 'Emma'?

EMMA: Oh, please do! I just wanted to say … *(trails off, trying to find the right words).*

JOHN: Yes?

EMMA: Just that … if there is anything – ever – that we can do to thank you for your support and your help … we are very much in your debt.

JOHN waves her thanks away as he leaves the room. But then turns.

JOHN: Come to think of it … if you did want to show your gratitude, there are a couple of things.

ROBERT: Yes?

EMMA: Of course!

JOHN: Firstly – Robert. Never tell anyone again that I come from Yorkshire. There's only so much that a proud Lancashire man can cope with.

They all laugh

JOHN: And - Emma?
EMMA: Yes?
JOHN: Given your proclivities for singing, I'd like you to take up a position within the Christian Israelite choir. We need more sopranos. And rehearsals are only three times a week.
EMMA: Oh. But we'll be living over in Stalybridge.
JOHN: Nonsense. It's only a half-hour's walk at the most. And you'll thoroughly enjoy singing praises to the Lord with the others.
EMMA: But it might be …
JOHN: I won't take no for an answer. It will do you the world of good. And it will be a spiritually uplifting way to demonstrate your gratitude – both to me, but more importantly to our Creator for all that he has bestowed upon you in life. (*He grins*).
EMMA: (*Dismally*) Yes, of course, Uncle John.

JOHN leaves the room.

EMMA: (*To ROBERT*) Oh, why on earth did I harp on about repaying his generosity?!
ROBERT: (*Cheerfully*) It won't be so bad, Emma.
EMMA: Well! It won't be you singing dirges with those po-faced old … Quick - Robert; I need an excuse not to have to join them!
ROBERT: I can't think of any. He's right … it's not even that long a walk away from where we'll be living in Stalybridge.
TOM: Looks like you can't get out of that one, love.
EMMA: Oh! But I can't! It would kill me!

EMMA is quiet for a minute, thinking. TOM and ROBERT look at each other and shrug.

EMMA: No. I've got it. The answer.
ROBERT: What?

EMMA: I need babies. Lots of them. Straight away.

ROBERT: *(Blushing furiously)* Well … well, I don't know if …

TOM: Blimey, Emma! Can't yer wait a few more days before yer start fiddlin' around with that sort of thing?

---ENDS---

7. THE BREAD RIOT

Bread Riots in Stalybridge. The building on the left being looted was Robert's first shop on Melbourne Street.

CONTEXT:

In 1862, King Cotton (Manchester) was experiencing a crisis as a result of the American Civil War. President Lincoln had declared a blockade on cotton being shipped to the UK from the south of the USA, in the hope of sapping the enemy's economic strength, which was still reliant on the cotton slave plantations. The effect of this, however, proved to be terrible for the poorest who worked in the cotton mills of south east Lancashire.

Although most of the working class felt solidarity with America's black slave population, by the winter of 1862 there were 7,000 unemployed cotton mill workers in Stalybridge alone and people were slowly starving. By now, Robert may have been only a 'simple grocer' but he was asked to chair a meeting on the American Civil War, which was attended by 500 people in the town.

The Poor Law existed to help the most desperate people out but, because of the sheer volume of people needing handouts in Stalybridge, the central committee in Manchester decreed that a system of 'tickets' should be introduced in order to obtain food in the town. Those who wanted assistance were also required to attend sewing or practical 'schools'. Clothing handouts were 'stamped' with the Poor Law mark, adding a further element of shame and misery for the town's residents.

During the winter of 1862–63, those worst affected – mainly the young Irish people of Stalybridge - began to riot, demanding bread and attacking the property of Poor Law guardians who were also the rich masters of the town. The unrest went on for several days, with the Riot Act being read as the disorder spread into Ashton, Dukinfield and Hyde. Armed troops on horseback (hussars) from Manchester galloped into the streets of Stalybridge to quell the disturbance as shops were looted and the Poor Law Relief Store – just a few doors away from Robert and Emma's shop – was set on fire.

By this time, Robert and Emma had been running their grocer's shop and tea trading business on Princess Street in the town for 15 years. They had nine surviving children, with another one to follow. Our relatives recall being told that, in order to stop his shop from being targeted, Robert threw bread and other provisions down to the crowds in the street.

Following the Bread Riots/Cotton Famine, Robert became a local councillor, later being appointed as a magistrate. But long before the Cotton Famine, he had developed a keen interest in British foreign policy and was a supporter of the diplomat and pro-Ottoman Turkophile, David Urquhart. In 1869, Robert was called to Parliament as an expert witness on the secret ballot and whether its introduction would ensure that the poor were less likely to turn to civil disobedience or to revolutionary politics.

STALYBRIDGE, MARCH 1863

FIVE PM IN THE LIVING ROOM ABOVE ROBERT STANLEY'S GROCER'S SHOP ON PRINCESS STREET, THE

MAIN STREET OF STALYBRIDGE. THIS IS THE LIVING
ROOM FOR A FAMILY OF ELEVEN - BARELY TIDY AT
THE BEST OF TIMES - BUT TODAY IT IS MORE CHAOTIC
THAN EVER. ALONGSIDE THE USUAL WASHING
HANGING DOWN FROM PULLEYS, THERE ARE BOXES
AND CARTONS STACKED UP AGAINST THE WALLS,
UNDER THE TABLE AND ON TOP OF FURNITURE,
FILLED WITH ALL MANNER OF GROCERY PRODUCTS
SUCH AS TEA, VEGETABLES, JARS AND PACKETS. NEXT
DOOR WE CAN HEAR THE CHATTER OF SIX OF THE
CHILDREN (ALL UNDER THE AGE OF TEN) AND THE
OCCASIONAL CRY FROM A BABY. IN THIS ROOM WE
HAVE **ROBERT STANLEY,** AGED 43, THE MOST
DISTINGUISHED LOOKING GROCER IN LANCASHIRE,
AND HIS WIFE, **EMMA STANLEY,** AGED 45. EMMA IS
LOOKING MORE DISHEVELLED THAN USUAL; HER
HAIR IS FALLING OUT OF ITS BUN. **WILL STANLEY,**
AGED 15, IS THEIR ELDEST AND A SERIOUS LOOKING
YOUNG MAN, WHEREAS **THOMAS STANLEY,** AGED 12,
IS A GOOD-LOOKING LAD BUT APT TO PLAY THE FOOL.
ANNIE STANLEY, AGED 13, THEIR ELDEST DAUGHTER,
IS PRACTICAL, BUT ALREADY DREAMING OF A LIFE
BEYOND PAROCHIAL STALYBRIDGE.

EACH MEMBER OF THE FAMILY IS BUSY MOVING
NEW BOXES INTO THE ROOM AND STACKING THEM
SPEEDILY, BUT CAREFULLY. THOMAS, HOWEVER, IS
DOING HIS BEST TO SHIRK. HE MUNCHES AN APPLE
QUIETLY WHILST SNEAKING LOOKS OUT OF THE
WINDOW.

EMMA: I'm glad you're not going to the Lodge tonight, Robert.

They all pause, straining to listen. We hear a faint sound of shouting.

ROBERT: I'd not leave you with what's going on over in Castle
Hall. This is how outright civil disobedience starts.
EMMA: You can understand why they're all so angry. This new
Poor Law thing.

ROBERT: I'm not impressed myself – at Manchester - imposing their rules on us, but there's ways and means and…

WILL: Forcing people to have tickets instead of money to buy food.

ANNIE: It's insulting. It's because those Manchester gents think the poor people here can't be trusted not to buy beer with their poor relief.

ROBERT: I've every sympathy with that view. Will – make sure the 'Closed' sign is showing on the shop front.

WILL: Aye.

ANNIE: But, Dad! The way that they're making them walk 'round, wearing those second-hand clothes with Poor Law labels stitched all over them!

WILL leaves the room to fetch more boxes.

EMMA: I think it's a bit rotten that they're making everyone who's out of work go back to those schools they've set up. Sewing and carpentry and what-not. It's …

ANNIE: It's degrading, is what it is.

ROBERT: *(As he heaves a box on top of the dresser)* Idle hands are the devil's workshop.

THOMAS rolls his eyes.

THOMAS: It's cruel, it is. Making anyone go back to school.

ROBERT: They should be thankful for any sort of learning. In my day a man had to take whatever learning he could find. Make the most of it.

EMMA: Mind your frock, Annie – you'll rip it on the nails on that box if you carry it like that.

ANNIE: Oooh … another rip of this frock and we'll have to be asking for new togs from the Poor Relief store for me!

EMMA: Oh, we'll never come to that.

THOMAS: I'd die if I had to wear those sorts of togs.

ROBERT: Don't be stupid, Thomas. Of course you wouldn't die.

THOMAS: No, I would. Really.

ROBERT: Stupid. Better a Relief Store label than freezing to death because you've only got rags, I say.

ANNIE: That Manchester committee lot should just write 'I'm poor and I'm desperate' on these poor families' foreheads and have done with it!

ROBERT: *(Passing ANNIE a box of apples)* Here – under the chair there. Well, whatever their reasoning, there's never any reason for the sort of shenanigans that they've been up to during the last few hours.

THOMAS: Attacking Old Bayley's carriage! I'd like to have seen that!

ROBERT: *Mister* Bayley to you. And there's never any justification for civil disobedience.

ANNIE: Not even Peterloo?

ROBERT: Peterloo was not about civil disobedience. Everyone from 'round here knows that.

WILL: *(Entering the room again, carrying a tea chest)* What was it all about then? Peterloo?

ROBERT: Lack of … of strategy and forward planning on … the part of the authorities.

WILL: Funny, I heard that it was because the rich toffs were wanting to get their own back on the working man.

ROBERT: You listen to some of the sillier customers too much. Anyway. Civil disobedience can always be prevented if the correct men are in power.

THOMAS: *(Finishing his apple and tossing the core onto the fire)* Well, I'm all for a bit of civil disobedience when it means we get to shut up shop a bit earlier!

EMMA: Don't sound so gleeful, lad. We're making no profit.

ROBERT: Not even breaking even.

EMMA: Exactly. No one can afford even the basics. It's crippling everyone, this cotton famine. I don't know how much longer this can go on for.

WILL: Yes, and you're the first to moan about having to eat tripe instead of meat, Thomas Stanley.

THOMAS: Euggh. Tripe. It's like eating the inside of a dead cat.

ANNIE: Thomas, don't be revolting.

THOMAS: Or … or dog sick.

EMMA: (Sternly) Thomas! You should consider yourself lucky to be having anything more than bread and water right now. There's folks in this town that'd murder for what you get to eat.

ROBERT: And that's the sort of thing that I'm worried about. Thomas, shift yourself. Come on, help me with bringing the last of these boxes up the stairs.

WILL: About time he did something.

ROBERT: We've practically emptied the shop now. Too much temptation for them today if we leave anything on show.

THOMAS: Do I have to? I've already swept the entire floor downstairs after we shut up. Can't Will help with carrying up the rest?

WILL: No – I'm whacked enough, after barricading the back door!

ROBERT is ignoring them both as he fetches another box into the room and passes it to THOMAS.

ROBERT: Now, come on, Thomas; stack them neatly at least, so they don't topple. If a job's worth doing…

THOMAS: *(Groans to himself)* It's worth doing properly. And why can't James Henry help out? He's ten years old. He's a right big girl's blouse, he is.

ANNIE: He's looking after the little ones. Sulking because he says it's my job to do that. But I don't see why the eldest girl always has to get landed with the kids all of the time.

EMMA: Fact of life, Annie. Get used to it. I had to.

WILL: He's not you know. Looking after them. They're all doing tossing in there.

ROBERT: They're what?

WILL: Gambling.

ROBERT: *(Stops what he is doing and stares at him)* Gambling? What on earth…?

WILL: Not proper gambling. They've just got a set of tatty old cards

THOMAS: They've not got any money or anything. Only pretend.

ROBERT: I don't even want pretend gambling going on under this roof!

THOMAS: It's just a bit of a game…

ROBERT: A game! Six of our own children under the age of ten engaged in gambling!

WILL: Well, the two babies can only just sit and gawp really …

ANNIE: And James Henry only uses old buttons. There's no harm in it …

THOMAS: Though Baby Bob did nearly choke to death on a button last week. Went blue, he did. I had to shake him upside down.

EMMA: What? When was this?

ROBERT: Gambling is illegal! Whether you're using money or not!

EMMA: I had no idea about this sort of …

ROBERT: And this is exactly the sort of attitude that leads to rack and ruin! *(To EMMA)* I need to sort the lot of them out! *(Moves to go next door, but EMMA stops him)*

EMMA: I think we've got bigger problems to deal with right now. The shouting from over Castle Hall way … it's getting worse.

ROBERT: *(Stops)* I suppose. These need moving over. *(He moves more boxes)*

WILL: If that James Henry carries on with his gambling habit, he'll be sent down for hard labour by the time he's 11.

EMMA: Annie – at least go and take the buttons off Baby Bob, will you?

ANNIE leaves the room.

THOMAS: The Stalybridge magistrates are still sending little kids to prison, kids much younger than our James Henry is, you know.

ROBERT: *(Shaking his head as he moves about the room)* It does need addressing; they're sneaky little scoundrels some of these children on our streets, but hard labour is a bit…

There is a noise from outside, on the street.

WILL: Someone's banging on the front door.

THOMAS moves over to the window and opens it, looking down.

THOMAS: It's for you, Dad. It's little Peter Grimbsy.

ROBERT: *(Goes to the window)* Young Peter – hello!

PETER: *(Voice from outside)* Dad said tell yer 'cause there's a mob at the end of Market Street. Comin' down this way.

ROBERT: Ah – thank you.

PETER: You know they smashed up Mister Bayley's factory before?

ROBERT: Oh dear. I knew about his cab, not about his factory.

PETER: Well, me dad said just to let yers know. Maybe they're after all the Relief Committee members now. Like what you are.

EMMA: *(Has joined them at the window – calls down)* But Mr Stanley isn't on the Poor Relief Committee!

PETER: Well … Mr Stanley spends half of his life in meetings and committees about the town, doesn't he?

ROBERT: Well, a fair bit but …

PETER: They're all as thick as pigmuck, the Irish, me dad says. So, they'll be after anyone on committees.

ROBERT: Right, well. Thank you, Peter. Tell your father thank you, too.

PETER: Ta. And Mrs Stanley, me mam says she'll be in th' shop as soon as she can, to pay off us stuff. She says she's sorry, but none of us 'ave any work now an' …

EMMA: Tell her it's not a problem. As long as it takes.

PETER: She 'ates bein' on the tick, she does.

EMMA: I know. You get back off home now – quick!

ROBERT: *(Under his breath)* 'As long as it takes' – honestly.

EMMA: Oh, hush.

ANNIE RE-ENTERS THE ROOM. ROBERT turns away from the window and as he does so, THOMAS leans further out.

THOMAS: Peter! Catch! *(He throws an apple down to PETER)*

PETER: Oooh! Ta, Thomas!

ROBERT: *(Under his breath)* There goes yet more of my profits.

EMMA: *(Going back to moving boxes)* Thomas, that was very kind of you. They're starving to death, that lot. Look like skeletons.

ANNIE: Mam … just thinking … I really don't think the downstairs doors will hold, if...

EMMA: Your dad and Will shoved those tea chests in front. They'll hold alright.

ANNIE: It's the back door I'm worried about; Dad's never repaired it and …

ROBERT: Alright! I have enough to do without foreseeing armed raiders attacking my own home, thank you very much!

WILL: Stop yarking, Annie. Didn't you hear me with the hammer? I nailed some planks across it.

ROBERT: Well, well. Points for initiative, Will.

THOMAS: And for stupidity. If there's a blummin' fire, we can't get out!

WILL: I thought of that, Mr Smarty-pants. I brought the ladder inside.

ANNIE: Oh, Mam! If there's a fire!

EMMA: Don't be silly.

THOMAS: Hope you're right. I don't want to die getting frazzled to death in a fire like Mrs Collingwood's burned-up baby last week.

EMMA: Thomas! Don't say such things!

THOMAS: Well, there's far too many babies getting burned to death over Castle Hall way, so you've got to ask yourself…

ROBERT: (*Cutting him off*) Thomas, will you please stop jabbering and help me with the last of these boxes.

THOMAS: And if there is a fire, I'm going to jump out of the side window there and straight into the river.

WILL: Idiot. It's that shallow, you'll break your neck. With any luck.

EMMA: Boys – please! (*She has stopped moving boxes for a minute and is leaning against the wall, tired.*) Robert, I can't bear this, just waiting to see if …

ROBERT: (*Looking at the clock*) The clerk will be with the mayor. They'll have sent a message on to Ashton already.

WILL: They should have set up a barracks there. Talked about it enough.

ROBERT: It'll happen fairly soon, I think … and with any luck the soldiers will be here in the next half hour or so.

THOMAS: (Gleefully) It's just like we're having our own revolution here in Stalybridge – building barricades and calling in the soldiers!

WILL: You read too much Dickens.

THOMAS: They'll be ravishing the place before we know it!

ROBERT: I think you'll find that the correct word is 'ravaging'.

ANNIE: They're… (*She jumps back from the window and shouts to the others*) They're coming – 'round the corner!

All rush to the window to see, as there is a loud smash of glass. Then another. Then more. Screaming and hooting – laughter and whistles and 'Down with the guardians' and 'Up their arses with their tickets'.

EMMA: The language! It's disgraceful!

WILL: Both ends – look! They're coming down the top end of the street too!

More sound of breaking glass.

ANNIE: Mam! That wasn't our windows, was it?

WILL: No. Next door but two … no, three… by the looks of it. Bayley's… they like their Old Bayley, don't they?

ROBERT: Confound those people! What on earth do they think they're doing?

Cries of 'Stuff your tickets!' and 'We're after you, Bayley'

WILL: They're nicking stuff! See – that fella there…

EMMA: Oh, Lord – look! Robert – see! They're in at our old shop! Oh – they're pulling everything out!

THOMAS: They're throwing it to each other! Weeee!

ALICE: And opposite – see at the tobacconists! They've got boxes of it out!

ROBERT: This is … And it's not just – see now, Rigby - the butchers!

WILL: Oh, they'll not mess with Mrs Rigby – she's terrifying …

ALICE: Actually, you're right; she's threatening them with a meat cleaver – look!

THOMAS: She'll lop their heads off!

EMMA: Thomas!

WILL: Dad – look! The Poor Relief store, too – why on earth are they going for that place?

THOMAS: I thought they hated those clothes.

EMMA: Annie – bread. Quick! Where did you put the bread?

ANNIE: Why…?

EMMA: Just…. (*Gesturing wildly at her*) Get it!

ANNIE: It's under the table… (*She dashes to the table to drag a basket out*) Here Mam – but it's stale. I was going to give it the birds.

EMMA: The birds can fend for themselves. The people don't seem to be able to.

ROBERT: (*Looking back from the window, suddenly realising what she's going to do*) Why! My clever little wife!

EMMA: Less of the 'little' if you don't mind.

WILL: Look – they've got inside the Poor Relief Store. They're… they're chucking clothes down to each other!

ROBERT: These people are… This is absolutely…

THOMAS: Woah! That's a whole pile of trousers! And jackets and shirts and…

ROBERT: I've seen it all now.

THOMAS: Oooh, catch them missus! Or your bloomers are gonna get all mucky in the puddles!

EMMA: (*Turning around from the basket of bread*) Thomas!

ANNIE: Mam, I'm going to check on the little ones. They'll be proper scared.

ANNIE leaves the room.

ROBERT: So, now we have a riot; we have thieving and looting on the streets of Stalybridge! Where are those blasted hussars?!

EMMA: Robert, your language!

ROBERT: Sorry.

There are voices directly under them now, shouting up to the family; most sound Irish.

MALE: Oi! Gawpers! Haven't yer never seen people tekkin' back the town before?!

THOMAS: *(Yelling back at him)* You're a bunch of lunatics going mental!

MALE: Cheeky young bleeder!

THOMAS: Cheeky yourself!

MALE: I'll come up there right now and punch yer filthy gob in, so I will!

FEMALE: Well, if we *are* lunatics – we're tekkin' over the asylum!

THOMAS: I'll kick you both into the river!

EMMA grabs THOMAS and pulls him away from the window.

EMMA: Thomas! Come with me! You can look after the babies!

THOMAS scowls as EMMA drags him off.

ROBERT: *(Calling down to the man)* I'm so sorry for my son's rudeness.

MALE: Sorry, 'ee says!

ROBERT: Can I presume that all of this consternation is the result of the Poor Law impositions?

FEMALE: Oooh – get him! 'Can I presume'! Mr la-di-da!

MALE: Aye. Yer can presume right!

ROBERT: The thing is, the Poor Law is a government directive and as such –

MALE: I don't give a tinker's cuss about no government directive!

FEMALE: They're not the ones who've had to suffer, so they're not!

MALE: They're not the ones seein' their bairns dyin'!

ROBERT: I do understand that it must appear that …

MALE: An' you're not exactly goin' hungry, are yer? Bet you've got a load of grub and whatnot in there! Filthy rich grocer!

ROBERT: *(His accent suddenly becomes rather Welsh)* Not at all! I've known plenty hard times myself, you know. I was born in Cardiff.

MALE: I don't care where yer were born!

ROBERT: We were a family of twelve and times were so terrible that I was sent up here to work, at the age of ten.

FEMALE: Then why aren't yer down 'ere with us? Ahh - yer afraid of the law, so yer are!

EMMA: *(Now back at the window, calls down to them)* But we also have fourteen mouths ourselves to feed up here!

ROBERT: *(Whispers to EMMA)* Fourteen? Have you got something to tell me?

EMMA: *(Whispers back)* No – for once. I'm including the two cats.

MALE: He's afraid of the law, alright! Coward!

THOMAS has now snuck back into the room and is at the window again – he starts yelling down at them.

THOMAS: No-one calls my dad a coward! You pair of filthy morons!

ROBERT: Thomas! *(Yanks him by the collar and away from the window, cuffing him around the head)*

FEMALE: Hah! At least the kid's gotta bit of spirit in him!

MALE: I'll not be called a 'filthy moron' by anyone – kid or not! Come on down here, me laddo, and I'll show yer 'oo's boss, so I will!

ROBERT: *(Now back at the window)* Sorry for my lad there!

MALE: Too late for that. See that little spark of a flame there? That'll be your shop next…

EMMA: Robert! They're setting light to the Poor Relief store!

ROBERT: Where are those damned soldiers?

MALE: *(Muffled)* Hey – you lot! Get over here! Try givin' this grocer's a lick of the flames!

ANNIE: *(Now at the window – calling down to them)* Sir! I'm so sorry, sir, about my brother! He's got a quick tongue - he doesn't mean what he says!

MALE: Send him down 'ere!

ANNIE: That's not a good idea.

FEMALE: Why?

ANNIE: He was dropped on his head when he was a baby … he's had a queer way about him ever since.

MALE: 'Oo cares if 'ee's an imbecile! Send 'im down!

ANNIE: When he's got his dander up, there's no stopping him! He gets so violent; he once nearly killed a policeman!

FEMALE: But he only looks about twelve …

121

ANNIE: He is! But it's like he's... possessed! And at night-time we have to put a dog collar around his neck and chain him to the wall! We had to get a priest in to exorcise his evil spirits.

WILL: *(Joining in)* But it didn't work! He nearly bit the priest's nose off!

MALE: *(Uncertain)* Well...

ANNIE: I'm so sorry. I know how hungry you are – please, take this.

ANNIE throws a loaf down to them.

FEMALE: That'll do!

MALE: Any more?

The family begin to throw the loaves down. Cries of 'Bread's up!' and 'Supper over here!'

ANNIE: *(To EMMA)* That's all the bread gone, Mam.

THOMAS: *(From the corner, where ROBERT shoved him)* Huh. It's that stale I hope they all break their teeth on it!

EMMA: They're still asking for more, Robert.

ROBERT: Oh, I don't ... we can't throw the whole of our stock down there.

EMMA: Some tea?

ROBERT: I'd rather not. Ah. Yes. That box in the corner over there *(Directing WILL)* Yes, the big box on the left. That's right.

ANNIE fetches the tea, WILL helping her.

THOMAS: *(From the corner, sulking)* And Annie – I'm going to start telling people that you have to shave your chin every night. And then ... then no man will ever want to marry you!

ANNIE: Oh, be quiet.

EMMA: Yes, you should be grateful to your sister for getting you out of a tight spot, Thomas.

THOMAS: But it's ...

EMMA: Now get back next door again and see to the children before I throw *you* out of the window!

(THOMAS skulks out of the room. The rest of the family begin to throw the tea down. Cries of 'Tea!' and 'More over here!')

EMMA: There's more of them coming over – we don't have enough!

ROBERT: There's that basket of bits and bobs on the front counter we can use; Will - it's next to the clock there.

ROBERT: *(Tossing items out of the window)* I'm afraid that's all … we've a family of … er … fourteen here ourselves and times are hard!

Cries of 'More!' and 'Liar!' from the crowd. Then another distinct voice is heard shouting at the rest of the crowd. This is BILLY THE BRUISER, notorious criminal and Stalybridge's champion bare knuckle fighter.

BILLY: *(Shouting)* Ah – leave this place alone! It's Mr Stanley an' his family, so it is. Don't you be spreadin' fire anywhere near 'im!

Cries of 'He'll be loaded!' and 'There'll be more where that came from!'

WILL: (Excitedly) It's Billy the Bruiser!

EMMA: Who?

WILL: The bare-knuckle champion of Stalybridge!

EMMA: Oh….

BILLY: *(Shouting back at the crowd)* I mean it! Leave 'em alone - or you'll have me to deal with… go on, off wi' yer!

WILL: Did you see that right hook?! See that! He's famous for that!

EMMA: That man went down like a …

ANNIE: I'm sure he must be dead.

BILLY: Go on! Move on! Stanley's one of the good 'uns. If yer want to be smashin' stuff up, the others are goin' up to Bayley's house. Go on!

The crowd turns to move down the street and towards Cocker Hill and Mr Bayley's mansion.

ROBERT: *(Calling after BILLY)* Thank you, Billy!

As the crowd gradually quietens, we hear a lone teenager's voice from outside.

TEEN: *(Trailing after the crowd)* Bloody mustard! He chucked me a jar of bloody mustard! I hoped I'd get better than that![26]
EMMA: Robert - why on earth was Billy the Bruiser defending us?
ROBERT: Well…
WILL: *(Answering for him)* Billy can't read. And he was in the shop one day showing this letter – it said that he'd been summoned to court for one of his fights.
ANNIE: Dad read it out for him. And then he looked up some legal advice for him.
ROBERT: Got him off with just a piddling little fine.
EMMA: Why on earth would you help someone like Billy the Bruiser?
ROBERT: His mother's a lovely old lady. But she's bed ridden.
EMMA: And?
ROBERT: If Billy went to prison, she's got no other soul in the world to look after her. She'd be in the workhouse straight away.
EMMA: You big softie.
ANNIE: I don't think … It looks like the fire in the store hasn't properly caught.[27]
WILL: They're so stupid, they can't even light a fire properly.
ROBERT: Thank goodness – and - ah! At last! The hussars are here!

The sound of horses' hooves in the distance and shrieks from the crowd.

WILL: Ooh. Look at them go! That'll sort the men from the boys!
EMMA: Oh! Oh! The violence! Those soldiers, they're being far too…
ANNIE: And their swords, Mam; they're actually trying to use them against people.
EMMA: They're slashing them at people! *(Emma clutches her daughter)*.
WILL: I'm going to get Thomas – he has to see this!

---

[26] This is an actual phrase uttered by one of the rioters. He caught a jar of mustard that one of the shopkeepers had thrown out of the window and he was rather disappointed. His words were reported in the national newspapers and in the government inquiry.
[27] The fire did not catch and the shop was saved, although many of the items had been stolen.

ROBERT: Stay where you are, Will. Thomas has enough silly ideas in his head without being party to this!

EMMA: Oh – we can't have a Peterloo! Not in Stalybridge!

ROBERT: Well … let's hope the soldiers can restrain themselves.

ANNIE: I wonder if any of the crowd made it up to old Bayley's house?

EMMA: I hope not. She's terrible poorly, is Mrs Bayley. It'd kill her, this sort of thing.[28]

ROBERT: Old Bayley can be a bit of a rogue at times - but his wife does a lot for the poor.

ANNIE: Shall I… the little ones. Mam - if they're looking out their window they'll be frightened out of their wits.

EMMA: Yes. (*Distracted, mesmerised at the scenes outside*) They're very quiet…

WILL: That's because James Henry will have had them all taking bets on how many people get stabbed.

EMMA: Oh, don't!

WILL: Well, it's true. He's on his way to turning the younger ones in the Stanley family into a den that'd rival Fagin's.

ROBERT: I'll deal with the children and their gambling problem tomorrow. They'll… (*He trails off*)

The family stay at the window, quiet for a while as they watch the rest of the scene play out. Finally, ROBERT stirs himself.

ROBERT: I'm going to move the furniture back and head down to the town hall. See if there's anything that I can do to help.

ALICE: Look how fast the soldiers have moved them back! They're legging it back to Castle Hall.

EMMA: Yes… Yes – Will. Help your dad. Walk over to the town hall with him. They could do with a few more level heads down there.

WILL: (*Stirs himself, away from the window*) You know what, Dad? I think you'd be a far better councillor than that lot at the town hall are.

---

[28] The crowd did make it to Bayley's home and smashed the windows. Mrs Bayley died not long afterwards – apparently as a result of the distress.

ANNIE: And you'd be a much better mayor than this one we've got.

WILL: Yes. Useless, he is.

EMMA: Ha! Robert Stanley the Mayor – that'll be the day!

ROBERT: *(Offended)* Well, thank you my dear.

EMMA: Oh – you know I'm only teasing. You'd make a wonderful mayor.

EMMA kisses him on the cheek; WILL and ANNIE pull faces at each other and depart on seeing this display of parental affection.

ROBERT: I can't see a mere grocer ever being elected as mayor.

EMMA: In the future, Robert, I think it will be more about a man's courage and intelligence.

ROBERT: *(Self-deprecating)* Ah. That rules me out then.

EMMA: And the cunning, too. You've got that.

ROBERT: What on earth do you mean?

EMMA: I know exactly why you were so explicit about which tea we should throw down to the crowd.

ROBERT: Yes?

EMMA: Because that particular batch was the one you said was contaminated.

ROBERT: Was it?

EMMA: Yes. You said this morning that it was only useful for the cabbage patch!

ROBERT: I'd forgotten all about that.

EMMA: Of course.

ROBERT: I don't know what you are insinuating, my dear.

EMMA: You! Attempting to poison a bunch of rabble-rousers and thugs!

ROBERT: *(Holds his hands up in mock surrender)* Ah well, you know what I always say: Waste not …

EMMA: Want not.

EMMA laughs a sigh of relief and exhaustion. ROBERT pulls her to him and kisses her.

---ENDS---

8. FROM MAGISTRATE TO MAYOR

CONTEXT:

By 1874, Robert Stanley was something of a civic hero. Having withstood the Bread Riots during the Lancashire Cotton Famine of 1861–63, he had become a local councillor and a magistrate. As working men were slowly being given the vote, Robert set up an Anti-Screw Association which sought to protect them from unscrupulous factory owners, who often bribed and threatened them to 'vote for their man'. Robert had been called to Parliament in 1869 as an expert witness about whether the secret ballot would be the best way to protect the working class from such practises. Following the Great Hunger (or 'Potato Famine') of 1845-1849, towns across Manchester had experienced a huge influx of Irish immigrants and by 1868 nearly 50 per cent of Stalybridge residents were Irish. During this year, the area had again exploded in riots. This time the violence was caused by the anti-Roman Catholic William Murphy, who travelled to England from Northern Ireland to preach against the Roman Catholic church.

Looking towards Stalybridge Town Hall, just a few hundred yards from Robert's shop and home

During these years, Robert was working hard to build up his successful grocery shop and his tea trading business, frequently travelling to Manchester where he also had an office at the Old Corn Exchange. As well as sitting as a magistrate at the Petty Sessions three times a week, he became heavily involved with Stalybridge civic life. He led the committee that built the new Victoria Market Hall, was one of the original trustees that created the new Stamford Park and was a key member of the Joint Waterworks Committee with Ashton

128

– building the new reservoir at Dovestones in order to supply fresh water to the town - marking him out as a 'municipal socialist'. In addition to this, he was a member of various other council committees, a Freemason and leader of the local Conservative Association.

This scene imagines the domestic life of Robert and Emma and considers the background to his appointment as mayor.

ROBERT'S HOME; GROCER'S SHOP, PRINCESS STREET, STALYBRIDGE, JULY 1874.

TEA-TIME ON A MONDAY AT THE STANLEYS' HOME IN THEIR GROCER'S SHOP. IN THE COOKING AREA, DOWNSTAIRS FROM THE SHOP, **EMMA STANLEY**, AGED 48, IS PREPARING A MEAL ON THE RANGE. EMMA HAS NOW GIVEN BIRTH TO ELEVEN CHILDREN BUT IS STILL AS SPRIGHTLY AND AS TRIM AS EVER. HER SECOND ELDEST DAUGHTER, **MARY-JANE**, AGED 19, IS SITTING IN A ROCKING CHAIR, PEERING NEAR-SIGHTEDLY AT ONE OF THE MANY JOTTERS WHICH ARE PILED ON HER LAP. **SARAH**, AGED 13, IS A PRETTY GIRL – AND PERHAPS RATHER AWARE OF THIS, AS SHE BRUSHES HER DARK HAIR AND GAZES AT HERSELF IN THE MIRROR.

The bang of a door and the sound of a raspberry being blown outside in the yard. EMMA stands with her hands on her hips and tuts, shaking her head.

SARAH: Honestly! All you did was ask her to bring the rest of the washing in, Mam. Our Em might be older than me, but she acts like such a baby.
EMMA: Good job your father isn't home yet to have seen that performance.
SARAH She's a hot-headed little cat. She'll take it out on the little ones in the yard now. Hopefully Bob will bite her.
EMMA: Sarah, stop gawping at yourself in the mirror and get that washing folded.

129

SARAH rolls her eyes and dumps her hairbrush down. She goes over to the washing. EMMA continues with making the meal on the range.

SARAH: Can't you help, Mary-Jane?

MARY-JANE: I've got so many jotters here to mark! Ask one of the boys.

EMMA: Ha. It's not worth the arguing, trying to get them in here for anything other than being fed.

MARY-JANE: (*Sighs and stands up, taking a sheet with Sarah*) If I must. Oh, but my back… Now, no, stand over there! Get yourself in order. We can't fold it like that. No, to your right, not to your left. Honestly!

SARAH: Mary-Jane, you're such a pain. You're like a sergeant major. I'm glad that I'm not in your class.

MARY-JANE: If you were, I'd have you standing in the corner with a big dunce's hat for most of the time.

SARAH: I don't see why I have to still go to school anyway. I'm old enough not to be there anymore. Our Em's allowed to stay home now!

EMMA: She's 15 and you're 13. You need to do at least another year.

SARAH: There's no point! What do I need to learn if I'm going to be married and have a family? It's just silly.

MARY-JANE: Sillier wanting children, if you ask me. All the work that they create. Plus, they're noisy and smelly. They sap all of your energy, grow fat on your wellbeing … and they have no manners whatsoever.

EMMA: There are days that I agree with you on that, young lady.

MARY-JANE: Mr Thompson says that children are no better than parasites.

EMMA: You're keen on that Mr Thompson, aren't you?

MARY-JANE: I'm no such thing! I just appreciate his views.

SARAH: See! Even the teachers hate children. School is a horrible place.

MARY-JANE: Mr Thompson teaches arithmetic. It's a thankless task in this town. People here are very slow-witted.

EMMA: It's not something that I've noticed. Our customers are usually pretty sharp on checking if they've been short-changed.

MARY-JANE: That's because their talent only goes so far as the absolute basics of mathematics. The mark of true intelligence is whether you can calculate in the abstract.

SARAH: I want to die of boredom just listening to you.

MARY-JANE: *(Yanking the sheet violently towards her so that SARAH stumbles)* Put a child from Castle Hall up against a monkey from the zoo and give them some basic algebra and the monkey would win every time.

EMMA: I think you need to get out of teaching yourself, with that attitude.

MARY-JANE: Not quite yet. And at least I'm not working in one of the mills or selling tripe in the fish market.

SARAH: I think our Em has the most sensible idea for a job. Making dresses.

MARY-JANE: Lucrative, too.

SARAH: People pay lots of money for frocks.

MARY-JANE: Yes, so long as we don't educate women and continue to encourage them to think that the only joy to be had in life is to be bound up in a swathe of silk with a dead duck draped across their head … then certainly. There's money to be made.

EMMA: I'd give my eye-teeth for a dead-duck hat.

SARAH: Well, Mary-Jane won't ever buy you one.

EMMA: Honestly, though, I don't know where you get your views from, Mary-Jane. I really don't.

MARY-JANE: Probably Dad. Speak of the devil.

ROBERT opens the back door and enters.

ROBERT: There appears to be a problem outside. I have just had to reprimand two of my brawling children.

SARAH: Our Em will have caused it.

ROBERT: Perhaps. She was holding a pillowcase over John's head. He claimed that she was trying to suffocate him.

SARAH: She probably was.

EMMA: She just snapped a few minutes ago.

ROBERT: What brought that on?

EMMA: I just asked her to bring the rest of the washing in off the line. She'd just sat down to do one of her lady's fashion drawings.

ROBERT: Ah. That's an arts-orientated mind. Never easy to live with a creative. Look at the Shellys!

MARY-JANE: You make Em's interest in designing fashions for brainless ladies of leisure sound rather loftier than it actually is.

ROBERT: I would have thought that you would encourage another female into a profession, Mary-Jane.

MARY-JANE: Profession! Designing fripperies can hardly be deemed to be a 'profession'.

SARAH: It is, if you're skilled and ladies want to buy these things.

MARY-JANE: We should use our brains to do good! I'd rather use mine to help the female cause!

ROBERT: Well, I'm sorry to tell you this, Mary-Jane, but I feel that far too many females in Stalybridge are rather a lost cause.

EMMA: Oh dear. More drunken women up in court again?

ROBERT: Oh, yes. I need to sit down. Mrs Fox again.

EMMA: Uh-oh. Rosanna Fox and her rivers of gin.[29] Sarah – make your father some tea. Quick.

ROBERT: *(Hanging up his hat and sitting down)* It was that bad today, I need something stronger than tea. Might go down The Feathers later.

EMMA: Not good then?

ROBERT: No. Four hours! Listening to a throng of hoi polloi plead innocence. Not one of them admitted the error of their ways! Not one!

MARY-JANE: Hardly surprising when they know that they're going to have the book thrown at them. There's no mercy for people these days.

ROBERT: Now, Mary-Jane, you know that that's completely untrue.

EMMA: She doesn't mean …

ROBERT: Because when I've been the lead magistrate on sentencing, I've always done my best to give folk the option of a fine or of a sentence.

MARY-JANE: No, I didn't mean that.

ROBERT: Good.

---

[29] Rosanna Fox was the most notorious drunken woman in Stalybridge. Like many others, she appeared countless times before the magistrates. See *His Own Man* for more information on the problem of women and alcohol during this era.

MARY-JANE: Everyone knows that you're far more fair-minded than the rich magistrates, the sorts who have no idea what it's like to go without a meal.

ROBERT: Speaking of which, when's tea ready?

EMMA: Bit later than usual.

MARY-JANE: Thomas hadn't lit the fire like Mam asked him to.

EMMA: Asked him to light it whilst I went over to the market, getting ready for the Stamford Park bazaar.[30] We've got a lovely lot of cheeses for our stall.

MARY-JANE: He can't even do a simple task like lighting a fire. Thinks it's woman's work. That it's beneath him.

ROBERT: He said that?

MARY-JANE: He doesn't need to say it. I know our Thomas.

SARAH passes ROBERT a cup of tea. He sips it.

ROBERT: Ah. Good blend, that one. Very nice.

MARY-JANE: So, what unfortunates had to lay their lives open to you in front of half of Stalybridge today then, Dad?

EMMA: Yes, I think it's terrible the way that any Tom, Dick or Harry can just roll up to the courtroom and listen to all of the gory details.[31]

MARY-JANE: People have a peculiar way of getting their fancies.

EMMA: They like their stories.

MARY-JANE: I don't know why they can't just pick up a good book.

ROBERT: The sorts who turn up to court to have a snigger at the expense of others, Mary-Jane, couldn't tell you half of their ABCs. Read a book? Ha.

SARAH: That's true. Bessie Cronkshaw and all of her brothers and sisters go to watch what's happening in court. And they're all very backward.

ROBERT: I think I've seen them. They should be in school.

---

[30] The people of the area were offered cheap land by the Earl of Stamford in order to build a park. They raised the money through various efforts, including bazaars. Robert was appointed as one of the original trustees of Stamford Park. See *His Own Man* for more information on Robert and municipal socialism.

[31] Concerns over what we would refer to as 'rubber-necking' and of children being exposed to cases involving illegitimacy and indecency frequently appeared in the local newspapers. See *His Own Man* for more instances.

SARAH: They usually go to the Saturday court. They take a bag of Bull's Eyes and share it amongst themselves. Bessie says it's a lark.

EMMA: I can't imagine why their mother allows that! It's so … common, gawping at the lot of unfortunate people.

ROBERT: I've tried to speak to the other magistrates about this sort of thing, but until I've got the mayor on-side, nothing is going to change.

MARY-JANE: So, why won't he stop members of the public going in?

ROBERT: It's always been the tradition of the land: a public hearing. But things are changing now. Lancashire seems to be one of the very few counties where the court isn't closed for the more … unsavoury cases.

EMMA: Well, surely some of the details …

MARY-JANE: I can only imagine …

SARAH: (*Excitedly*) That's why the Cronkshaws go! It's the details!

EMMA: … that these people have to give out … It's not fit for the ears of children!

ROBERT: It's usually just a case of some lout who's given his wife a black eye. Or some drunken woman who's stolen a mackerel or a pair of stays.

SARAH: Imagine – stealing a pair of stays! *(SARAH happens to be holding one of EMMA'S stays and waggles it at MARY-JANE, who rolls her eyes)*

ROBERT: Nothing that our children won't already have been exposed to by listening to the more gossipy customers in the shop.

SARAH: I do love our shop. Sometimes, if we're lucky, we get people trying to thieve from us! That's always a bit exciting!

EMMA: 'Lucky'!

ROBERT: Don't be ridiculous, Sarah. These people are the scourge of all hard-working shopkeepers.

SARAH: Well, I always think it's quite exciting, watching Dad performing a citizen's arrest.

ROBERT: Ah, yes. I've not had the chance to do that for a while though. It's your mother who does it more these days.

EMMA: Can't be helped. You're in the court so much.

SARAH: Mrs Furrows from the drapers said that she's never known a woman catch so many thieves as our mam.

EMMA: Oh, she's forever saying that …

SARAH: That time when mum trapped that man who took the flour by hitting him on the head with a bucket and then wrapping him in the rug by the door!

MARY-JANE: And getting four of us to sit on him until the constable came.

ROBERT: Heh. Your mother is an argument for the future recruitment of women into the constabulary.

EMMA: I don't think a woman would ever be so foolish as to want to do a job like that, Robert.

MARY-JANE: Indeed. You'll be saying we're stupid enough to want to join the army next.

ROBERT: Your mother catches the thieves and I have to sentence them. What a to-do.

SARAH: Mind you, the stories that Bessie tells us from court are rather different to what you tell us, Dad.

ROBERT: Oh yes?

SARAH: Like the servant girl in the pub – the one whose baby you said died 'by accident' the other week. Bessie said it wasn't an accident at all.

ROBERT: Oh?

SARAH: Yes. Bessie said no one knew that the girl was having a baby. And that she had it all on her own in her room above the pub.

ROBERT: Did she now?

SARAH. Yes. And Bessie said that the girl deliberately dropped it on its head and then stuffed it up the water closet pipe when it was dead.[32]

EMMA: Robert! They shouldn't be hearing things like this!

ROBERT: No, they shouldn't. We need to stop all of this.

EMMA: They're learning all sorts that they don't need to know.

ROBERT: I'll corner the mayor again. The problem is, he believes that public humiliation is an essential ingredient of justice.

MARY-JANE: That's a medieval attitude!

---

[32] A true case from 1874. Robert, though, ruled that the girl did not deliberately kill the illegitimate baby. But because of the serious nature of the case, it had to be referred to the criminal court, where the unfortunate girl was sentenced to prison with hard labour. See *His Own Man* for details of this, and other unhappy cases heard by Robert.

ROBERT: To be fair, the mayor's not so keen on children attending the hearings anyway. But that's mostly because they snigger such a lot. He finds it hard to keep order.

MARY-JANE: He should try it with a class of 40 of the little monkeys.

SARAH: I heard that he finds it hard to keep order because of whatever's in that bottle he's always sipping from.

EMMA: That's enough, Sarah.

SARAH: Well, I don't like this mayor. He's always sending little children to prison. With hard labour!

ROBERT: I agree, he doesn't have the best...

MARY-JANE: It's true. Like, Tommy Morgan – the eight-year-old lad from Castle Hall that he gave three months with hard labour to.[33]

ROBERT: Ah, yes. Not good.

MARY-JANE: I teach his sister. She told me that Tommy was nearly killed by a load of falling bricks last week.

EMMA: Goodness!

MARY-JANE: He'd been with the prison-gang and they were building a wall at a sewage works. It collapsed on him. He can't walk now. They don't know if he ever will.

EMMA: Well, we've had him thieving from our shop, I know, but there's never any justification for ...

MARY-JANE: Eight years old! Hard labour!

ROBERT: We need to sort out this kind of thing. Flogging is the best bet in these cases.

MARY-JANE: Well, I'm completely against flogging for children too!

EMMA: I'm not a fan of it myself. Not from a stranger. Different if it's the parent doing the discipline.

MARY-JANE: No - all of this is an outrage in a modern society! And half of these chaps alongside you who are doling out these sentences call themselves 'Liberals'!

ROBERT: The thing is, most of the other magistrates think that with these sorts of children ... prison is a treat for them.

MARY-JANE: A treat!

---

[33] During Robert's first term as mayor, from 1874-75, the practise of this in Stalybridge was raised in Parliament. See *His Own Man* for more on how and why this came about.

ROBERT: Yes – a bed and some food and quieter nights than they get in their own homes.

SARAH: They make it sound quite pleasant. I might like to try my hand at prison, one of these days.

MARY-JANE: You will soon enough, if you keep wittering on about getting married and having a family like you do.

EMMA: Oh, you're a silly pair.

ROBERT: But the mayor needs tackling on this one. It's tricky; he's more interested in going off on his shooting parties up on the moor.

EMMA: It's no wonder that crime is on the up here! So, this is why I have to manage the shop on my own – and I never see my husband because he's in court half of the time!

MARY-JANE: Well, I think that this particular mayor has never been interested in anything other than feathering his own nest.

ROBERT: Now, now. That's a bit …

SARAH: I thought they didn't pay people who were councillors and mayors and magistrates?[34]

EMMA: They don't. But there are all sorts of other advantages to being a councillor or a mayor. Other money-making opportunities can come your way.

ROBERT: Huh. Well, I've never been anything other than out of pocket since I became a councillor.

MARY-JANE: Plus, power attracts them. They're all power-crazy, these men.

ROBERT: (*Ignoring her*) Anyway, if we paid men to do this line of work, we'd attract the wrong sorts. Men of lower classes, who are only in it for the money.

MARY-JANE: As opposed to men of the upper classes who are only in it for the status. And the backhanders.

EMMA: (*Smiling, shaking her head*) She has a point.

ROBERT: And then there's the prize idiots like me who are clearly in it for entirely the wrong reasons.

MARY-JANE: Poor old Dad.

---

[34] During the 19th century, councillors in England were not paid for their duties. In fact, many of them paid for various civic buildings and made other local gifts i.e. Robert was the first mayor to wear Stalybridge's new mayoral gown and chains, which was a personal donation to the borough by his fellow (mostly wealthy) councillors.

ROBERT: Yes, to them, I'll always be the lower-class odd bod. The interloper councillor and magistrate.

SARAH: Daniel Shawcross's dad calls you 'Snooping Stanley'.

ROBERT: Oh, I've heard it all: 'sticky beak,' 'nosey parker', 'intermeddler'. Doesn't faze me in the slightest.

SARAH: Well, it annoys me when Daniel says it.

ROBERT: No, if anything, it motivates me. Although, I am thinking of calling it a day.

EMMA suddenly stops bustling about with the pots and pans and turns to stare at him.

MARY-JANE: Really?

ROBERT: I think so. I've done ten years. It's never-ending. Council, court, council, court.

MARY-JANE: I don't believe it.

EMMA: Tires me out, just watching you. Never mind all of the extra work 'round…

ROBERT: I barely get time to read the papers in between all of that and the shop and the going to Manchester for the tea side of things.

EMMA: You're like a bear with a sore head when you've not read your newspapers.

MARY-JANE: But you'll never … if you stepped down … you're the fairest chap we've got. Everyone says that.

SARAH: Apart from Daniel Shawcross's dad.

EMMA: Well, he's as common as muck.

SARAH: Actually, I'd be sad too. I like you being a councillor. You're a bit of a hero.

EMMA: Oh, don't you two be encouraging him! I'd like my husband back! There's too much to be doing on my own 'round here.

ROBERT: Well…

EMMA: And the other men in this family are neither use nor ornament. (*Takes her pinafore off and hands it to Robert*) Yes. I for one will be glad if you step down.

ROBERT: Oh, here we go. I don't know why you always leave the bread for me to do.

EMMA: Because I'm getting arthritis. And you're good at kneading the dough.

ROBERT: *(Tying the pinafore around his waist.)* Well, I don't mind this little job. I always imagine the dough to be Mr Gladstone. Our Prime Minister is sorely in need of a good pummelling.

MARY-JANE: Or you could imagine Mrs Whatmough. Your favourite customer.

ROBERT: Urggh. Don't get me started. "There's a rat's whisker in this batch of cornflour, Mr Stanley.' 'No, Mrs Whatmough, that's one of your own whiskers.'

SARAH: Oh, Daddy, you do look like such a big girl's blouse in that pinny!

ROBERT: How dare you! I'll have you know that I'm a dainty little fairy of a girl! See! *(Starts prancing around the kitchen, waving a wooden spoon)* This is my fairy wand and I shall dance the Sugar Plum Fairy for you!

SARAH shrieks with laughter and tries to yank the spoon off him. ROBERT twirls away from her and whacks EMMA on the bottom with the spoon. At that exact moment, the door opens and a man – COUNCILLOR SHAW - is standing on the threshold. He has removed his top hat, revealing a perfectly bald head and his mouth is hanging open in shock.

COUNCILLOR SHAW: I do apologise. Thought I heard a 'Come in'.

ROBERT: *(Mortified, hastily untying the pinafore and shoving the spoon back at EMMA)* Not to worry, Jim; I was just, erm, helping Emma out with kneading the dough.

SARAH: And pretending that he's murdering the Prime Minister and Mrs Whatmough!

EMMA: Sarah! Seen and not heard!

ROBERT: Ha-ha! Ah, well – this isn't normally the course of events of an evening at my house. You've caught us in a rare moment of…

COUNCILLOR SHAW: Uh – domestic levity?

ROBERT: That's the one. Now … can we offer you a cup of tea?

COUNCILLOR SHAW: No. Can't stay. Just wanted to … have you heard the news?

ROBERT: No, I've not had a second to look at the papers today.

COUNCILLOR SHAW: No, no – not that. Local news. Mayor's stepping down.

ROBERT: Fernihough? Is he? Now? What on earth for?

COUNCILLOR SHAW: No – not now. Not now. At the election. November.

ROBERT: Really?

COUNCILLOR SHAW: Doesn't want to stand again. Had enough.

MARY-JANE: I'll bet it's more likely because he knows the country's going to kick the Liberals out!

COUNCILLOR SHAW: Not far off, Miss Stanley. Us Conservatives look to be in with a good shot for the first time in a long stretch.

ROBERT: Fernihough's wanting to jump before he's pushed.

COUNCILLOR SHAW: Exactly. And Councillor Stanley, you're the Conservative Chairman here.

ROBERT: Yes?

COUNCILLOR SHAW: And we think you're the best man for the job…

ROBERT: Yes …

COUNCILLOR SHAW: So, you'll accept the nomination - for mayor? After the elections?

ROBERT: Me? Why… Goodness. It's not something that I thought I'd be... not what I thought people would…

COUNCILLOR SHAW: Why ever not?

ROBERT: Well, I'm just a grocer. I don't have the same sort of credentials that you fellows on the council have. You know. The background. The same sort of … education. Trade and the like.

COUNCILLOR SHAW: Codswallop! Best man for the job.

ROBERT: Well, thank you, that's incredibly… But - the thing is, I've never heard of a tradesman such as myself being appointed mayor.

COUNCILLOR SHAW: Times are a-changing! And we'll throw our weight behind you. We'll make it a first. Put Stalybridge on the map!

MARY-JANE: For something good for a change!

ROBERT: Well … I …

COUNCILLOR SHAW: Come on! No finer fellow. And ... you'll be making history!

MARY-JANE: This all makes perfect sense.

COUNCILLOR SHAW: Your daughter is right. And you're always saying that logic should prevail.

ROBERT: Hmm. Yes. Well. Put like that... it's hard to refuse. Alright then.

He puts his hand out to COUNCILLOR SHAW and then realises that it's covered in flour, so he grabs a cloth and cleans it. They shake on it.

COUNCILLOR SHAW: Now. Let's keep it under our hats. Button your lips. Your good ladies', too.

MARY-JANE rolls her eyes. SARAH mimes 'button lip'.

ROBERT: Yes. Goodbye. Have a good evening and... thank you. Thank you indeed.

COUNCILLOR SHAW leaves.

ROBERT: Well. That's a turn up for the books!

SARAH: Oh ... this is so exciting! I can't wait to tell everyone at school; I shall burst keeping a secret like that!

ROBERT: Well, don't get too excited for now. It may never happen.

MARY-JANE: Oh, fiddlesticks. Of course it will happen. Our dad! The mayor!

EMMA: (*Utterly despondent – to herself whilst gripping the wooden spoon*) And just when I thought I might be getting him back.

SARAH And he'll be the first grocer-sugar-plum mayor in the history of the land! And fair justice shall prevail! But... oh... (*She rushes to the window*)

MARY-JANE: What? (*Following her*)

SARAH: Looks like Our Em is trying to drown our Bob in the water-barrel!

ROBERT: Give me that! (*Yanks the spoon off EMMA*). I'll dispense my own form of justice in this house!

ROBERT *dashes out of the house, whilst* EMMA *moves to the fireplace and bangs her head slowly against the wall.*

---ENDS---

9. THE MAYOR FOR TEA

CONTEXT:

In November 1874, Robert was elected as the ninth mayor of Stalybridge at the age of 46. Although he had never been criticised in the press and was extremely popular, the local newspapers bemoaned the fact that for the first time ever a man from the lower classes – a mere grocer, who was 'too thin' and too young - had gained the most important post in the town.

After moving to the town in 1847, Robert joined the Anglican Old St George's Church and became the leader of the local Conservative Association. At this time, the Conservative (or 'Tory') Party was very much the party of the working-classes – as opposed to the Liberal Party, which represented those with new wealth, and which called for a faster pace of reform in society. Robert's views on political reform were interesting; he held grave concerns that working men were susceptible to voting recklessly (i.e. for the redistribution of wealth and for new socialist notions) if they were not given a decent – and a political – education. He believed in individualism, self-improvement, hard work and that a man's homelife should not be subject to over-interference from the state. Despite this, he was very much a 'municipal socialist' in terms of creating civic improvements for the working classes to enjoy.

As a magistrate, Robert showed sound judgement and impartiality. Unlike many of his peers, he insisted on using the either/or system of offering a fine or a prison sentence. During the first year of his office, Stalybridge achieved national notoriety when a question was raised in Parliament about the sentencing of a seven-year-old boy to an adult prison 'with hard labour'. It turned out that the local newspaper had inaccurately reported on the case.

Robert was elected as mayor again in 1875 and, during his second term, his growing interest in defending the Ottoman Empire led to him refusing to call a meeting to condemn 'the Bulgarian Atrocities' (where Ottoman Muslims were accused of slaughtering hundreds of Christians). This raised questions in Parliament and was commented on by the then Prime Minister, Disraeli. Robert's action was followed by other mayors across the land but, for the first time ever, he was severely condemned by many of the 'great and good' in the local area. This scene pictures what one of his first days as mayor of Stalybridge might have been like.

STALYBRIDGE TOWN HALL, NOVEMBER 25TH 1874

A TUESDAY MORNING AT THE END OF NOVEMBER. **ROBERT STANLEY,** AGED 46, IS SITTING AT A WRITING DESK IN AN UPSTAIRS ROOM AT THE TOWN HALL - THE MAYOR'S OFFICE. HE IS WEARING A NAVY-BLUE SUIT - NOT HIS FINEST - AND THERE IS A GROCER'S OVERALL HANGING ON THE COAT RACK NEXT TO THE DOOR. ROBERT HAS BEEN IN HIS NEW POST FOR TWO WEEKS. WE HEAR HEAVY RAIN OUTSIDE AND THE SOUND OF HORSES' HOOVES CLOPPING, ACCOMPANIED BY THE OCCASIONAL WHINNY AND DISTANT SHOUTS OF MEN CALLING OUT FROM THE MARKET AREA. ROBERT HAS AN OPEN DIARY AND AN INK PEN AT THE READY, AND NEXT TO HIM AT A SMALL TABLE SITS **ADAM BLETCHLEY,** AGED 41, THE TOWN CLERK. BLETCHLEY HAS GINGER, WAVY LOCKS, COIFFURED CAREFULLY, ALONG WITH A BUSHY MOUSTACHE. HE HAS VARIOUS COUNCIL BOOKS PILED UP IN FRONT OF HIM AND IS READING OUT THE NEXT FEW WEEKS' UPCOMING EVENTS TO ROBERT.

BLETCHLEY: …and Monday coming you have the Sanitary Committee; then Tuesday, the Highways Committee; and Wednesday, over in Ashton in the afternoon, you have the Joint Waterworks Board.

ROBERT: Urgh – over in Ashton again? Wednesdays are the Petty Sessions and then I'll have to get over to Ashton. That's a whole day gone from the shop, as that Ashton lot never shut up gabbing and…

BLETCHLEY: I'm afraid so.

ROBERT: I hate coming back from there in the evenings. The contrast between the quality of the Ashton gas lighting and ours...

BLETCHLEY: It's not good.

ROBERT: And the cost! The gas company have clearly been ripping us off. I'll be pushing for us to go municipal and take the dratted thing over.

BLETCHLEY: Always a thorny issue and sure to get on the wick of Napoleon Ives.[35] Easy to do though, that - irritating our esteemed gas inspector.

ROBERT: He's something of a pedant.

BLETCHLEY: Heh. But even he can't rival *you* for attention to details, Mr Mayor.

ROBERT: How so?

BLETCHLEY: Well... counting the number of gas lights out. Or the number of courtyard taps leaking, or however many sewer gullies are... [36]

ROBERT: I take your point, thank you. I'm a dreadful bore, obsessed with minor details.

BLETCHLEY: Not at all! If it wasn't for you, I doubt very much that the new Victoria Market Hall would have been built at all! And then you almost single-handedly steered the creation of the reservoir up at Dovestones.

ROBERT: Well...

BLETCHLEY: Not to mention how important your trusteeship of the new Stamford Park has been. Plus, you're the fairest of all our magistrates, your unique contributions to the School Board, and then there's...

ROBERT: *(Raising an eyebrow)* Very nice to hear, Mr Bletchley, but I have very little say in whether you will receive a pay increase this year.

BLETCHLEY: Ha. Well. One can but try. Right. Back to business. On Thursday we have the Finance Committee. Then, Friday, the Watch Committee.

---

[35] Napoleon Ives caused much merriment within the council, due to his pedantic stances. He later seemed to learn from the errors of his ways and also became mayor of Stalybridge. More Ives-related incidents are related in *His Own Man.*

[36] Robert did indeed patrol Stalybridge, counting faulty gas lamps, sewer gullies and dripping taps. See *His Own Man.*

ROBERT: But on Monday, Wednesday and Saturday mornings I have my magisterial duties at the Petty Sessions! How on earth did the other mayors manage all of this workload?

BLETCHLEY: Well, you're the ninth mayor of Stalybridge and yet the first to have held down a full-time job.

ROBERT: That's a scandal in itself

BLETCHLEY: The other mayors were always either 'men of leisure', as they say, or had at least 100 employees to delegate to.

ROBERT: I can see why I was the first tradesman ever to achieve this post. No one else to date has been crackers enough to attempt it!

BLETCHLEY: It certainly sounds more glamorous than the reality, I'm afraid.

ROBERT: Not to mention the loss of my income whilst I'm away from the shop.

BLETCHLEY: I'm sure that Mrs Stanley is an excellent first mate at the helm of Stanley and Sons.

ROBERT: Oh, certainly. And thankfully our older children help out.

BLETCHLEY: Will they follow you into the trade?

ROBERT: Goodness, I hope not. I can't see independent grocery shops lasting much into the next century. Mark my words, all these big London consumer stores will gobble up the small ones.

BLETCHLEY: You think?

ROBERT: Oh yes. They'll build gigantic shops and drive down prices. And then local people will switch their loyalties and soon the likes of Stalybridge will become ghost towns.

BLETCHLEY: Goodness, but you're full of the joys of spring today.

ROBERT: Hmph. All that I'm saying is that it's not a very lucrative business, grocery. And set to decline.

BLETCHLEY: Mirroring the fortunes of our Empire, it seems!

ROBERT: Sadly. Still, at least our Queen seems to be in far bolder spirits these days.

BLETCHLEY: Ah, yes. I believe we have a certain Scot to thank for that…

ROBERT: Oh, don't let's go bashing that poor fellow like everyone else does. If he's cheering the Queen up, then she jolly well deserves it.

BLETCHLEY: I think it's more about *how* the chap is cheering the Queen up that people object to…

ROBERT: Anyway.

BLETCHLEY: Yes. Onto the council agenda. I've added the horrible railway station death as another item.[37] That poor woman – they were walking round with a bucket and picking up bits of her from…

ROBERT: *(Holds his hand up)* Let's not go over the details.

BLETCHLEY: Fair enough. But this issue gets everyone very angry about that outrageous railway company and the danger they're putting us all in.

ROBERT: Indeed. All the councillors will start ranting and raving in the meeting. So, I'm going to prepare a letter for the Home Office beforehand - from the town council. Save us some time

BLETCHLEY: Usually the councillors sit and agree on the words…

BLETCHLEY eyes ROBERT, whose face is set.

BLETCHLEY: Very well… *(Scribbles a note)* Then, next up. On Saturday, you have morning coffee with St Paul's Ladies' Guild.

ROBERT: Urgh. Really? It will be nothing more than a host of gossips surrounded by dry cake and inferior coffee blends.

BLETCHLEY: I'm afraid you have no choice in the matter. St Paul's Ladies always hold an annual high tea to welcome in the new mayor.

ROBERT: I have very little patience for these female-led fripperies.

BLETCHLEY: Well, they'll have a list of burning issues for you! I've heard they've organised a campaign to allow perambulators into Dukinfield Cemetery.

---

[37] Several deaths had occurred on Stalybridge's railway line, due to overcrowding and lack of safe places for passengers. Just before Robert became mayor, a woman was hit by the London express train. The newspapers reported her death in gruesome detail. Robert chaired a public meeting about it and a government inquiry was held. Eventually an improved station was built for the town. *See His Own Man* for more.

ROBERT: Goodness. A campaign about perambulatory access. But these ladies do occupy themselves with the serious and important issues of the day, don't they?

BLETCHLEY: Heh.

ROBERT: At least there will be the Annual Pensioner Tea Party to look forward to at some point. I much prefer that. We have over two hundred attending these days.

BLETCHLEY: The longer these old people live, the more it's costing the town council though. Maybe we should hold the Pensioner Tea Party next to the railway line.

ROBERT: I'll pretend I didn't hear that.

BLETCHLEY: Only a joke. (*Shuffles his papers*) Doesn't your father travel up from Cardiff every year for the tea party?[38]

ROBERT: He does indeed. He's 86 now. I've just received a letter from him today saying that he's looking forward to seeing me in the new Stalybridge mayoral robes.[39]

BLETCHLY: A proper cause for celebration for him.

ROBERT: Ah, yes. We must hide the gin! And keep him away from some of the more attractive octogenarians. He's a bit of a charmer.

BLETCHLEY: Well, along with the flirting, the pensioners might also be rioting.

ROBERT: How so?

BLETCHLEY: I've heard that the Pensioner's Committee has already booked Reverend Joseph Rayner Stephens to speak.

ROBERT: Yes, he's just reached his own threescore and ten, so he qualifies as a pensioner now himself.

BLETCHLEY: I remember his rabble rousing very well from when I was a small child.

ROBERT: Yes, I saw him yesterday and he said that he's very much looking forward to his entitlement to a pensioners' free tea party.[40]

BLETCHLEY: Do you think that he'll urge the pensioners to form a revolutionary guard? Get them arrested for sedition?

---

[38] We have no information on Robert's father, William, after his move to Cardiff. However, a chance reading of the Stalybridge Reporter in 1875 mentioned that he had travelled from Wales for this occasion.

[39] Robert was the first mayor of Stalybridge to wear full mayoral robes, along with a chain, paid for from donations made by some of the wealthier councillors on the town council.

[40] The famous Joseph Rayner Stephens did indeed address the Pensioner's Tea Party during Robert's first year as mayor. He called Robert the 'wisest man in the town'. See *His Own Man*.

ROBERT: Hmm. Well, that would certainly be more fun to observe than the Ladies of St Paul's Coffee Morning will be.

BLETCHLEY: I realise that it's not really up your street, but it's important that you pacify St. Pauls, given that you yourself attend Old St George's.[41]

ROBERT: It was bad enough when we had the Battle of the Two Saint Georges![42] It's hardly a good example of Christianity, this sort of thing.

BLETCHLEY: Well, regardless …

ROBERT: Thank goodness for Reverend Jelly-Dudley at our church.[43] He's a thoroughly good egg and puts up with no nonsense from ladies trying to dictate to us, with their perambulatory access and whatnot.

BLETCHLEY: He does have a rather silly name though.

ROBERT: Yes, it is a very silly name. Ha! Jelly-Dudley, the good egg! Thank goodness he is of the low church inclination. Mrs Stanley isn't too big a fan of church in general.

BLETCHLEY: No?

ROBERT: No. When we met, I was a member of the Christian Israelite church.

BLETCHLEY: Ah, the beardies.

ROBERT: Yes, that's what the locals called us. And Emma said their various rules and regulations ended up putting her off churches for life!

BLETCHLEY: Not you, though?

ROBERT: No. I feel that a bit of order and direction is a good thing for most human beings. Emma is the sort, though, who manages quite well without it. Great initiative and work ethic.

BLETCHLEY: She seems to manage your shop very well, given all the time that you dedicate to the town council. It's always bustling, so my wife says.

---

[41] The 'churching the mayor' tradition occurred on the first Sunday after an election, where a procession of all councillors and local dignitaries would travel to the church that the mayor attended himself. More on this tradition and on the speech that Robert gave can be found in *His Own Man*.

[42] For numerous reasons, two St George's churches were built next to each other ('Old' St George's was known as 'Cocker Hill Chapel') and the vicar of the 'new' church decided to attempt a takeover bid of the 'old' church. For many months, doors were locked and subsequently smashed down. Hundreds of Stalybridge folk turned up every day to watch the rather outrageous spectacle, which achieved national attention. See *Two Into One Will Go*, by P. Denby.

[43] Yes, this was his real name.

ROBERT: True. Stanley and Sons seems to be rather more popular than Mr Pickering's grocer's or Mr Doxey's.

BLETCHLEY: Well, Mr Doxey needs to sort out the dust balls in the corners of his shop window. I wouldn't want to eat anything from there.

ROBERT: Indeed. And Mr Pickering has never really gained back some of his trade since he was in court for tea contamination.[44]

BLETCHLEY: Poor chap. Tea dealers and traders are at the mercy of these unscrupulous darkies from Africa.[45]

ROBERT: *(A bit ruffled)* Well, I'm not sure where you're buying your tea from, Mr Bletchley. The British public mainly favour Ceylonian or leaves from China.

BLETCHLEY: To be honest, Mr Mayor, I'm not much of a tea drinker. I prefer to take a little coffee.

ROBERT: *(Appalled)* Coffee, Mr Bletchley! A terrible potion! Gives the brain far too much stimulation and rots the gut! Leave the coffee consumption to the dandies of London town, I say, or to the ladies of St Paul's.

BLETCHLEY: I'm afraid it's too late. I'm quite the addict.

ROBERT: Well, we shall soon knock that one out of you. I'll fetch you a sample of my finest Gunpowder Tea. Wakes a man up of a morning without sending him off to work acting like a giddy kipper.

BLETCHLEY: Well, if it's a free sample, Mr Mayor, I'm game. The wages that the borough pay me are far from impressive.

ROBERT: Huh, they're a far sight more impressive than mine. I get paid diddly-squat![46]

BLETCHLEY: Yes, but you get to wear a very fine and very new gown, and to have the respect and esteem of the entire borough.

ROBERT: Hmmm. Be that as it may, it is a good deal – a great deal - of hard work in addition to running a shop and a tea trading business.

BLETCHLEY: Returning to the tea – did Captain Arrowsmith not finger the dodgy foreigner who sold Mr Pickering the duff tea?

---

[44] William Pickering was 'up in court' for buying contaminated tea. Tea contamination was a serious problem throughout Britain at this time.

[45] The term 'Darkies' was unfortunately, a commonly used adjective to describe anyone who was not a white, European during this period in British history. Plenty more derogative words and images existed of course.

[46] Councillors and mayors were unpaid for their work. This was one of the reasons why town councils were entirely dominated by wealthy men until this point.

ROBERT: (*Shaking his head*) Mr Bletchley, I was ten years old when I first began observing the tea trade at my Uncle John's shop.

BLETCHLEY: So young!

ROBERT: Yes. And from my 37 years in this business, I can assure you that the largest portion of tea contamination comes from the English side.

BLETCHLEY: Really?

ROBERT: Certainly. And there is really no excuse for selling a batch that contained steel filings and white powder or whatever else they found in it.

BLETCHLEY: Well, Captain Arrowsmith and his crew at the police station do seem to have issued many notices under the Adulteration Act. But people don't like all these new inspectorates.

ROBERT: It's a shame, because whilst I'm all for the rights to privacy, when it comes to issues of justice and public safety, I'm with the inspectors, every time.

BLETCHLEY: So, how is it that even good chaps like Pickering end up with contaminated tea?

ROBERT: Well, there is far too much negligent purchasing of tea batches. Most folk like Pickering don't take the time and effort to truly understand the tea trade.

BLETCHLEY: I see.

ROBERT: I'd offered to share my own experience with Pickering before he got into that mess. But perhaps he was more concerned with 'profit at any cost'. Certainly not interested in fraternal bonds of businessmen.

BLETCHLEY: Not on the square, then?

ROBERT: Not in any square that I'm associated with.

BLETCHLEY: That's Stamford and Warrington Lodge, isn't it?[47]

ROBERT: Yes. Although Pickering could well be involved with one of the newer, brassier Lodges. He's a Liberal. They never like to admit that there's something to learn.

BLETCHLEY: So, what sort of advice would you give on preventing tea contamination?

ROBERT: Ah, yes. (*Clears throat*) First of all, find a reliable company. One with a noble cause behind it; philanthropically

---

[47] Membership of the Masons was almost a prerequisite for civic life in Victorian Britain. Jamie Gilham has written extensively on this issue in *Victorian Muslim* in relation to Quilliam's Masonic allegiances.

driven. Perhaps favour them with, say, 50 per cent of your purchases. I like to use Twinings.

BLETCHLEY: Very good.

ROBERT: Then - don't go for a rock-bottom price; these men who end up with contamination, they often buy cheap – in bulk - and then charge the usual price.

BLETCHLEY: So, the customer is unaware of the huge profit that the shopkeeper would get?

ROBERT: Precisely. Result? A poisoned customer and a ruined reputation for the tradesman.

BLETCHLEY: Hmmm.

ROBERT: Then, for the other 50 per cent of your tea purchases, use trusted individual traders.

BLETCHLEY: Like…?

ROBERT: For example, I've developed relationships with several chaps from abroad on the floor of the Corn Exchange. Men devoted to the cultivation of high-quality teas.

BLETCHLEY: They must carry a higher price, then?

ROBERT: Certainly. But this then assures you of a genuine respect for the tea itself. And for those involved in buying and selling it.

BLETCHLEY: It must take a lot of time, building relationships.

ROBERT: It does. But it pays off.

BLETCHLEY: I imagine that you must need to be very passionate about your product.

ROBERT: Oh, yes. You must get to know the ins and outs and the history of the plants and of the people in these regions. Even the religion has a bearing on the success of your trade.

BLETCHLEY: The religion?

ROBERT: Oh, yes. Well, in the case of Chinamen, I have had little interaction with them personally. Primarily, I work directly with Turkish traders. Sometimes Ceylonians. A lot of Levantine tea traders in Manchester, too.[48]

BLETCHLEY: But aren't that lot Muhammedans? Aren't they a bunch of brigands?

ROBERT: (*Appalled*) Not at all! Certainly not the Mussulman tea-trader. He is no brigand.

---

[48] The Levant is equivalent to the historical region of Syria but in a wider sense includes all the eastern Mediterranean.

BLETCHLEY: Well, I've never heard anyone put it any differently about the Muhammedans!

ROBERT: Well, I can assure you … I have spent many hours in the company of such tea-traders, and they are honest men. And in comparison to the British traders, they care far more about the price that a tea farmer's family is paid.

BLETCHLEY: I should never have thought it.

ROBERT: One fellow that I regularly buy from at the Corn Exchange – a Mr Rafiq – I trust him that much, that I pay him upfront before I even receive the tea.

BLETCHLEY: Goodness!

ROBERT: And I've also struck up great friendships with Levantine traders in Manchester. I need them for translation work with the newer traders that I meet from overseas.

BLETCHLEY: But how can you be certain that they're not all in cahoots? That they're not taking you for a fool?

ROBERT: (*Stands up and walks to the window; there is shouting outside – an argument between two market traders*) You see, these people are often far more welcoming and offer much more hospitality than native Englishmen. For every single foreign tea trader I work with, I am invited to their homes in Manchester.

BLETCHLEY: That must be…

ROBERT: Fascinating. It is. I've met their wives and children – some of them have more than one wife, you know. And there is no finer method of deciding whether a man can be trusted than by seeing how he runs his household.

BLETCHLEY: I'd be worried in those parts of Manchester that they'd rob me and leave me for dead!

ROBERT: Oh, Bletchley. You need to get out of Stalybridge a bit more. Plus, I always say that if you talk to someone about their faith, you can gauge quite well…

BLETCHLEY: A chit-chat about religion with them!

ROBERT: Why not? Rafiq and I have had many conversations about the similarities between Christianity and his Muhammedan beliefs.

BLETCHLEY: Well…

ROBERT: And after my first visit to his home in Rusholme, he returned to Turkey for some time. When he came back, he brought with him a letter of greeting for me from the tea farmer himself.

BLETCHLEY: The tea farmer? He could write?

ROBERT: Yes. I think Rafiq prefers to work with farmers who are literate. He likes to have things in writing for them so that both parties are fully legally protected by any arrangement.

BLETCHLEY: That seems most...

ROBERT: Principled of him. And then, next - the fellow that bags up and transports the tea from the farmer for Rafiq - he sent me a copy of the Qur'an.

BLETCHLEY: The what?

ROBERT: Their holy book; the book of the Mussulmen.

(ROBERT *wanders back to his chair and sits down, tapping his fountain pen against his notebook*)

BLETCHLEY: Goodness! Why would he send you such a book?

ROBERT: Because Rafiq told him that he had met this English fellow in Manchester who had shown interest in their beliefs.

BLETCHLEY: What a strange - and unusual – gesture for a man who had never met you.

ROBERT: Not so strange when you have met as many Turks and as many Mussulmen as I have. In fact, Rafiq's next action was even more generous.

BLETCHLEY: Let me guess: Rafiq gave you a batch of the finest quality tea – for free!

ROBERT: Ha-ha! No.

BLETCHLEY: He … brought you a new wife back from Turkey?

ROBERT: (*Scowling*) Don't be ridiculous.

BLETCHLEY: My apologies.

ROBERT: Does Mrs Stanley look like the kind of woman who'd put up with that sort of thing?

BLETCHLEY: Heh. No.

ROBERT: No, he bought me another copy of the Qur'an.

BLETCHLEY: Wasn't one copy sufficient?

ROBERT: Perhaps - if I could read Arabic! Indeed, I do read Hebrew, but Arabic is something that I have not yet learned. It's on my retirement list, though.

BLETCHLEY: Mine is to learn to play the trumpet. *(He mimes playing the trumpet. ROBERT eyes him strangely)*

ROBERT: Well, it's a good job we're all different. And you see, their religion was written down for them – they say - directly from God through the mouth of their Prophet Muhammad.

BLETCHLEY: Ah.

ROBERT: That it was given to them in the Arabic language. This is why they say that the Muhammadian religion is far closer to God than Christianity is.

BLETCHLEY: Is that what they say?

ROBERT: Yes. They say that our English Bible has been translated from dozens of different languages, from very many different versions, and remains very far from any original truths that God gave to us.

BLETCHLEY: Do they really?

ROBERT: Yes. They believe in the same God as us, you see. They believe that there are three people 'of God' or 'of the book'. The Jews, then the Christians and then them – the Muhammedans.

BLETCHLEY: Well, I never knew that.

ROBERT: And they believe in exactly the same prophets as Christians and Jews, but they say that there was an end prophet after Jesus – their Muhammad.

BLETCHLEY: So, Christ is a prophet for them?

ROBERT: Yes, the most special of all prophets – until Muhammad. But they do not believe, as Christians do, that Jesus Christ was God incarnate.

BLETCHLEY: Ah, a significant theological differentiation there.

ROBERT: Oh, yes. But nonetheless, I shall let you know more about it all when I have finished reading the Qur'an.

BLETCHLEY: But I thought you couldn't read Arabic.

ROBERT: Apologies, that's what I meant to say – this second copy of their holy book was an English translation.

BLETCHLEY: How quaint! That someone wanted to do that. Translate it into English.

ROBERT: Well, it's a very popular subject these days, Mr Bletchley. Even Queen Victoria is said to be interested in the subject of the Muhammedan religion.

BLETCHLEY: I suppose it must help her understand how certain elements of the Empire behave.

ROBERT: There is that.

BLETCHLEY: I mean, I thought it was Hindoo fighting Hindoo, until I read that there were various religions out there, trying to lop each other's heads off.[49]

ROBERT: *(Ignoring him)* One of the problems, though, is that these English translations of their book are always carried out by Christians. So, invariably, they're setting out to prove that the Muhammedans are misled!

BLETCHLEY: Hmm. Some of these churchmen wouldn't want you to be reading an unfiltered version, I imagine.

ROBERT: Indeed. But, alas, I cannot see me finding any time soon to read the book.

BLETCHLEY: *(Sighs, looking at the clock).* Time is always the issue.

ROBERT: I've already had it for a year, and I have only broken into the first two chapters.

BLETCHLEY: Our time is not our own!

ROBERT: *(Pointing his fountain pen at BLETCHLEY)* And the way that you are flinging tea parties and council committees at me, I might as well abandon all hope of even picking it up for another two or three years or so!

BLETCHLEY: Don't you think that perhaps these men were being rather too … thoughtful?

ROBERT: *(Puzzled)* How so?

BLETCHLEY: I mean, what if they're aiming to get you to take an oath of their own - for you to become the first Mussulman mayor in Britain!

ROBERT: Ha! Ha-ha! Imagine what Reverend Jelly-Dudley would say to that!

BLETCHLEY: *(Grinning)* Especially after you were claiming your Christianity so fiercely in front of half of Stalybridge at your Churching last week!

ROBERT: Perhaps I should lend the Reverend Jelly-Dudley my copy of the Qur'an. He is certainly a man with more time on his hands than I.

---

[49] There was general confusion around the word (spelled) 'Hindoo' in Britain at this time. It was usually used to refer to anyone who was from the Indian sub-continent.

BLETCHLEY: And on that note, Mr Mayor – back to business.

ROBERT sighs and opens his notebook again.

ROBERT: Go on.

BLETCHLEY: You need to jot down Tuesday: 'Pianoforte serenade 6 pm at the Town Hall'. Wednesday – 'Meeting with the gas inspectors at 1 pm' and then 'Town meeting with regards to the death at Stalybridge station'.

ROBERT: Did we invite the railway company to attend? To provide an explanation? To vent our disgust at them in public?

BLETCHLEY: We did. No reply so far.

ROBERT: Hmph. I cannot bear these rich, pompous idiots who run the train companies, who don't give a tinker's cuss about mutilating our townsfolk.

BLETCHLEY: They certainly think that they're a cut above the rest of us.

ROBERT: Yes, I'd like to stick a fatwa on them.[50]

BLETCHLEY: I'm sorry?

ROBERT: Nothing, nothing.

---ENDS---

---

[50] A fatwa is an important legal opinion made by a Muslim qualified in Sharia Law.

10. FOREIGN MATTERS IN THE PUB

CONTEXT:

In 1881, Robert Stanley became landlord and owner of the New Inn, a pub on the border between Ashton and Stalybridge. Pub life was a crucial part of culture in these mill towns, providing warmth, cheer

The New Inn today, Ashton under Lyne

and a much-needed chance to relax and socialise.

The Stanley family still ran the grocer's and tea business in Stalybridge, but now chose to base themselves in the living quarters of the inn. Robert would have played a big role in managing the pub, but even so, it is likely that he now had more time to spend at Manchester's Old Corn Exchange in terms of the tea-trading business. It seems that during this time, he got to know more Muslims engaged in various international trades. Robert's knowledge of the Ottoman Empire and of Islam certainly increased at this point in his life. He wrote letters to the Sultan/Caliph (ruler of the Ottoman Empire) outlining the need for an English-Muslim translation of the Qur'an and advising him on agricultural and military issues. Following his letters to *The Crescent* – Britain's first Islamic magazine - Robert also met the country's most famous Muslim convert – Sheikh William 'Abdullah' Quilliam.

In the 1891 census, Robert and Emma were living with several of their adult children at the New Inn; Thomas, Mary-Jane and Sarah. Their youngest, Alice, had recently married and moved out. In 1897, Robert sold the pub to Cardwell's Brewery in Hulme, Manchester. Whilst it is highly unlikely that Robert was a follower of the Temperance movement (given his decision to purchase and live over a pub), as he drew closer to Islam it seems obvious that the close association with pub life did not sit comfortably with him. A year later, in 1898, the family were pub-free; they had moved to Manchester and Robert had said Shahada, becoming a Muslim.

This scene imagines some of the discussions that might have taken place when Robert had decided to sell the pub and move to Manchester.

ASHTON-UNDER-LYNE, OCTOBER 1896

MID-MORNING IN THE LARGE KITCHEN OF THE NEW INN. THREE WOMEN ARE SITTING AT THE KITCHEN TABLE. THERE ARE SEVERAL OTHER LARGE TABLES AROUND THE KITCHEN, ONE HOLDING A SLAB OF NON-DESCRIPT MEAT AND ANOTHER HAS SEVERAL BOXES OF EGGS, BREAD, BUTTER AND MILK. THERE ARE DOZENS OF POTS AND PANS HANGING FROM A RACK AND AN ENORMOUS RANGE OVEN. **EMMA STANLEY,** AGED 70, HAS NOW BEEN THE PUB LANDLADY FOR SEVENTEEN YEARS. SHE HAS AGED WELL BUT LOOKS IN NEED OF A REST. **MARY-JANE,** AGED 38, REMAINS UNCHANGED: A TEACHER, SHE WEARS SPECTACLES AND CONSTANTLY PULLS THEM ON AND OFF IN ORDER TO LOOK AT THINGS. SHE LOOKS EVERY INCH 'THE SPINSTER SISTER', BUT REVELS IN THIS ROLE. **ALICE STANLEY,** AGED 25, IS THE YOUNGEST CHILD AND STILL LOOKS FAR MORE CHILDLIKE THAN HER YEARS. SHE IS IN THE FIRST FLUSHES OF EARLY MARRIED LIFE.

EMMA: What's your father doing up there? I've shouted him a dozen times.
MARY-JANE: Bang the gong.
EMMA: No. Thomas is having a sleep – he only went to bed at one.
MARY-JANE: I think Dad went up to write a letter.
EMMA: No doubt. He doesn't like writing his letters down here. Says the smell of the beer clings to the stationery.
ALICE: I don't suppose Queen Victoria would appreciate her correspondence smelling like a brewery.

EMMA: Oh, you don't think he's writing to the Queen again, do you?

MARY-JANE: She must have a proper little collection of them by now. I bet she's made a scrapbook up of Mr Stanley's letters ... and shows them round the Court.

ALICE: Maybe that's why the country's gone to pot. She's been showing them to the Prime Minister. They've all been following Dad's advice.

EMMA: We shouldn't make fun.

ALICE: Actually, I think the Queen has been spared today. He was grumbling on before ... along the lines of 'Bring Back Disraeli'.

MARY-JANE: Either that or it'll be one of his 'Send Mrs Fawcett and her dim-witted suffragist troops off to prison!' letters.

ALICE: They proper get him angry, those women, don't they? I've never understood why.

MARY-JANE: Because he's a dinosaur!

EMMA: Mary-Jane ...

MARY-JANE: Well, I'm sorry, Mother, but there are certain subjects that he becomes very irrational over.

EMMA: There's some things he gets worse about as he gets older.

MARY-JANE: I mean, he's always criticising women for being too directed by their emotions – but he's incapable of having a calm discussion about female suffrage. His logic goes to pot.

ALICE: Same if you mention Oscar Wilde.

EMMA: Or where the post office should be located in Stalybridge.

MARY-JANE: Oh – and all of this new 'wireless communication' of Mr Marconi's; Dad thinks it'll result in a world filled with imbeciles who are rendered incapable of reading a book.

ALICE: And the way he chunners on about foreign affairs. Joe says that Dad's got it all wrong on Afghanistan.

MARY-JANE: Your Joe's as bad as Dad. Give a man a newspaper and the mention of a possible conflict and they're all suddenly experts. Even when – like Dad and Joe - they've never left the shores of this country!

ALICE: It does seem a little bit ... unusual to be so interested in foreign affairs. And to have never left the country.

EMMA: Well, where on earth would your Dad have gotten money to go travelling with?

ALICE: Uncle John; everyone knows how rich *he* was.

EMMA: Oh, yes. But he'd never have stumped up any cash for foreign exploits.

MARY-JANE: But I thought that his son – Deane, wasn't it? - was killed in South Africa?

ALICE: Was he? I never knew that.

MARY-JANE: Yes. He fell off his horse hunting for diamonds. Yet another man come to a nasty end thanks to the love of money.

EMMA: Yes, well, Deane was another one with silly ideas. Like your dad, a bit too obsessed with the Turks. Gave him some funny views on things, those towels did.

ALICE: *(Puzzled)* What?

EMMA: Ran that Turkish towel company.

MARY-JANE: I'm not sure how providing cotton towelling products can result in funny views; diamonds might send someone silly, maybe, but…

ALICE: I don't see why Uncle John couldn't have paid for Dad to travel too.

EMMA: Deane was John Stanley's son and your dad was just his nephew.

ALICE: Hmm. I suppose your children always come first in life.

EMMA: They do. Although your dad came a pretty good second when it came to your Uncle John. They always shared an interest in religion.

MARY-JANE: Well, I suppose, to give him his due, Uncle John helped you and Dad out quite a bit, didn't he? Getting you the shop and everything.

EMMA: Exactly. And we were grateful enough for that without us having to hanker after foreign adventures.

ALICE: You've never seemed the sort, Mam.

EMMA: No. But I'd be quite grateful if someone made an effort to take me to Blackpool to see the new tower. That's quite far enough for me, thank you very much.

MARY-JANE: Not an unreasonable thing to ask, Mother. I'll remind Dad.

ALICE: So, if Dad had been offered the money to go travelling – would he have done it?

EMMA: Maybe. But not if I had had anything to say about it. Stuck in Stalybridge on my own, bringing up eleven children!

MARY-JANE: True, travel is a male prerogative, as well as something available only to the wealthy. Oscar Wilde, for example. Imagine if he'd been a common working man!

ALICE: Yes – imagine!

MARY-JANE: His life would have been in ruins after he left prison. But because he's got a bob or two, he scarpers abroad and starts up a new life on the Continent.

EMMA: Hmm, well. If Oscar Wilde had been a common working man, he wouldn't be in prison in the first place.

ALICE: Why?

EMMA: Well, the things that these chattering classes get up to - the queer ideas that they get in their heads - too much time on their hands, if you ask me.

ALICE: Oh, Mother! I quite like Mr Wilde's work. He's written some excellent things.

EMMA: I don't doubt that he has. But there's something not quite…

ALICE: It's a shame I can't share his work with my students. They'd probably learn a thing or two.

MARY-JANE: That's what folk are scared of. That the likes of Oscar Wilde will educate children in completely the wrong way.

ALICE: It's all very silly. Mind you, Joe is completely against Mr Wilde's sort of 'lifestyle'; thinks he should be birched.

EMMA: Well, I wouldn't go that far, but I'd not have him free to be roaming around and corrupting young boys.

MARY-JANE: Corrupting young boys? Honestly! I'm surrounded by dinosaurs! Dad and your Joe, Alice - and even Mum with her…

EMMA: Mary-Jane, I don't know where you get your radical notions from, but they're certainly not from this house.

MARY-JANE: This pub, you mean. Oh, I must say that I'm looking forward to living in a proper house again.

ALICE: Well, I'm only sorry that I can't come with you. But marital duties call.

EMMA: *(Waving her hand)* So they should. And whilst I'm glad that our Mary-Jane has the sense not to get married and that she prefers to stay with her parents…

MARY-JANE: Heh – I'll take that as a compliment.

MARY-JANE picks up her mother's hand and kisses it.

EMMA: ... No, I wouldn't have thought that our Thomas would still be living with us at the age of 44.

MARY-JANE: Well, we're just a port in the storm for our Thomas. He gets to have a nice job, bed and board and the chance to save up a bob or two before he runs off again in a couple of years and blows it all on his adventures.

EMMA: Aye. He likes his three women running 'round after him, seeing to his every need.

ALICE: Well, I don't run about after him. I've got Joe to look after!

EMMA: Oh, I don't mean you – I mean Maria. *(She stands up to fetch the teacups)* Maria's paid to help out with the housework and making the pies and whatnot. But I'm always telling her not to be seeing to our Thomas.

MARY-JANE: Well, I think she probably ignores your advice, Mother. She's often 'seeing' to him.

EMMA is not listening as she has her head in the cupboard, looking for a tin of biscuits. ALICE mouths 'Really?' to her sister, who nods. ALICE looks shocked. EMMA brings out the biscuit tin, rattling it.

EMMA: *(Opening tin)* Thought so! That Thomas! There's only two left!

ALICE: Anyway. On Thomas. Have you decided if he's going to be going with you to Manchester?

ROBERT, aged 67, enters. He is as smartly dressed as ever in his black suit and is carrying a small parcel of letters and a box of ink pens. He places them on the table.

ROBERT: No, Thomas is most certainly not coming to Manchester. About time he stood on his own two feet. Ah, I thought I heard the sound of a kettle. And biscuits, too!

EMMA: No biscuits. Thomas.

ROBERT: Typical. Where is he?

MARY-JANE: Still in bed.

ROBERT: What? The beer delivery arrives at eleven!

MARY-JANE: I can help.

ROBERT: No fear, I shall go up and throw cold water in his face if he sleeps in any longer. He's no idea what hard work means.

ALICE: So, what are his plans for when you go to Manchester?

ROBERT: Haven't a clue. Probably involves mooning around and entering into a state of shiftless unemployment again.

ALICE: Joe was wondering whether you'd take him on as an agent with the tea business, like you've done with our John.

ROBERT: I'd happily do that, Alice - if he showed any ounce of initiative or common sense. It would have done Thomas the world of good to settle down with a family like our John did. Responsibility.

EMMA: Well, you were the one who encouraged Thomas to go off on his travels.

ROBERT: Yes, but I thought it would be the making of him! If I had had the chance of that - to travel and to enlighten myself further about the world - I would have seized the day!

MARY-JANE: Funnily enough, we were just saying that.

ROBERT: I'd have made the most of it!

EMMA: Well, I'm very sorry that we hampered your progress, dear.

ROBERT: (*Kisses her on the head*) I didn't mean it like that. Now someone pour me a brew before we stew it.

MARY-JANE: We were also saying before, Dad, that most men just read the newspapers about overseas affairs. And then formulate their ill-informed opinions without ever having travelled.

ROBERT: Oh yes?

MARY-JANE: Yes. But our Thomas has done the opposite hasn't he? He spends his money on foreign travel and still comes back utterly ignorant and vacuous.

ROBERT: (*Chuckles to himself*) Oh, get back in the knife drawer, Miss Stanley.

EMMA pours the tea and hands out small pieces of biscuits.

ROBERT: Goodness me, broken biscuits. It's like the days of the Cotton Famine and the Bread Riots all over again.

EMMA: Thank goodness we don't see that sort of monkey-business anymore.

ROBERT: Well, they'll be seeing it in Russia soon – mark my words!

EMMA: *(Rolling her eyes)* Blummin' Russia.

ROBERT: Now, what's on the agenda for you ladies today?

ALICE: I'm off to Jowett's on Penny Meadow to buy a new jacket for school.

EMMA: And we're about to start the pies. Maria's day off.

MARY-JANE: Urgh. I hate faffing around with meat.

EMMA: So, we're just waiting for the butcher's boy. I'm a bit worried he'll have mucked the order up.

ROBERT: Why would he do that?

EMMA: Because we've not used Fitter's before.

ROBERT: And that will make Mr Fitter more vigilant. They won't want to lose the new business.

ALICE: So, why have you dropped Patterson's? You've always used Mr Patterson.

EMMA: Oh, it's some experiment of your father's.

ROBERT: It's not an 'experiment'. And Patterson has had more than enough out of us over the years. He's talking about buying one of those new motor cars.

MARY-JANE: *(To Alice)* Dad's been reading about the benefits of this meat that the Mussulmen eat – 'halal', isn't it called?

ROBERT: That's right. We'll be using Mr Fitter's meat in the pies. Instead of Patterson's. Fitter is Jewish.

ALICE: Won't that upset the punters? I can't imagine anyone being persuaded by exotic dishes. Whether Jewish or from a Mussulman!

ROBERT: Alice – this meat tastes nicer.

ALICE: Really?

ROBERT: Jewish fellows like Fitter slaughter the animal in much the same way as the Mussulman does. A calmer manner. The blood drains from the animal's throat and …

MARY-JANE: *(Holding her hand up)*. Please. You know I don't like talking about how things are killed.

ROBERT: I could understand that if you chose to only eat vegetables. But …

EMMA: Change the subject, Robert.

ROBERT: Anyway. We used to eat the same sort of meat many years ago. Just before you were born, Mary-Jane.

ALICE: Where would we have gotten halal meat from 'round these parts?

ROBERT: Like I said, it's the same as the kosher meat that the Jews eat. When I worked in Uncle John's shop, we sold kosher there. It was a Christian Israelite shop.

EMMA: It was back in the day when we had to attend the Christian Israelite Sanctuary. They'd only eat kosher.

MARY-JANE: Ah, yes. After Uncle John paid for your wedding … and for our shop.

EMMA: *(Looks heavenward)* Urgh. All those regulations on what you could - and couldn't - eat and drink.

ALICE: So, when did you stop going?

EMMA: After Uncle John died. It was rather a blessing.

ROBERT: Emma!

EMMA: Well! *You* didn't have to sing in that choïr with all their rules for women; *(to her daughters)* we could only wear blue or yellow, no mirrors allowed and some of them wore veils…

MARY-JANE: No! How ridiculous!

ROBERT: They were only following what the Bible teaches.

ALICE: Is that why you won't have your photo taken, Mam?

EMMA: No. Just don't like gawping at pictures of myself.[51]

MARY-JANE: There aren't many Christian Israelites left in Ashton, now.

EMMA: Lots of folk fell away from it, after their prophet went to Australia. Uncle John's wife, Mary …

MARY-JANE: *(To Alice)* Aunt Mary was nearly thirty years younger than Uncle John.

ALICE: Urgh.

EMMA: … She had their children baptised in the Church of England, only days after he died.

MARY-JANE: Bit of a spiritual insurance policy, no doubt.

ROBERT: *(Ignoring them)* Anyway. We'll be buying the meat from Mr Fitter. It's both kosher and halal.

ALICE: But, Dad - is this for … kindliness reasons – for the animals? Or…

---

[51] Although we do have photographs of Robert and of his children, there are no photographs of Emma.

166

ROBERT: (*Ducking the issue*) Various, but…

MARY-JANE: But, wait a minute. What about pork? I thought that the Jews don't eat pork? So, is that the same for the Moslems?

ROBERT: Yes. Both religions follow the letter of the law on dietary requirements. From the book of Leviticus. A pig is a thoroughly unclean animal. And I for one, no longer wish to consume it.

MARY-JANE: I suspect that the pig is an enormous fan of the Jewish and the Moslem religions, then.

EMMA: Wait a minute! Pork … we didn't discuss that, Robert, not having pork sausages. I like my pork sausages!

ROBERT: (*Dismissively*) Oh, we'll be fine with beef sausages.

EMMA: Well, I'm not happy about that!

There is silence for a moment. ROBERT deliberately ignores EMMA's remark.

ALICE: They don't drink alcohol either, do they? The Muhammedans.

ROBERT: They don't.

EMMA: Well, at least they'll have less sick to clean up outside of *their* front doorsteps then. Sixteen years of that, we've had.

MARY-JANE: But Dad, as for the pies – what if the customers notice the difference? In the taste?

ROBERT: Believe me, if anything, it's a better taste. They'll be happier.

EMMA: But they'll be able to tell!

MARY-JANE: Maybe we can put a notice up: 'Your pies now contain Moslem meat and all proceeds from the sale of your pie will go to re-building the failing Ottoman Empire.'

ROBERT: Sarcasm is the lowest form of wit.

ALICE: I don't understand though, Dad; if you're trying to sell the pub, why bother experimenting with the meat?

ROBERT: (*Vaguely*) Oh, you know, start as you mean to go on.

ALICE screws up her face, puzzled and mouths at MARY-JANE, 'What?' MARY-JANE shrugs.

ROBERT: Anyway. The sale is due to go through with the brewery in 8 to 12 weeks. So, the impact of changing the meat is hardly of any consequence.

EMMA: Maybe not to you, but…

ROBERT: *(Holds his hand up in a 'stop' gesture and speaks loudly)* I've said what I have to say!

There is an uncomfortable silence. EMMA is patently unhappy. She stands up stiffly, takes the tea pot and plonks it down hard on the counter.

EMMA: *(To herself but deliberately loudly)* Next thing, he'll be wanting to experiment with taking the alcohol out of the beer!

MARY-JANE and ALICE catch each other's eye, trying to assess the severity of the situation.

ALICE: *(Changing the subject)* So, who is your letter to, Dad? The Queen?

ROBERT: Ha – no. I'm giving the Queen a rest. *(Trying to be jocular)* She'd become far too dependent on my advice.

EMMA: *(Under her breath)* Perish the thought.

ROBERT: And, anyway, she has a fine new advisor now. One Abdul Karim - a Mussulman from India who is apparently causing waves amongst her courtiers because he is teaching her Urdu and lessons from the holy Qur'an.[52]

MARY-JANE: It strikes me that our Queen is one of those women who cannot survive without a man to lean on. Hardly the strong female leader that everyone talks about.

ALICE: Who're you writing to then, Dad? The Prime Minister? The Pope?

ROBERT: If you're really interested – and you don't need to pretend that you are…

ALICE: *(Trying to change the atmosphere)* Oh – I am!

ROBERT: It's to the Caliph. Or the Sultan, as he is also known.

ALICE: Is that the same person as the Amir? I thought you'd already written to the Amir.

---

[52] See *Victoria and Abdul*, by Shrabani Basu.

ROBERT: No – goodness, Alice! Fancy not knowing the difference between the Amir and the Caliph! You're a teacher!

ALICE: Perhaps. But we're only mere mortals. We can't know everything.

ROBERT: I might be better teaching your children myself at this rate, despite the fact that I never had any formal schooling.

ALICE: You'd not be able to cope with the lack of discipline, Dad.

MARY-JANE: True. You can only cane them these days, Dad. You can't tie them to a post anymore and flog them.

ROBERT: More's the pity. No, the *Amir* is the leader of Afghanistan – a very-forward thinking man, Abd-ar-Rahman. And the *Caliph* is over Turkey – over the entire Ottoman Empire. His name is Abdul Hamid Khan the Second.

ALICE: Oh, I see. So why are you writing to him?

ROBERT: Just responding to something that I read about his current problems. That I saw written in this. (*Waves a copy of The Crescent at her*).

ALICE: What's that?

ROBERT: (*A bit puffed-up*) Ah … The Crescent. It's the first publication produced for all Moslems in the world. The publisher goes by the name of a Mister William Quilliam. Resides in Liverpool. A highly esteemed lawyer.

EMMA: (*Her back is still turned*) 'Highly esteemed' – the chap is from Liverpool. Ha!

MARY-JANE: (*To Alice*). He became a Mussulman. Now goes by the name of 'Abdullah Quilliam'.

ROBERT: I see you've been reading my publications again.

MARY-JANE: It pays to be kept well-informed about the latest issues that our menfolk are discussing in their smoking rooms and in their clubs.

ROBERT: (*Chuckling*) Ah – a spy in our midst!

MARY-ANNE: If you like. But I've seen him mentioned many a time in the Manchester Guardian, too.[53]

---

[53] Although named the 'Manchester Guardian', the prominence of the city meant that this newspaper was one of Britain's main national newspapers. Later on, the 'Manchester' part of its title was dropped and it is now the same 'Guardian' newspaper as today.

ROBERT: He's very highly regarded. The Caliph himself has appointed Quilliam as the head of the religion in the British Isles. 'Sheikh ul Islam' is his title.

EMMA: *(Turning around now and sitting back down. Arms folded.)* Very grand. Did he get a medal too?

ROBERT: *(Ignoring her)* Anyway. There's a Turkish tea-trader, chap I often see on the floor of the Corn Exchange; he always gives me his copies of The Crescent, once he's read them.

MARY-JANE: It's quite an interesting read, actually.

ROBERT: And it's far less biased about how British foreign policy affects the Moslem populations of the world than … the likes of The Guardian or The Times.

ALICE picks up the magazine and pauses as she reads

ALICE: Quite a wide variation in content; geological formations on the Isle of Man … Freemasons and … goodness! Polygamy?

MARY-JANE: Hmm. There's only so much you can read about Mr Quilliam's love of rocks. He is quite the bore when it comes to geology.

ROBERT: Heh. He's a member of the Royal Geographical Society. I've attended one of his lectures at the Secular Hall in Manchester on the subject.

MARY-JANE: He tries to tell 'jokes' in his publications too. I'm not fond of how he likes to poke fun at women.

ROBERT: Oh, Mary-Jane; it's very gentle humour *(ROBERT pokes her sleeve gently as if to emphasise this)*.

ALICE: So, anyway, Dad. *(Handing 'The Crescent' back to him)* What's your letter about? Can you read us a bit of it?

ROBERT: Oh, I don't want to cause you to fall asleep.

MARY-JANE: Don't worry. You can't possibly be as tedious as your Mr Quilliam and his rocks.

ROBERT: *(Giving her a look, he takes the letter from his top pocket)*. Well, alright then. Here's an extract: *'It would certainly be a wise decision for His Royal Highness to investigate the current practise of agricultural chemistry, as recommended by the scientist Mr Ville. If His Royal Highness is able to improve the quality of the soil, then Turkey should surely be able to improve its army numbers, to the tune of at least fifty thousand more men in the military.*

His Royal Highness, therefore, might also like to look into sending some of his finest scholars to Germany's world-famous agricultural schools.'

EMMA: *(Half-snorting).* Well, I'm sure that he will feel very enlightened, after receiving that.

ALICE: But, Dad - don't you think that he'd know that sort of thing already?

ROBERT: You'd be surprised. There are an awful lot of powerful men who are surrounded by advisors, fellows who lack intelligence and who are not well-read.

MARY-JANE: That's very true. Men who are awarded such positions as an accident of birth as opposed to merit.

ALICE: But, don't you think that the Caliph would find it a little bit... I mean – a man from the north of England sending him information on how to run his troops?

EMMA: *(Arms folded, looking at ROBERT directly).* What if he thinks that you're some sort of a ... spy?

ROBERT: Not at all! The information that I'm outlining for him is clearly designed to be helpful.

EMMA: Well. *(Standing up again and beginning to sweep the kitchen floor.)* Just don't go sending your letter from the post office here, Robert. Mr Proudfoot the Postmaster is a nosey so and so.

ROBERT: I'll post it in Manchester, like I always do.

EMMA: Good.

ROBERT: Yes. There's folks round here who don't take kindly to people who have different opinions about the world.

MARY-JANE: There certainly are.

ROBERT: And that's another reason I'll be glad to move away.

MARY-JANE: Yes, and the sooner I can start going to more social affairs for women - that don't involve flower arranging and beetle drives - the better!

ALICE: Well, I'll miss you all. There's only Bob and our Em near me now. Won't you miss us, Mother?

EMMA: Well, we're only a hop and a skip away on the train. And if we find a house in Rusholme... *(eyeballs Robert)*

ROBERT: *(Nods)* I'm onto it, don't worry.

EMMA: ... We'll be right next to John and Martha and the little ones.

MARY-JANE: *(Standing up and taking the broom from EMMA, directing her to sit down.)* It'll certainly help our John, having Dad nearby to help him on the tea side of things.

EMMA: We're supposed to be retiring!

MARY-JANE: So, sit down for a minute and start practising!

ROBERT: Yes, sit down, Emma. Oh, it won't be long … John just needs a bit of help with improving in terms of his manner with customers.

MARY-JANE: *(To ALICE)* John doesn't like talking to all the foreigners like Dad does.

EMMA: *(Finally sitting down and picking her teacup up.)* He's never liked talking to foreigners, has our John.

ROBERT: I know, and it's ridiculous. I don't know who he gets it from.

EMMA: Well, I'm with our John. It's embarrassing when you can't understand foreigners' accents.

ROBERT: Ridiculous! I had to put up with it in the court room in Stalybridge! People that were jabbering away like monkeys and from only down the road in Castle Hall. Could hardly understand a word they said.

EMMA: Some folk just aren't comfortable with those from different places.

ROBERT: Very silly. People are people. We all need to listen to each other more, to learn from one another. That's what I try to do.

MARY-JANE: Unless it's Oscar Wilde.

ALICE: Or the Archbishop of Canterbury.

MARY-JANE: Or the suffragists.

ALICE: Or the Bulgarians.

MARY-JANE: Ooh, yes, we'd forgotten about the Bulgarians. And the Greeks!

ROBERT: Alright, alright, that's enough.

MARY-JANE: *(Still chuckling)* But, Dad – if the Caliph decides to write back, how will he know our new address in Manchester?

ROBERT: Oh … good point. I'd better give him my Corn Exchange address. Yes… *(He looks around at the kitchen and nods slowly)* Yes, I shall be sorry to see the back of this place, in some ways.

EMMA: Well, I for one won't be. I never wanted to be a pub landlady. And sixteen years is enough for anyone.

ROBERT: Still, it's been a nice little earner for us in many ways. A shame, though, that Thomas never showed any aptitude for it.

MARY-JANE: He's never shown much aptitude for anything, other than mysterious adventures abroad that involved losing several hundred pounds.

ROBERT: Still. Living in Manchester… We'll meet far more interesting people.

MARY-JANE: No doubt Dad will be bringing all his Turkish and Levantine tea-trader friends home for a spot of supper with us! That should be a bit of … fun.

EMMA: Well, he'd better find himself one of those halal butchers, because I won't be cutting the throats of some poor animal and saying a prayer over it – just to please his dinner guests.

ROBERT: *(Rolling his eyes)* Emma – there are one or two butchers like that in the Rusholme area. And we'll get plenty of invitations to go to the houses of my fellow tea traders. A very hospitable lot, most Mussulmen and folk from the East.

EMMA: Wonderful. I'll dust my veil off and walk twenty paces behind you.

ROBERT: Now, that's where John got it from!

EMMA: What?

ROBERT: His silly notions of how foreigners behave.

EMMA: Hmph. Well. We'll have been married for 50 years in just a few months. So, if you think that all of a sudden I'll be like one of these women who…

ROBERT: I'd never think that, dear. Oh, that reminds me. Our Golden Anniversary Tea Party at Belle Vue. As well as the usuals from Stalybridge, I've invited some tea traders – chaps from the Levant and Turkey in Rusholme.

EMMA: Well, that'll save us a bob or two.

ROBERT: How so?

EMMA: Because that'll stop the Stalybridge lot coming. I can't see any of them wanting to be at a party that involves no pork, no bacon, no beef and no alcohol. It'll be a laugh a minute.

MARY-JANE: Might I suggest, Dad, that as a special Golden Wedding treat, you take Mother to see Blackpool Tower instead?

ALICE: What a lovely idea – go on, Dad!

ROBERT: Not likely. The mood she's in, she'll shove me off the top!

---ENDS---

11. THE FAMOUS MR QUILLIAM

CONTEXT:

William Quilliam was born on the Isle of Man in 1855 and was some 28 years younger than Robert Stanley. His family were wealthy, middle-class Wesleyan Methodists who were strong proponents of the temperance movement. Quilliam became a lawyer based in Liverpool and did his bit for the suffering poor of the city, taking on many of their cases for free. Unlike Robert, his family wealth enabled him to travel overseas and in 1886, he converted to Islam following a trip to Morocco. He set up the Liverpool Muslim Institute (LMI)

Inside the Liverpool Mosque c. 1898

along with two magazines - *The Crescent* and *The Islamic Review* - which were shipped around the world to existing Muslims and to new converts. During 1889, he founded the first mosque in Britain at Brougham Terrace in Liverpool.[54] He was a champion of Ottoman Islam and, in 1890, the Sultan (or Caliph) of the Ottoman Empire, Abdul Hamid Khan II, proclaimed Quilliam as 'Sheikh al-Islam' – the spiritual leader of Muslims in Britain. Quilliam and the LMI also set up a boys' and a girls' school, and the Medina Orphanage, which raised destitute children in the Islamic faith but also aimed to restore the reputation and wellbeing of their mothers. Quilliam was a fierce critic of the hypocrisy of men's attitudes towards women in Victorian England and felt that Islam provided at least one answer to this – that of polygamy. He himself was in polygamous relationships for most of his adult life and had children by two of his three wives - Hannah Quilliam and Mary Lyon.

---

[54] During the same year, Britain's first purpose-built mosque – Shah Jahan Mosque - was founded in Woking, Surrey by a non-Muslim. The two mosques therefore, appeared at the same time and are friendly rivals for the title of 'First UK Mosque'.

Whilst Quilliam frequently railed against the actions of British Christianity at home as well as overseas, he was at ease with incorporating Christian traditions into British Islam, such as hymn singing accompanied by an organ and holding enormous Christmas Day parties for the poor of Liverpool. Quilliam brought a record number of white British men and women to Islam and on 22nd April 1898, Robert Stanley said Shahada at the Liverpool mosque in the presence of the Sheikh.[55]

This extract imagines the scene shortly after Robert said Shahada – becoming Brother Robert 'Reschid' Stanley.

THE LIVERPOOL MUSLIM INSTITUTE, 22ND APRIL 1898.

MID-AFTERNOON IN A COSY STUDY AT BROUGHAM TERRACE, LIVERPOOL. A FIRE IS BURNING IN THE GRATE AND **WILLIAM 'ABDULLAH' QUILLIAM,** AGED 42, ENTERS, ALONG WITH **ROBERT STANLEY,** AGED 69. THEY ARE JUST RETURNING FROM PRAYERS, WHERE ROBERT HAS FORMALLY ACCEPTED ISLAM IN FRONT OF THE OTHER WORSHIPPERS. THE ROOM IS RICHLY DECORATED WITH ALL MANNER OF COLOURFUL OBJECTS AND FURNISHINGS: PAINTINGS AND MURALS AND TURKISH CARPETS. QUILLIAM GESTURES FOR ROBERT TO SIT DOWN ON A SOFA AND HE SITS ACROSS FROM HIM, AT HIS DESK. HE IS A HANDSOME MAN WITH A LONG BEARD AND WEARS A RED FEZ ALONGSIDE THE USUAL VICTORIAN MIDDLE-CLASS DARK SUIT AND WAISTCOAT. A SMALL MONKEY ('MR BARNUM'), WHO WEARS HIS OWN TINY FEZ, IS PERCHED ON HIS SHOULDER. ROBERT LOOKS DAPPER IN HIS SUNDAY BEST. HIS BEARD IS NOW ENTIRELY WHITE, AND HE IS ALSO WEARING A RED FEZ.

---

[55] To become a Muslim, a person needs to say 'Shahada' – this is usually said in Arabic but can be said in any other language. It translates as, 'There is no god but God, and Muhammed is the messenger of God'.

QUILLIAM: *(Clapping his hands)* So, Brother Reschid; you've formally accepted Islam!

ROBERT: Yes. It was an honour doing it in your presence.

QUILLIAM: No. The honour is all mine.

ROBERT: Thank you. And … I really feel no different. About any of this.

QUILLIAM: And why should you? By saying Shahada, we simply mark a return to our natural state.

ROBERT: Yes…

QUILLIAM: Christianity – or any other religion – has only been a mere diversion. You've simply come back to where you were always meant to be.

ROBERT: Well, I'm glad to have been shepherded in this direction. I'm almost seventy years of age, so I don't have many more innings left to run.

QUILLIAM: Brother Reschid, let's have no more of your morbidity on this joyous day! Now, *(He takes a pen and paper from his desk)* for this week's *The Crescent*, I shall add your name to the roll call of the faithful.

ROBERT: Excellent, Sheikh.

QUILLIAM: *(Pointing the pen at him)* And from now on, please, just address me as Brother. Or Abdullah.

ROBERT: I couldn't…

QUILLIAM: No. None of this Sheikh business. It was all very flattering, of course, for the Caliph to have granted me the title, but in Islam we focus on fraternal bonds and on equality.

ROBERT: If you…

QUILLIAM: I insist. Let's keep the grand titles for the newspapers. And for the folk who are all too easily impressed with that sort of thing.

ROBERT: *(Nodding)* Of course.

QUILLIAM: But I wish to refer to you as 'Justice of the Peace' and 'His Worship the Mayor' in my publications.

ROBERT: Former mayor - it should be former mayor.

QUILLIAM: If that's what you prefer.

ROBERT: Yes. And if I can be referred to as Brother Reschid only here in the mosque…?

QUILLIAM: *(Scribbling notes)* Of course. I take it that your family are still rather ... confused about your new direction?

ROBERT: Hmm, yes, there is some confusion. And some 'concern'. Especially amongst my wife and daughters.

QUILLIAM: Oh dear. The women can be all too ready to listen to idle gossip.

ROBERT: I'm afraid so.

QUILLIAM: Let's get them over here to Liverpool. We can introduce them to Sister Fatima, previously known as Miss Frances Cates. The first native British woman to accept Islam here!

ROBERT: Ah, yes, I've already had the pleasure of meeting Fatima Cates already. Only nineteen when she decided to follow Islam, wasn't she?

QUILLIAM: Indeed. A brave soul. And she'd soon reduce any of their fears or anxieties about your decision.

ROBERT: Perhaps. But the only thing is, the women from my hometown of Stalybridge are not ... easily impressed by strangers!

QUILLIAM: Ah, yes. Mill town women can be rather opposed to anything a little bit different - not that I'm saying that your women are simple factory-workers...

ROBERT: No, *(Rather quickly)* not one of them! Although we don't look down our noses at the millworkers, of course.

QUILLIAM: Of course.

ROBERT: Although I prefer that sort of attitude in comparison to the sentiments displayed by my sons. They are extremely hostile and suspicious towards my interest in Islam.

QUILLIAM: Hmm. We often come across jealousy masquerading as suspicion. (He *picks up his Qur'an and waves it for emphasis*) The Prophet Muhammed – peace be upon him – said that, *"Envy makes the life of a jealous person bleak."*

ROBERT: Jealousy?

QUILLIAM: Often. Perhaps because the other person has found deep happiness.

ROBERT: That would never have occurred to me.

QUILLIAM: I've seen it a lot. So, how many Moslems do your sons know?

ROBERT: Ho – well, between the five of them, the grand total of ... none!

QUILLIAM: But we can't expect a person born in this country, with no exposure to Moslems and no knowledge of Islam, to instantly understand what you're doing.

ROBERT: Indeed.

QUILLIAM: Especially with some of the rubbish that the papers write!

ROBERT: True. I shall have to invite you to tea, Sheikh, er … I … Abdullah, so that you can work your magic upon them!

QUILLIAM: I'd be delighted.

ROBERT: And if you bring Mr Barnum, here, *(Robert nods at the monkey)* he will do a good job at working *his* magic on my grandchildren. Everybody loves a pet monkey.

QUILLIAM: Mr Barnum deserves a medal for his services towards winning suspicious people over to the cause of Islam.

ROBERT: I can imagine that he does.

QUILLIAM: In fact, I think that Mr Barnum's charms are far more powerful than any treatises that I write, or any lectures that I give!

ROBERT: The Christian church should follow your example. If they introduced a few cuddly animals into the pews, their congregational numbers would not be dwindling half so much.

MR BARNUM chatters grumpily at ROBERT.

QUILLIAM: Ha! I don't think that Mr Barnum likes being referred to as a 'cuddly animal'. He's convinced that he's a fully-grown man, you know.

ROBERT: He almost looks it, with that tiny fez of his.[56]

QUILLIAM: And your own - new - fez looks rather magnificent on you, I must say. A perfect fit.

ROBERT: It feels … somewhat small. Or perhaps my head is growing bigger these days with all the splendid things you keep saying about me to people.

They both laugh.

---

[56] Although we do not know the name of Quilliam's monkey, the name 'Mr Barnum' suits him and was chosen because Quilliam and the other Muslims enjoyed a trip to Barnum's circus when it visited Liverpool. Quilliam's granddaughter remembered the monkey very well and said that it used to wear a miniature fez.

ROBERT: I was wondering what my dear old father would have made of seeing his son wearing a fez.

QUILLIAM: Yes?

ROBERT: He was a hatter, you see. Specialised in beaver hats, before they fell out of vogue. After that, our family fell on hard times.

QUILLIAM: Ah, yes, the whims of fashion.

ROBERT: Still, the fez covers the baldness – so it's a very positive thing!

They both chuckle

QUILLIAM: Now, here…

QUILLIAM reaches into his pocket and takes out a small box, handing it to ROBERT, who opens it.

QUILLIAM: …is your official membership pin. May I formally welcome you to the Liverpool Moslem Institute, my dear Brother Reschid!

ROBERT: Goodness, but what a…! *(He holds a jewelled tie pin up, so he can see it more clearly)* My eyes really are not what they used to be… What is …?[57]

QUILLIAM: They're rubies. From Constantinople. From the Caliph. My favourite jewel; they glow with warmth and welcome.

ROBERT: Yes, a very precious gem. And yet the only women I've ever known named Ruby happen to have been rather coarse and extremely common.[58]

QUILLIAM: *(Laughing merrily)* Oh, Brother Reschid! Thankfully I have known several highly esteemed and intelligent ladies named Ruby.

ROBERT: Well, I'm glad that someone has.

They both chuckle away.

---

[57] After my grandmother Edith died, we found a tie pin of this description in her jewellery box. After consulting experts with knowledge of the Liverpool Muslim Institute, is seems clear that it was some sort of a membership pin.

[58] Robert's great x4 granddaughter is named Ruby. And has a good sense of humour!

ROBERT: So, sent from the Caliph, you say?

QUILLIAM: A most generous sponsor of our work. He's grateful, too, for the advice that you've provided the Ottoman Empire with: agricultural, military, industrial.[59]

ROBERT: Not at all. I'm just a foolish old man who likes to write letters.

QUILLIAM: Nonsense. You are one of the most prolific writers and campaigners that we have had the privilege to join us!

ROBERT: Really, I have much to learn. I hope that you'll all be patient with your old Brother Bob.

QUILLIAM: Ha! I shall certainly call you 'Brother Bob' if you like. And you can call me 'Brother Will'. Or 'Brother Bill'.

ROBERT: The Brothers Bob and Bill!

QUILLIAM: We sound like a dreadful Wild West show!

They both laugh. The monkey is getting irritated with all the merriment and leaps down off Quilliam's shoulder, scurrying away.

ROBERT: Oh dear. I think we've upset Mr Barnum.

QUILLIAM: Never mind him. He's a vain little creature and hates it when he's not the centre of attention.

ROBERT is pulling at his lapel, attempting to fasten the pin.

QUILLIAM: I wouldn't do that if I were you. Not casting aspersions on my fellow Liverpudlians, but…

ROBERT: Perhaps best not to wear it outside of the mosque, then?

QUILLIAM: Yes. And best not to venture outside here in your fez.

ROBERT: Hmm. Negative attention?

QUILLIAM: Yes. I'm sure that you've heard about the attacks on the mosque here. As well as on ourselves.

ROBERT: The windows being broken - and people threw black puddings at you when you were delivering a lecture, didn't they?

---

[59] Before Robert converted, he had written to the Caliph on several occasions, providing him with advice on various matters – which the Caliph acknowledged and followed. See previous scene 'Foreign Matters in the Pub' as well as *His Own Man.*

QUILLIAM: Tip of the iceberg stuff. Sister Fatima has – yet again – had horse dung rubbed in her face by local youths.[60] Despicable.

ROBERT: Outrageous! The police?

QUILLIAM: We reported it, but Fatima didn't get a chance to look at the scoundrels properly.

ROBERT: The poor woman!

QUILLIAM: Yes, but Fatima bears it most nobly. Says that if she wasn't a Moslem, they could well have attacked her for another reason.

ROBERT: Dear, dear.

QUILLIAM: Such as, you know, a woman coming to this part of town on her own, or because she's carrying books or what-not.

ROBERT: A courageous attitude on her part. But … the cowards!

QUILLIAM: Yes. And these attacks are another reason why I rarely wear the traditional Ottoman robes outside of these walls.

ROBERT: It's sad that you have to think like this.

QUILLIAM: True, but aside from that, I'm a lawyer trying to help the city's poor - most of them would run a mile if they saw me in my Moslem attire.

ROBERT: Yes, I imagine they would feel more naturally inclined to trust more conservative attire.

QUILLIAM: Boring though it is.

ROBERT: It makes me think, though. We white men who are Moslems, can easily blend into the British way of life through our clothes.

QUILLIAM: Yes.

ROBERT: But our Moslem friends of colour walking around in Britain, they can't suddenly change their skin colour in order to hide from thugs and hoodlums.

QUILLIAM: Certainly! And even more reason to counter some of the despicable views towards foreigners and towards Moslems.

ROBERT: Born of fear and lack of education.

QUILLIAM: Indeed. I do find, though, that just by staying calm, we can sometimes win such people over.

ROBERT: Yes?

---

[60] This is true. Attacks on the mosque had always taken place, but they increased in intensity in relation to international matters. The women – and the inspirational Frances 'Fatima' Cates – were unfortunately very vulnerable targets.

QUILLIAM: Last week I was giving a lecture; there were shouts of abuse and one fellow even brought a trumpet to blast on, to drown me out.

ROBERT: Silly fool.

QUILLIAM: But I stayed my course and afterwards two chaps came up to me to apologise for their previous thoughts towards Moslems. They showed me their pockets – full of stones.

ROBERT: What?!

QUILLIAM: Yes, they had intended to throw them at me, either when I was speaking, or afterwards.[61]

ROBERT: This is just intolerable.

QUILLIAM: Sadly, this country has a shameful reputation for persecution of those that they deem to be heretics. The poor Quakers, for example.

ROBERT: Indeed.

QUILLIAM: There are dozens of groups who have been mistreated, simply because they dared to have different religious beliefs. The same with those folks you grew up amongst – the Christian Israelites over in Ashton!

ROBERT: Precisely. And my Qur'an tells me that those of different faiths should never be treated with prejudice or violence.

QUILLIAM: Absolutely! It doesn't matter how wrong or misguided people are – we're all made in the image of Allah.

ROBERT: Yes. And I learned much from the Christian Israelites about the origins of the Abrahamic faith. I owe them a great deal.

QUILLIAM: So, how is it, Brother Reschid, that you have come to be so well-informed on religion, history and geography? Have you travelled far with your business in the tea trade?

ROBERT: Quite a distance. I once reached Portsmouth.

QUILLIAM: Portsmouth?

ROBERT: Yes. Dreadful place. Full of feckless idlers. And the French.

They both burst out laughing. MR BARNUM – now under the table – chunners in disgust.

---

[61] This actually happened to Quilliam, as reported in *The Crescent.*

183

QUILLIAM: He hates us enjoying ourselves! But be serious ... your travels?

ROBERT: I am being serious. Portsmouth has marked the extent of my geographical pursuits.

QUILLIAM: No!

ROBERT: Yes. I've travelled to London many times, of course; the most memorable being when I was called as a witness to Parliament on whether the secret ballot should be introduced.[62]

QUILLIAM: Really? So, you were successful in persuading them to adopt it, then!

ROBERT: Not exactly. I warned against it.

QUILLIAM: Goodness!

ROBERT: Not for want of equity, I hasten to add.

QUILLIAM: So...

ROBERT: Well, I felt that for local elections the secret ballot was preferable. I myself had been defending working men from bribery and violence when they voted against their masters' wishes in public.

QUILLIAM: Ah. I see.

ROBERT: But for the national elections, I was against the secret ballot.

QUILLIAM: Why? Because voting in secret is somehow ... unmanly?

ROBERT: No. Because I have seen how ill-informed most working men are. No education whatsoever on matters of politics.

QUILLIAM: It's certainly never been taught since public schooling was introduced.

ROBERT: Meaning that the average chap is far too easily persuaded to vote for all manner of riff raff. Charlatans who play on the working-class man's misery and poverty. Predators who can persuade him towards foolish notions.

QUILLIAM: Such as?

ROBERT: Such as the redistribution of wealth.

QUILLIAM: Ah, yes. Always sounds so delicious when you have nothing to your name.

ROBERT: Or they will vote for a man simply because he looks and sounds impressive. If these votes are allowed to take place in secret -

---

[62] See *His Own Man* for an analysis of Robert's contribution to the 1869 parliamentary select committee on voting reform. This led to the Ballot Act 1872.

without being held to account publicly - a man will, all too often, vote stupidly.

QUILLIAM: You think so?

ROBERT: Yes. They will vote stupidly, selfishly, as a way of 'getting the boot' into those who have always held power, or simply towards those who are wealthy. To those that have come to represent their dissatisfaction with their own lot in life.

QUILLIAM: I see what you're saying.

ROBERT: And then ridiculous, egotistical, talentless men will be voted into power. And after that? The people will be unable to make good the damage that they have done.

QUILLIAM: So, did the politicians and the ministers listen to these views of yours?

ROBERT: Certainly. I was there for hours. They asked me around three hundred questions. The foreign secretary himself came over and shook my hand. To thank me.

QUILLIAM: Impressive.

ROBERT: For all the good it did.

QUILLIAM: Well, the Liberals were under pressure to adopt the secret ballot, weren't they?

ROBERT: Exactly. And whilst at the local level it has certainly helped protect the common man from being bribed for his vote, I do fear that in years to come the people…

QUILLIAM: If left uneducated…

ROBERT: … will one day vote disastrously as a result of being preyed upon by the more sinister sort of politician. The grubby little men, the sort who say things like, 'I speak as I find'.

QUILLIAM: I hope that you're wrong. But perhaps we won't be around to see such havoc.

ROBERT: Probably not. No one would want to listen to the 'I told you so' fellow, at any rate!

QUILLIAM: Ha! Indeed not. It seems, though, that Britain is quite the wrong country for a revolution. The general population prefers conservatism and plodding along.

ROBERT: There is a lot to be said for it.

QUILLIAM: I am guessing that you're not a fan of the suffragists or of wanting to see the enfranchisement of women just yet.

ROBERT: Goodness, no! I am far too old to be able to cope with the thought of the secret ballot AND women being able to vote!

They both burst out laughing again.

QUILLIAM: Ha-ha – oh! Ow! Ow! *(He swipes under the table)*
ROBERT: What on earth is it?
QUILLIAM: You naughty little thing!

The monkey dashes across the room and climbs the curtain, perching himself at the top of the rail.

QUILLIAM: Mr Barnum nipped my ankle! Nasty little thing!
ROBERT: Perhaps he's a suffragist sympathiser.
QUILLIAM: Well, so am I! He should have bitten you, instead, Brother!
ROBERT: I suspect he doesn't like us chuckling. My daughter, Sarah, was like that; she'd sulk for hours if people were having fun and she wasn't at the centre of it. Rather like a monkey.
QUILLIAM: Oh dear.
ROBERT: Thankfully, she is far more attractive than a monkey. Easily the prettiest of my daughters. Nothing of the marmoset about her face and figure.
QUILLIAM: It can be a concern, though, as a father. When you have a very attractive daughter.
ROBERT: True. Although she is a rather young widow now. So, less to worry about, now that her respectability is ensured.
QUILLIAM: It would be good to meet your family soon. It also … might set their minds at ease, to meet me.
ROBERT: And to find that you are not a total monster!
QUILLIAM: Indeed!
ROBERT: Yes. We shall invite you to tea in Rusholme.
QUILLIAM: Splendid.
ROBERT: It's just Emma and I and two of our daughters; Sarah, whom I just mentioned, and Mary-Jane, who has never married. My other eight children are in and around Stalybridge and Ashton and what not.

QUILLIAM: Good. I shall travel over to Manchester as soon as I can.

ROBERT: I shall speak to Emma about dates.

QUILLIAM: And we shall do it when I am back from Sierra Leone.[63] We have extensive relations with the local Moslem community there.

ROBERT: Yes, I've been reading about it in The Crescent.

QUILLIAM: The new mosque is coming along nicely; I am increasingly tempted to settle overseas, if I am to be truthful with you.

ROBERT: So why do you remain here?

QUILLIAM: Ah, the family. My children – the schools here cannot be rivalled by overseas institutions.

ROBERT: A British education can be a fine thing.

QUILLIAM: And then there's my commitments as a lawyer, of course.

ROBERT: Your attitude is admirable. I have heard of no one else in this city who works for the poor for no payment, as you do.

QUILLIAM: But these desperate people need the help! And, practically speaking, the other paid work that I do - representing the wealthy and the like - I do need it, to pay the bills. Two households to keep, Brother Bob!

ROBERT: Ah, yes.

QUILLIAM: And most importantly of all, the need to bring Islam to the British Isles.

ROBERT: Of course.

QUILLIAM: Speaking of which; would you like to accompany me on a stroll to our Boys' School? We can pop into the Medina Orphanage, too, if you like.

ROBERT: That sounds excellent.

QUILLIAM: Good. But we must leave our fezzes here.

ROBERT: Ah, in case any local youths want to try a bit of target practise on us?

QUILLIAM: Yes. In Islam we don't have to turn the other cheek as Christians do. But it wouldn't look good, would it? A magistrate

---

[63] In *The Crescent*, Quilliam frequently mentioned the Liverpool Muslims' link with Muslims in Sierra Leone and South Africa. He spent much time travelling during these years and was particularly fond of the mosque in Sierra Leone and helped to obtain funding from the Amir in order to open it.

and a lawyer being arrested for kicking a group of young hoodlums half to death!

They both laugh. Mr BARNUM swears at them in monkey language. They both stand up. QUILLIAM rubs his ankle.

ROBERT: Does your wife not like to accompany you on your travels overseas?
QUILLIAM: Wives, you mean. I have two of them.
ROBERT: Oh! Apologies … yes.
QUILLIAM: Perhaps naively, I thought that having two families would allow me to escape the monotony of the usual British norms of family life. But alas no!
ROBERT: No?
QUILLIAM: No. A man is still not permitted to sit and indulge himself in a Qur'anic text of an evening without being called upon to rehang a lampshade or to oil a squeaking hinge or some such nonsense.
ROBERT: I'm a little confused … are you not yet divorced from your first wife, then?
QUILLIAM: Goodness, no. No, my fellow; I'm sure you've read the various articles I've written about polygamy.
ROBERT: Oh! Of course. I didn't realise that you yourself…
QUILLIAM: That's probably because you don't live in Liverpool. Everyone here seems to be aware of it.
ROBERT: I've not yet met anyone – in Britain – who has taken more than one wife. Legally speaking, I mean.
QUILLIAM: Well, I suppose it's still not caught on much yet. But I hope to change all of that.
ROBERT: No … in Manchester I've met several travellers – traders – from the Orient who have taken one wife in Manchester and who have another family at home in the Levant or wherever.[64]
QUILLIAM: So, Brother Reschid, what are your thoughts, about taking more than one wife?

QUILLIAM takes both coats off the coat stand and hands ROBERT his.

---

[64] Syria, but sometimes used to mean the broader, eastern Mediterranean region.

188

ROBERT: *(Putting his coat on)* In the Qur'an… Surely, the contextual information is all-important on whatever view we take on it.

QUILLIAM: Go on.

ROBERT: The cultural and societal conditions behind why the Prophet – peace be upon him – took several wives.

QUILLIAM: Yes?

ROBERT: Because he had wealth. And he could help to provide for them when they were left as widows etcetera, etcetera.

QUILLIAM: Indeed.

ROBERT: So, it seems to me that the practise is entirely acceptable - if not to say productive - to wider society, when such conditions can be fulfilled.

QUILLIAM: But if these practises - as you say - are productive and even beneficial to the community, why have the men of Britain not embraced polygamy yet?

ROBERT: Well…

QUILLIAM: *(Interrupts him, growing passionate)* I mean, we quite freely adopt the fashion of whiskers, the high collar, the new line of waistcoat at the drop of a hat, don't we? Why have other men of England not followed the example of Islam?

ROBERT: Perhaps … perhaps for two reasons.

QUILLIAM: Yes?

ROBERT: Well, the example of the Prophet – peace be upon him – and your own example are entirely driven by compassion.

QUILLIAM: And?

ROBERT: And – as your work with the children of the Medina Orphanage has demonstrated - women and children need to be helped and protected in such an anti-female society as this one. But…

QUILLIAM: But?

ROBERT: But unfortunately, the average British man does not see this. He turns a blind eye to their distresses. He would not seek to take on another wife and family in order to help them.

QUILLIAM: *(Stroking his beard)* True. Sadly true. And your second reason?

ROBERT: My wife, Abdullah.

QUILLIAM: How so?

ROBERT: And all the other women of England who are of the same mindset! They're terrifying – and they'd never stand for it!

They both guffaw again. The monkey shrieks at them.

QUILLIAM: Oh, do be quiet, you little horror. Well, you must bring Mrs Stanley here to meet both my wives, Brother Reschid.
ROBERT: I shall attempt to do so.
QUILLIAM: Very different creatures, both of them. And yet, somehow, they manage to accommodate each other - as well as myself.
ROBERT: Excellent.
QUILLIAM: Yes. They will tell you – and Mrs Stanley – that they reap the benefits of our extended family life and arrangements.
ROBERT: So, do they never come into conflict with each other?
QUILLIAM: Well … Hannah and Mary, as I said, are made of quite different stuff; one is more the genteel housewife and the other a … rather more colourful actress. She performs at the Liverpool Empire, you know.
ROBERT: Goodness; how very interesting.
QUILLIAM: Yes. So, I'll admit that the potential for personality clashes has always been there.
ROBERT: And how do you prevent them from occurring?
QUILLIAM: Oh, simply in the same manner as all Englishmen do with the two most important women in their lives.
ROBERT: Yes?
QUILLIAM: as they do with their own mother and their wife….
ROBERT: And that is...?
QUILLIAM: Keep them in separate houses. Preferably separate towns! The less they see of each other - the better!

Both roar with laughter. Mr BARNUM screeches, then jumps down from the curtain rail and flees from the room.

---ENDS---

William Abdullah Quilliam –
Sheikh ul-Islam of the British
Isles

12. PEAS IN HIS POCKETS

EMMA STANLEY'S MONOLOGUE

CONTEXT:

In 1897, Robert and Emma moved to Rusholme, in Manchester's Chorlton district, with their two daughters, Mary-Jane and Sarah. For a family that had always lived in Stalybridge and Ashton and was fiercely devoted to the area, this was quite an unusual relocation to make in their twilight years. Their youngest son, John, was already living in that part of Manchester with his family and was a partner in Robert's tea business, which was based at the Old Corn Exchange in the city. Shortly after the move, the couple celebrated their golden wedding anniversary; a tea party was held for friends and family at Belle Vue Gardens.

The Stanley's house was in this row, Upper Brooke St, Rusholme

Two months later, though, John died at the age of 35, leaving a wife, three small children and one 'on the way'. One of these children – George – moved in with his grandparents and another – Marguerite - went to live with Robert's youngest daughter, Alice, in the village of Uppermill. Presumably this was because Robert's newly widowed daughter-in-law was finding it hard to cope with so many mouths to feed after her husband's death.

This monologue imagines what Emma's thoughts and feelings might have been, two years after their move and a year after Robert's conversion to Islam.

MANCHESTER, APRIL 1899

EMMA STANLEY IS 73 YEARS OLD. SHE IS PROPPED UP
ON HER BED, HOLDING A COPY OF THE MANCHESTER
GUARDIAN. IT HAS SEVERAL LARGE HOLES IN IT. A
PAIR OF SEWING SCISSORS LIE ON THE NIGHTSTAND
NEXT TO HER, ALONG WITH A CUP OF TEA. ON A
NIGHTSTAND ON THE OTHER SIDE OF THE BED IS A
RED FEZ AND A COPY OF THE QUR'AN. SHE WEARS A
PAIR OF READING SPECTACLES AND LOOKS TIRED;
HER HAIR IS NOT AS FIRMLY FIXED AS IT USUALLY IS.
SHE WHEEZES WHEN SHE BECOMES OVER-ANIMATED.

I'm having a little rest and a read of the newspaper whilst they're all
out.

She pokes the newspaper.

Well, what's left of the newspaper, after Robert's got to it with the
scissors. He snips everything to bits, he does. Always done that.
Sends his 'items of interest' all over the show. Thinks it's his duty to
inform others. Quite kind of him, really. But…

She shakes the newspaper and peers through one of the holes.

It doesn't feel like that when you get a rare minute to yourself and
you want to read the thing! No, having young George here has been
a lot harder than I thought it would. It's … I'd just made his bed –
he'd wet it again – and I started having another one of those dizzy
spells, so I thought I'd have a little lie down whilst it's quiet. Read
the paper.

She folds the newspaper over so it's easier to manage.

I suppose I was thinking that … well. I've had eleven babies, so
having just the one child around the place would be a bit of a
breeze. But I'm 73 now. It tells on you, it does.

I'm not complaining, though. I've never been a complainer and I'm not starting now. I've got a lot to be grateful for in life. But it's certainly ended up, well…

She eyes the fez.

Rather different than I thought it'd be. Our retirement years, I mean.

But in the grand scheme of things, having a nine-year-old around isn't that much of a bother. No, I think we'd be alright – with all of these changes, I mean - if it weren't for other folks being gossips. Because, I mean, we've never been the subject of gossip, us Stanleys. But, oh, I'm sick to the back teeth of it all. Well, it's not here on our doorstep in Manchester, the tittle-tattle; what I mean is, you get it when you're over in Stalybridge. I've had that many folk say to me, *"Mrs Stanley! Now, that must have been a shock to the system!"* And the like. And sometimes they've even come out with proper ridiculous stuff, like *"So will you be joining him? Will you have to wear a veil?"* Jokes about harems and that. So much so that, even though I was the one against moving to Manchester, I'm glad we're here now. Every time we've gone back to Stalybridge since he joined the merry band of Moslems, it's become more and more difficult. I get fed up with having to button my lip and to carry on. Like none of it's of any consequence to me.

Oh, and the very religious sorts in Stalybridge - they're the worst. Think they're a cut above everyone else. They're horrified – you can tell. But they try and disguise it as something like … sympathy. Their expressions. Like they're constipated or something. What I call the 'someone's died' face.

She half-smiles and turns a page of the newspaper. A church bell chimes outside.

I'm not joking. I'm not. That's what it's like. Exactly the same expression that people plaster on their faces when someone dies. They did it when we lost the baby in '64. And then, just a few months ago, with John. A great big man of 35 he was, when he passed on, but they're always your babies, aren't they?

194

But the thing is – I think it's worse. With what's happened to Robert; peoples' reactions, I mean. Because there's no real sympathy in it all from them. They think we're all suffering a fate worse than death. Yes, not only is old Robert Stanley going to be burning in hell with the infidel, but he's a traitor to the British Empire, too. That sort of thing. Our Alice had it the other week in Stalybridge. From Reverend Booth, it was.

She turns another page of the newspaper. And sighs.

Alice said he'd been asking her about Robert, about him being over at the Liverpool mosque so much. And then suddenly he comes out with, *"If you turn your back on Christ, on the Day of Judgement, he'll turn his back on you. Your father should be mindful of that."* This all occurred in the queue at potato pie supper at the Conservative Association. Well, Alice just stood there with her mouth open because she couldn't believe how incredibly rude and, well, how out of place it was. There's not usually a lot of talk of God and eternal damnation in the queue for a potato pie supper at the Conservative Association. You're more likely to hear how badly Stalybridge Rovers are doing, or whether the beetroot looks a bit iffy, or whether Mrs Feathers on the corner of Ridge Hill Lane is charging men for more than just her laundry services. But no, bold as brass, the reverend was.

She reaches over to a cup of tea and takes a drink.

Ugh. Too weak. I've had 60-odd years of practise and I'm still nothing like as good as Robert is at brewing up. Anyway, so Alice says she's stood there in shock, but then Reverend Booth – who was next in the queue – just changes the subject and starts moaning, because he can't get the girl to serve him his potato pie. Starts complaining at the top of his voice that he's being 'overlooked'. Well, it turned out that the lass dishing-up the food had been a pupil of Alice's - Jenny Raddle. And she'd started serving Alice before the reverend. So, he says, *"Excuse me, young lady, I'm standing here with an empty plate,"* and she said *"Well, there you go. It's not nice having your back turned on you, is it? And didn't the Lord say, 'He who is first shall be last?"*

Well! That caused quite a to-do! Alice said that what made it even worse was that Jenny was shaking the potato pie ladle at the reverend as she spoke – trying to make a point, I suppose – and it splattered all over his waistcoat.

She starts chuckling to herself. But then a fit of coughing begins. She puts the newspaper down and reaches for a handkerchief, coughs into it for a few seconds and then tucks it back into her sleeve.

Oh, I shouldn't. I shouldn't be laughing at it all. I mean - wasn't it such forward behaviour of that Jenny! But anyway, the secretary of the Conservative Association - who'd seen all of this happen – sent her packing. Lost her job over it all. Well, Alice ran after the lass and caught up with her on Mottram Road and Jenny said she wasn't that bothered about it, because she'd had enough of working for the Conservatives anyway. That they all had these airs and graces there, and not one of them any better than they should be. She said that she'd known she'd done the right thing as soon as the chairman had shouted at her that she was a "brazen little yid".

She shakes her head and picks up the newspaper again.

"Brazen little yid". Of all the things! Because, apparently, Jenny's family are Jewish. And she said that she's had nearly two decades of people like Reverend Booth telling her that 'her people' were responsible for crucifying Christ. And she also said that the reverend was lucky she hadn't tipped an entire bowl of potato pie on his head. In the end – and this is very naughty - our Alice paid a little lad who does odd jobs in the kitchen there to sneak into the cloakroom and fill the reverend's coat pockets with a load of black peas. The really mushy ones. Oh, I know she shouldn't have done that, but she's one for carrying out her own forms of justice is Alice.

She chuckles to herself again and makes as if to reach for the handkerchief.

Can't help but smile at the thought of his face when he reached into his pocket for his Bible or whathaveyou. It's funny, though. I never knew that they were Jewish – the Raddles. So, I told Robert that –

not the bit about the reverend being rude, he would have gotten very cross over that – about the Jewish thing. Whether he knew. And he said, *"Hmm, that would fit; they probably changed their name from something like Radowanitz to Raddle"*. Apparently, a lot of them felt that they had to do that, to protect them from being persecuted over in Europe and Russia and the like. But they never really looked Jewish, the Raddles. Not like the Jews that you see here in Manchester. But perhaps they tried not to look *too* Jewish because of living in Stalybridge. It's not the kind of place where you'd deliberately stick your head above the parapet.

She reaches for her handkerchief again and coughs into it. Then blinks hard, several times.

All of that made me realise that I've never really had a proper conversation with a Jewish woman. Well, not knowingly. Or a Moslem woman, either, come to that. Although Robert keeps saying we should go and meet one of this Quilliam-fella's wives. Or one of the women in Liverpool who've converted. I'm not sure I really want to. Our Mary-Jane says they'll no doubt be an easily led lot. Just converting because their husbands forced them to. She says, *"Most women are far too sensible to keep wanting to change their religion. Men have got nothing better to think about than masterminding wars, using their religion as an excuse for it. Mr Quilliam probably selected all of his wives for being susceptible to fairy stories."* Robert got proper annoyed with her when she said that. He said – for starters - this Quilliam has only two wives and that even though the children are brought up as Muslims, the wives are still Christians. And then he said, given that Mary-Jane was such good chums with the Pankhurst ladies, that she should be more respectful of women's rights to choose how they live, and that Islam is far superior to Christianity, when it comes to logic. And that it treats women far better.
No, Robert's none too impressed with the fact that our Mary-Jane is 'round the corner at the Pankhurst's so much since we moved here. I'm not sure what I think of it all. I mean, don't get me wrong; they're very nice ladies, Emmeline and Christabel and Sylvia and … and … the other one whose name I can never remember. But everything comes back to "being a woman" for them. You can be

having a perfectly nice chat with them about the price of turnips or whathaveyou and you'll end up being carried off on a big discussion about how the turnips have only found their way to your cupboards because some poor woman died a premature death from growing them, or from contracting turnip-disease or something.

She shakes the newspaper.

Now, here's a natty little article that Robert has missed! The Archbishop of Canterbury criticising 'the religion of the Muhammedans'. Heh. I'll have to cut that one out for him myself. That'll keep him busy writing a few more letters.

She reaches for the scissors and snips round the article, her tongue poking out in concentration.

I shouldn't encourage him, really. I mean - this isn't exactly how I'd hoped to be spending my retirement, him being on the train to and from Liverpool half the time and bringing home a parade of foreigners: merchants, sailors and whatnot. And then your white converts - all of them a bit eccentric. Me having to feed and water them all. Oh, I don't want to sound resentful. Or jealous. I mean, I've never been the possessive sort. I've always let him have his meetings and his council and his committee whatnots. But you don't expect to have all of these new people come into your lives at our ages.

She places the cutting and the scissors back on the nightstand.

And it's the look that he gets when he's with them. His face sort of … lights up. Takes years off him. Makes me feel a bit funny, that. The thing is, none of them are my cup of tea. Well, not the convert ones, because most of them are the posh sorts. Oh, I've met various lords and ladies thanks to Robert's council stuff over the years, but you can never really relax around folk like that. Plus, all these converts ever want to natter about is their Mussulmen talk. Or they want to convince you to believe in what they believe in. I've nothing in common with them! I haven't! And it's the same with Mary-Jane's upper-crust friends who all meet up at the Pankhursts' house. I've nothing in common with them, either. None of them have ever scrubbed their own laundry. I mean, I grew up from the age of nine in domestic service, emptying chamber pots for others, lighting fires at five 'o clock in the morning in the freezing cold. All of that. Still, when you're talking to that Pankhurst lot, at least you can have a good moan about the menfolk.

Mind you, come to think about it, they're after their converts too, that lot. More women signing up for their causes. One of them – no more than thirty years old she was – said to me; "You should come along here more often, Mrs Stanley. We need more women of the working classes." Cheeky minx.

She puts the newspaper down and takes her glasses off.

Pointless trying to read this. Can't concentrate. Anyway. I should get up and put the tea on.

GO TO BLACK

Come up on EMMA, standing at the front room window. Morning. Hands on hips, looking out. The noise of barking outside and boys' laughter.

Would you look at those lads! What they're doing to that poor little dog! Cruel things.

She raps hard on the window and mimes at them to "clear off!"

If they carry on with any of that, I'll go and sort them out, I will. You didn't get any of that in Stalybridge. Well, not as much as you do here. Rotten bullies.

Pause.

I've been feeling a bit better this week. Not as many of those dizzy spells.

She picks up a copy of The Manchester Guardian off the dresser. Again, it is full of holes.

He's been snipping again. All the foreign things, by the looks of it. Well, with or without the holes, I can never make any sense of the foreign news. I can't keep track of it all – who's owning what country these days and all the different names confuse me. It's hard to remember the name of someone or something if you don't know them or if you've never been there. I can't even say that it's my age! I've always been like that with funny names. He got annoyed with me yesterday, because I said 'Armenia' instead of 'Afghanistan'. *"Well"*, I said, *"they both begin with A, don't they – and they're foreign!"* We don't have cross words very often. In fact, we have even less nowadays. He'd say that it's because he's a Moslem now. But I think it's more to do with us not running a shop or a pub. And he helps me 'round the house more than ever. Sweeping a room. Lighting a fire. Brewing up. He'll even press the linen without being asked to. No, there's many a wife doesn't see their husband for dust once they're into their retirement hours. They'll be off down the pub or to the Freemasons or something. Not Robert. He's happier reading a book or pottering around in the back yard with one of those exotic plants that his traveller friends bring back for him. He has his meetings over in Liverpool, of course, but he's more of a home-bird than ever, really. Having George with us helps. It's given him … well, I don't know what you call it, but I think it helps us both. In our spirits. Even though in my body - the lad fair tires me out! Little whirlwind.

Pause.

I do wish though, sometimes, that we'd had Marguerite here as well. But there's not enough room for another grandchild. And anyway, she's better off in Uppermill with our Alice and her Joe. Been good for her, them both being teachers. She's been awarded a place at Ashton Grammar! First in the family to have a grammar school education. And a girl to boot! Big smile on Mary-Jane's face when she heard that.

A short intake of breath. Then she coughs for a few seconds.

Speaking of education, we had our Will and his family 'round for Sunday dinner last week. Me and Sarah had made a lovely roast chicken. Halal meat, it was, too! Took some finding to get a full chicken of that sort. Anyway, just as we were serving it up, Robert was chatting about a couple of new tea deals he'd managed with an Indian chap he'd met at Mr Quilliam's mosque. Will said, *"Oh, so are there Moslems in India then? I thought they were all Hindoos."* and Robert was horrified.[65] Came out with the usual, *"What do they teach folk in school these days?"* and Will reminded him that he had been too old to have come under the 1870 Act and to go to school very much. And that maybe if his parents hadn't used him as child labour in their own grocer's business he'd have had a better education himself. Well … Robert's face! Although if he's anything like me, he was probably feeling a bit guilty, too. But then, he starts reminding everyone that *he* hadn't received a formal education and yet he'd made it his mission to go out there into the world to read and to educate himself.

Barking from outside. She goes to the window again.

Oh. It's alright. Not those grubby little lads again. It's just the dog. Attacking the rag and bone man. He's a grumpy swine, that chappie. Serves him right.

And then, Robert starts to regale us with all the sorts of different lessons the orphans study at Mr Quilliam's orphanage school. Telling us that the they're excellent little scholars and prize their education above all else because they've risen from the most horrible positions in society. But then Mary-Jane breaks in, saying that – as a teacher – she felt that this Moslem school and orphanage should not call it an education because the precise root of the word – as derived from the Latin, apparently – is to "draw out from within" and that she has read that Mr Quilliam and friends force the destitute women who give up their children to this orphanage to

---

[65] There was general confusion around the word (spelled) 'Hindoo' in Britain at this time. It was usually used to refer to anyone who was from the Indian sub-continent.

agree that they should be brought up as Moslems. So, Mary-Jane said, this was not an "education" – it was "proselytising and indoctrination".

She picks up the various scraps of unwanted newspaper and twists them into kindling.

Well, then it was no stopping them. Robert telling Mary-Jane that she'd obviously been spending too much time over at the Pankhursts' and with the Manchester Secular Society too, that she'd developed some very unbalanced notions. And her telling him that at least *she* was allowed to have an opinion amongst her friends – unlike *his* friends, like this Mr Quilliam, who just wants women to be there to sire children, be his bed fellows and to wander around with veils over their faces in case they tempt another man into lustful thinking. And then our Will blushing and telling Mary-Jane to lower her voice and stop being so raucous … He's become more and more … prudish he has, as he's gotten older, has Will.
I got quite upset at all of this. I don't know why they had to pick a mealtime to start a quarrel. By the time everyone had stopped arguing, the gravy had congealed, and the chicken had dried up. Sarah and I had done our best to make a nice Sunday lunch and there they all were, bickering over the sort of things that don't matter a jot to your ordinary folk. Robert, of course, couldn't even blame a glass of beer on his tetchiness as he's now completely sworn off the stuff. I mean, you try and do your best for your family and you try and set an example, but it's like they want to somehow spoil it for you.

GO TO BLACK.

Come up on EMMA, in the front room, sitting in an armchair next to a roaring fire. There is a vase of flowers on the mantlepiece, bundles of folded-up washing sitting on a chair and a small fez on the hearth, filled with pieces of kindling and rolled up newspaper.

I'm just having a little sit down after doing that bit of folding. Takes it out of me, it does, these days. The boys will be back from

Liverpool shortly. It's lovely weather, so I thought George needed to get out and about a bit. Besides, he's been mithering to go over there and meet Mr Quilliam and that monkey of his again. I don't mind him going. Means he can keep an eye on his grandad for me.

Pause.

Well, I must say, I've warmed to that Emmeline Pankhurst now. She's often asked me about Robert before, but never in a nosey way – not like your Stalybridge or your Ashton lot. No, she's always seemed to be more interested in listening to what I think, rather than telling me what I should be feeling. Yes, after how she was with me this week, I've decided she's a proper lady, she is. We bumped into each other outside the Infirmary. I'd just left Robert there.

She catches her breath and coughs. Pats her chest to calm herself down.

He'd been over at Liverpool last week and these horrible lads there had started following him. Throwing stones at him, after he'd come out of Mr Quilliam's place.[66] One of the stones hit him above the eye, cut him badly. And he'd come all the way back to Manchester on the train with this awful thing bleeding all over the place. When he got in, the silly old swine said that he'd just wanted to get home to his own bed and to sleep it off. But I said no, I'm not having that, so I dragged him across the road to the Infirmary. Well, if you live practically outside of it, you should make the most of it, shouldn't you? The doctor told me to go home whilst they stitched him up and to come back later when he was steadier on his feet … and … well. It was a terrible shock. To see your husband like that. It was the first time I'd ever seen him looking so poorly and so, well, old, I suppose. He's never gotten really 'old' - not Robert.
So, I was standing at the side of the Infirmary, trying to get my breath back and get my composure and all of that, when along comes Emmeline Pankhurst. Rushing past, arms filled with her usual purple and green rosettes and her banners, on her way to one of her

---

[66] There is no evidence of Robert ever being attacked for his beliefs, but the attacks on the Liverpool mosque and on women converts such as Frances 'Fatima' Cates are well-documented. The fear of attack and of abuse would have been very real for Robert's family.

disturbances – she's forever organising her disturbances - but she stopped when she saw me, asked me how I was doing. And so, I told her that Robert had had a bit of an accident.

Pause.

She took hold of my hand in both of hers. All concerned. I said, well, not to worry, it was obviously just a case of some nasty boys showing off to one another and she said, *"No! Would you excuse a girl who behaved like that?"* Which is true, I suppose. I mean, just look at all the outrage that her and her emancipation friends are faced with, just because no-one is used to a woman kicking up a fuss about something in public. She started saying something about how despicable it is when people do brutal things like that to others because of their beliefs. But my eyes started welling up, so she stopped talking. I think she realised I'm not one who likes to be seen crying. And so, she said, *"I'm going to call in on you. Check you're both alright. But tell Mr Stanley we're all this in together. Solidarity, Mrs Stanley, solidarity! We shall overcome!"* And with that, she was off again, on her way to throw a placard at a politician or whatever it is that the newspapers like to accuse her of doing. And then - the next day - she brought those flowers round.

Nods at the vase.

She arrived, with a daughter in tow who was yawning her head off. That Christabel, it was. Apparently, Christabel had just had another night in the prison cells for slapping a policeman at the Free Trade Hall. Anyway, Mrs Pankhurst said that she wouldn't come inside as no-one likes unannounced guests. But she thrust this big bunch of freesias at Robert and told him that a real man would happily accept flowers from a woman, that he shouldn't look so surprised.

She starts to laugh again but it turns into another coughing fit. She uses her handkerchief but this one goes on for a while.

Dear me, I shouldn't do that to myself. Then she left, telling me to try and not worry too much about the sorts of things that my "very original" husband gets up to. "Very original". His face when he heard her talking about him like that! *She made me sound like one of her bohemian friends*", he said afterwards. Mary-Jane said, *"Well, if the fez fits, Father."*

But I *am* worried about him. About it all. How can you not be?

Pause.

It's ridiculous, in a way. All those years where Robert was up against all sorts of low-life folk, like those thugs threatening the factory workers because of whatever way they'd voted and all of the drunkards and thieves he had to sentence when he was a magistrate - people who knew where we lived. But I never lay awake at night fretting over them coming to get him. I suppose I thought that, because he was upholding British law, that British law would protect him.

Now, I wonder if British law *would* protect him, because of whatever it is that he believes in these days? He says the police in Liverpool don't take the attacks on the mosque at all seriously. They don't even bother investigating. It's because people seem to think that these Moslem converts have turned their backs on Britain. Ridiculous! You only have to listen to him wittering on about the wonders of our Queen and the achievements of our country to know that. And apparently even Victoria herself has a favourite servant who's a Moslem. Chappie from India. He's teaching her his language and the Qur'an and all of that. Our Robert says that fact shows us all that he's in good company, says he's always known that the Queen has her head screwed on right.

Our Mary-Jane says that there is a current fad, a phase for being interested in Moslem society. But, maybe I'm the dinosaur – the dying out species. I've never been one for fads or causes. It strikes me that these days everyone seems to want to change their clothes or their hair or their religion or whatnot. One day you'll probably be able to choose whether you're a man or a woman. It wouldn't surprise me. And, well, if it cheered people up? If it didn't harm anyone, would it really matter? Heh. The very thought.

Pause.

But not me; I'll never change. And I don't imagine that I'll ever settle here in Manchester. No, Stalybridge, that's my place. No place like home, that's what they say. But the next time I probably get over there, it'll be when they put me in a box and wheel me over to St Paul's graveyard.

Ooh, I'm being morbid.

Takes a deep breath and coughs.

The dizziness… There, now. It's gone. It's alright. It's this chest. Weaker and weaker it's getting.

She stands up.

I'd better cheer myself up before they get back. I hope that Robert hasn't gone all giddy and treated the boy to another fez.

She nudges the fez containing the kindling with her foot.

Because the lad didn't look after this one, did he? His grandad brought it back for him the other week. A little one, like the ones their orphans wear. I found it by the side of George's bed yesterday in a bit of an unfortunate state. He'd been trying his hardest not to wet the bed. He tries his best – he really does but … but Robert had forgotten to put the chamber pot back in George's room, hadn't he? And the lad had gone and left his fez next to the bed. So, he was half-asleep, when he did it. He cried, he did, when I said that the water mark had ruined it. That it was all out of shape now. Bless him. I said, well, I'll not throw it out. We can dry it out a bit – and then we can use it for the kindling, can't we? And no one else in the world will have such a fancy kindling container, George! Then he perked up a bit. So, I …

She has a fit of coughing and has to steady herself, putting her hand against the wall.

Oooh, that's not good. It's really not getting any better, this chest. Anyway. Robert had clocked it – the fez – the next day. I'd put it on the windowsill to try and dry it out before I put the kindling into it. He'd picked it up and was looking at it. Asked me why it was damp. Well, I did think about telling a white lie but … No. So, I told him what George had gone and done when he was half asleep. And Robert didn't say anything at first – he was probably thinking it was his fault a bit. Because he knows it's his job to put the empty chamber pots back. But then he started chuckling away. Said, "I did wonder why it was a bit whiffy." Which was a relief – him laughing about it all - because I'd honestly been worrying that ruining a fez – and especially peeing in one – might be considered to be a mortal sin amongst Moslems. You know … very offensive to them. Or something.

Seems not, though. Seems you can still have a laugh about the silly little things in life. And you can't live without that, can you?

GO TO BLACK.

NOTE: Emma Stanley died on 4th January 1902. At the time of writing, I was not aware that Emmeline Pankhurst had actually signed Emma's death certificate – nor that Emma had died of bronchitis; this was discovered some weeks after these scripts were completed.

13. THE MAYOR AND THE SHOWGIRL

CONTEXT:
Following the death of his father, John, in 1898, nine-year-old George Stanley moved a short distance in Manchester to live with his grandparents, Robert and Emma. John died only seven months after his father, Robert, had converted to Islam. George's sister, Marguerite, aged ten, went to live with Robert's daughter, Alice, in Uppermill, and their other two brothers – one a new-born – stayed with their mother in nearby Chorlton.

Whilst we know next to nothing of George's life after he was brought up by his grandparents, it is quite likely that Robert 'Reschid' Stanley would have taken young George along to the Liverpool mosque on a number of occasions in order to meet Quilliam and see how Muslims worshipped.

Quilliam himself was in polygamous relationships for nearly all his adult life. His first wife, Hannah Quilliam, was from a well-off middle-class background. Together they had four children, all of them brought up as Muslims and given Muslim names. Before converting to Islam, Quilliam had also had a mistress – she was a 'showgirl' (his words) – named Mary Lyon who often appeared at the Liverpool Empire. Although she

THE LIVERPOOL MOSQUE
Moslem devotion led by the Sheik ul Islam

Quilliam in white, Robert is in the fez behind him

remained a Christian, they married in an Islamic ceremony and their children were brought up as Muslims and given Islamic names.

This scene envisages what it might have been like when young George accompanied his grandad to Liverpool.

LIVERPOOL DOCKSIDE, AUGUST 1899.

A HOT AUGUST DAY AT THE ALBERT DOCKS IN
LIVERPOOL. THE CRIES OF SEAGULLS ARE NEARLY
DROWNED OUT BY THE SHOUTS OF SAILORS, THE
CLANGING AND BANGING OF METAL CHAINS,
HAMMERS AND ACCOMPANYING THUDS AS CRATES ARE
LIFTED AND DROPPED. THE DOCK IS FILLED WITH
SHIPS AND SAILING CRAFT OF ALL SHAPES AND SIZES.
SHEIKH **ABDULLAH QUILLIAM,** AGED 43, IS LOOKING
OUT ACROSS THE DOCKS. HE IS SMARTLY DRESSED, AS
ANY WELL-TO-DO LAWYER WOULD BE. **ROBERT
STANLEY**, AGED 71, IS ALSO RESPECTABLY DRESSED
AND IS PERSPIRING SOMEWHAT, WIPING HIS BROW
WITH A HANDKERCHIEF AND FANNING HIMSELF WITH
HIS HAT FROM TIME TO TIME. **GEORGE STANLEY,**
AGED 9, HAS STRIPPED DOWN TO HIS SHIRT AND HAS
ATTEMPTED TO ROLL HIS TROUSER LEGS UP. HIS
STRANGE ENSEMBLE IS TOPPED OFF WITH A SMALL RED
FEZ AND HE IS FANNING HIMSELF WITH A LARGE FAN
EMBLAZONED WITH A COLOURFUL ARABIC DESIGN. HE
OCCASIONALLY REMEMBERS TO FAN HIS
GRANDFATHER WITH IT.

QUILLIAM: So, what do you think of your trip to the mighty port
of Liverpool, George? You've certainly brought the weather with
you.

GEORGE: Well – it's been a grand day so far. Thank you for my
fez, Mr Quilliam. And the fan, too. I can't wait to show the lads at
school. It'll tickle 'em pink.

QUILLIAM: (*Bursts out laughing*) Really! The things this boy comes
out with.

ROBERT: He's always spoken like that, has George. Nothing to do
with me.

GEORGE: I speak as I find.

ROBERT: Mind your manners, George. Your grandma said that I'm permitted to treat you to an ice-cream if you manage to reign your tongue in a bit.

GEORGE: Well, what would I eat my ice-cream with if I did *that*? My nose?

ROBERT sighs with exasperation. GEORGE fans him. Hard.

ROBERT: Now, George. Be careful with that fan. It's a special gift from the Sheikh, for your grandma.

QUILLIAM: So, tell me, young Mister Stanley – the ships. We've been on three of them now. Which did you prefer?

GEORGE: The blue one - 'The Harpoon'. The negro - I mean, the *chap* we met on there - was very kind to me. He gave me this little pocketknife!

GEORGE whips a not-so-small knife out of his pocket to show them.

ROBERT: Goodness! I didn't see him do that. You shouldn't have taken it, George; it looks quite a pricey little thing. We need to take it back to him.

QUILLIAM: No, no, Brother. It from was Ali - and a gift is a gift. He would be most offended if you tried to give it him back.

ROBERT: Yes, but…

QUILLIAM: Ali is an excellent man. But, George, why did you correct yourself then? When you began to describe Ali?

GEORGE: Well … because Grandma says it's not nice to talk about … to use certain words. To describe others. If they might not like those words themselves.

QUILLIAM: Yes?

GEORGE: And I had a funny feeling that Mr … Mr Ali wouldn't like to be called that.

QUILLIAM: You're correct. As is your grandma.

GEORGE: For example, my little brother has got the look of a sewer-rat, but it would be very cruel and unkind to say that to him.

QUILLIAM: Yes, it would.

GEORGE: Although we do say it behind his back instead.

QUILLIAM: (*Laughing*) Oh dear.

GEORGE: Grandma says that there are words we use - especially ones to describe people with different skin colours - that are not respectful. She says that some know-it-alls say that they're 'just words'. But they're not!

QUILLIAM: And I'm in complete agreement with her!

GEORGE: She says people who use words that hurt others are as common as muck.

QUILLIAM: Well, I have yet to meet your grandmother, George, but she only grows in my estimation, the more that I hear of her.

ROBERT: Emma is a rarity. She's always been more interested in what is in a man's heart than in his appearances. Or his material achievements.

GEORGE: Yes. So, I always have to be careful about calling my brother 'rat-face' when Grandma's about.

QUILLIAM: Very wise.

GEORGE: But Mr Quilliam; why are there so many men round this dock place falling over and singing and being very stupid?

QUILLIAM: Sadly, they're drunk. This is the effect of alcohol on the sailors. That's what it does to men and women alike.

GEORGE: Thought so. It happens at school.

ROBERT: (*Concerned*) What does?

GEORGE: We've got these twins in my class. Some mornings they turn up all intoxicated and that. And some days they're even sick with it.[67]

QUILLIAM: Goodness.

GEORGE: Yes. Their mam's too poor to give them a proper breakfast, so sometimes they have a few draughts of ale.

QUILLIAM: Terrible!

GEORGE: Yes. And one of them was once so bad with it that he was sick into his desk. Like this. (*GEORGE makes as though he is puking into his desk*)

ROBERT: That's quite enough, George! The Sheikh doesn't want to hear this sort of …

QUILLIAM: On the contrary. This is exactly the sort of thing that we need to be hearing about.

---

[67] In many areas of the country, beer was still cheaper than the cost of clean drinking water. It was very common for most children to be used to drinking alcohol, particularly in the poorest areas.

GEORGE: I can tell you much worse stories about Barnaby Grimshaw if you like.

ROBERT: *(Hastily)* No – we don't want to hear about Barnaby Grimshaw. Can you fan me a bit please, George? This sun is awfully hot now.

GEORGE attempts to fan his grandad as hard as he can by jumping up and down with it and waggling it at him.

QUILLIAM: *(To ROBERT)* But this sort of thing is a national scandal!

ROBERT: I know. That's better. Thank you, George.

QUILLIAM: We think of ourselves as a progressive nation because we no longer send tiny children down mines.

ROBERT: Indeed.

QUILLIAM: And yet we send them off to learn their ABC's whilst they're vomiting up the dregs of their parents' leftover tankards!

GEORGE: I concur! That's exactly what happens. And once, Barnaby Grimshaw did even much worse than that, in the corner of the…

ROBERT: That's enough, George. You did want that ice-cream, didn't you?

GEORGE: Yes. Sorry, Grandad.

Silence for several seconds.

QUILLIAM: Well, George, that Mr Ali who was so kind to you – he's coming to the mosque later for Salat al-Zuhr.[68] His crew are from Abyssinia. They're Moslems like us and…

GEORGE: Abyssinia in Africa? They've got Mussulmen in Africa?

QUILLIAM: Oh, yes. Many parts of Africa are far closer to the region where Islam began than we are here in Liverpool.

ROBERT: And our mosque has a close connection with Moslems in Sierra Leone.[69]

QUILLIAM: Yes. I've visited there myself, George. I've tried to persuade your grandfather to come with me but…

---

[68] Afternoon prayers.
[69] Quilliam's congregation had strong links with the mosque in Sierra Leone. See *His Own Man*.

ROBERT: I'm too old to be seafaring. I'd probably go rusty and seize up.

GEORGE: Silly. One day, Grandad, there will be big metal aeroflighter things and then you can fly over to Africa instead of having to go by boat!

ROBERT: I won't be around to see that sort of thing. You will, though.

QUILLIAM: Goodness, but you're in a maudlin mood today, Brother Reschid. Cheer up! The sun is shining; no need to be a party pooper!

ROBERT: My apologies. It was John's birthday today – George's father. It's only been a year since we lost him.

QUILLIAM: (*Puts a consoling hand on his arm*) Of course. Of course. It's against the laws of nature to lose one's child. Regardless of their age.

The two men nod and are silent for a few seconds, looking over the docks.

GEORGE: (*Trying to change the subject*) You know these dark sailors – do they think that you old white men … being Moslems, do they think you're all a bunch of lunatics?

QUILLIAM: (Laughing) Less of the old please, George! I'm nearly thirty years' younger than your grandfather. But, on the contrary, they're rather taken with the fact that native British men have adopted their faith.

ROBERT: They seem to feel that the mosque is some sort of a home away from home for them.

QUILLIAM: Yes. It's the native Christians in Britain that tend to have the negative reaction towards us being white and following Islam.

ROBERT: At the least, the mayor of Liverpool has always been very welcoming.

QUILLIAM: True. But he's in a minority. There remain many factions within the area, George, who like to verbally - and even physically - attack us.[70]

GEORGE: (*Very interested*) With knives? With guns?

---

[70] Quilliam was frequently verbally abused and threatened in public. He documented the attacks on other Muslims, both physically and in terms of vandalising the mosque. See *His Own Man*.

QUILLIAM: Well, usually it tends to be a shower of disgruntled youth. They collect outside the mosque and hurl abuse. Or stones.

ROBERT: Disgraceful. Lower class thugs!

GEORGE: That's awful! Why would they do that?

QUILLIAM: Well, many of the less educated amongst them feel threatened and frightened by anyone who dares to live their life a bit differently.

ROBERT: And ignorant, fearful people often turn to violence.

QUILLIAM: Plus, they don't like that white people consider people of different colours and creeds to be our equals. And that we socialise together.

GEORGE: That's just silly.

QUILLIAM: Of course it is. But these people – well, the ones who are youths or children - they don't know any better.

GEORGE: Well, they blummin' well should.

QUILLIAM: But think about it, George; if you've been mistreated by those in charge at the factory, the dockyard, in school, even at home, then you might be eager to find another group of people that you can look down upon.

GEORGE: I know what you mean.

QUILLIAM: Yes?

GEORGE: Yes. People at school are rotten to Barnaby Grimshaw, because he really smells. Even though those who're mean to him are just as mucky.

QUILLIAM: Exactly. And none are easier to look down upon than those of different races, creeds and religions.

GEORGE: They're very dim.

QUILLIAM: 'I might be poor' you tell yourself, 'but at least I'm not dark-skinned, or a Hindoo, or a woman.'

ROBERT: It makes such people feel better about their own lack of attributes. And it's the bully's mentality.

QUILLIAM: Precisely. And George, there are others too, who *have* had a superior education, but who are also against Moslems.

GEORGE: I bet they don't even know any Moslems!

QUILLIAM: Indeed!

ROBERT: And some of them fear the strength of some of the Moslem armies in countries that practise Islam.

GEORGE: Do they?

QUILLIAM: Yes. They fear that the Turks, for example, might side with other bold foreign powers, such as Germany, against the British Empire.

GEORGE: So, they think that you and Mr Quilliam might become traitors?

QUILLIAM: Well. That's how they perceive it, at any rate.

GEORGE: Well, all I can say is that people can be very, very stupid. *(He has had enough of the serious chat now)* May I get an ice-cream now, please? They're an ha'penny according to that sign over there.

ROBERT: What? That's a ridiculous price. In my day...

QUILLIAM: In your day, Robert – tell the truth; ice-creams didn't even exist. No man had yet invented how to keep flavoured blocks of ice from melting too fast.

GEORGE: Then I feel very sorry for you, Grandad. It was no way to live.

QUILLIAM: This shall be my treat, George. *(He hands him a coin)*

George thanks him and runs over to the ice-cream cart.

QUILLIAM: Now, Robert; did I hear you say that you were anticipating getting the 4 o'clock train back to Manchester?

ROBERT: Yes. Emma needs me back. We have the long-lost wanderer – our second son, Thomas – back from his latest expedition in the Highlands.

QUILLIAM: How delightful.

ROBERT: I'm not sure about that. Goodness knows what he's been doing up there. Probably flogging rainwater to the Scots, or one of his other half-baked money schemes.

QUILLIAM: Well, then, could I impose on you to do me a little favour on your way back to the train station?

ROBERT: Yes?

QUILLIAM: I had been hoping to do this myself, but I agreed early this morning to undertake a new case; a woman beaten severely by her husband.

ROBERT: Of course. What is it you need me to do?

QUILLIAM: I need this envelope dropping off at an address. It contains a considerable amount of money.

ROBERT: Not a problem. What's the address?

QUILLIAM: It is the… The Liverpool Empire.

ROBERT: The theatre?

QUILLIAM: Yes. The theatre. It's easy to find.

ROBERT: Oh yes, I know it.

QUILLIAM: It's the housekeeping – I meant to leave it the other day but completely forgot. It's for my wife, Mary. Not Hannah, my first wife, whom I know you've met. The other one. Mary. You've never met Mary. Not that there has been any reason for you not to have met her, of course.

ROBERT: Of course.

QUILLIAM: She's an actress.

ROBERT: Yes. You said previously.

QUILLIAM: Ah, yes. And as you know, both my wives are absolutely fine with each other – tolerant of each other – and our respective children spend many a happy hour playing together and chasing each other around.

ROBERT: Of course, Brother Abdullah. You don't have to…

QUILLIAM: And Mary just won't come to the mosque! She's a practising Christian still – but that's not why she won't come. She's actually very accepting of Islam, even though we were together before … before I converted.

A few seconds of silence as ROBERT deduces that QUILLIAM is referring to her previously being his mistress.

QUILLIAM: Yes, it's all very silly. But she's got it into her head the last few weeks that I perceive her to be some sort of a second wife in terms of status and suchlike.[71]

ROBERT: Oh.

QUILLIAM: Yes – and no amount of persuasion and sweet talk on my part can convince her otherwise.

ROBERT: Sometimes the females can dig their heels in a bit too much.

---

[71] Very little research has been conducted into the lives of Quilliam's three wives (later on in his life he also married the widow of his friend, Henri de Leon – whose name he also took on! See *His Own Man*). Because of this, it is all too easy to assume that they were easily led and rather vapid. Certainly, they lived their lives in the shadow of Quilliam, but he did not appear to be a man who liked to surround himself with anyone who lacked intelligence or who had a weak personality.

QUILLIAM: Quite. And, apparently, somebody has told her that when I give my lectures about polygamy, I explain that a man can take another wife if - *if* - the second female has fallen on hard times and needs looking after.

ROBERT: Hmm. Not helpful.

QUILLIAM: No. In fact, I suspect that the 'somebody' that told her this is my first wife,

ROBERT: Ah.

QUILLIAM: Anyway. So, Mary's now been having a few ... tantrums. Saying that I see her as some sort of a ... a charity case.

ROBERT: Oh dear.

QUILLIAM: Oh, I'll sort it out with her sooner or later. But she does need her household payments today and...

ROBERT: Abdullah, I understand completely. George and I will deliver it on our way back.

GEORGE comes running back – his treat is already half-eaten, and he is waving the coin at Quilliam. He has pink ice-cream all 'round his mouth and it is already dripping down his shirt. He is licking his hands.

GEORGE: Grandad! The ice-cream man said I didn't have to pay for it! Because I was with the Sheikh and the Sheikh helped his daughter out of a bad situation when she got arrested for beating up a sailor.

ROBERT: Oh.

GEORGE: Yes! She smashed the sailor's head in with a brick! But apparently *(mimics a Scouse accent)* that fella *"got what he had coming to him and no mistake".*

ROBERT: *(Murmurs)* Ah yes, the good people of Liverpool.

QUILLIAM: Now, now, Brother. Can't imagine it to be any different in Manchester!

GEORGE: And the ice-cream man says to tell you, Mr Quilliam, that he's going to stroll past your mosque on his way home today with his cart and see if any of your Mussulmen want cooling down from their too-spicy food. And he's got a right merry little bell, he says, and it'll complement all your wailing from the windows.

QUILLIAM: *(Sighs)* Yes. The good people of Liverpool.

AT THE LIVERPOOL EMPIRE. BACK STAGE.

A SMALL BUT COLOURFULLY DECORATED DRESSING ROOM; SPLASHES OF RED, GREEN AND GOLD. THE PLACE IS ELABORATELY DECORATED, WITH VELVET CURTAINS AT THE WINDOW AND GAUZY MATERIAL DRAPED AROUND THE FURNITURE. THERE IS A RED CHAISE LONGUE AND A LARGE PAINTING OF A SEMI-NAKED WOMAN ON THE WALL. **MARY LYON,** AGED 36, IS SOMETHING OF A STRAWBERRY-BLONDE BEAUTY. SHE IS STARING INTENTLY INTO A LARGE GOLD-BEDECKED MIRROR AND IS WEARING A ROBE WHILST FINISHING HER MAKE UP.

MARY: Enter!
GEORGE: *(Voice from outside)* Grandad?
ROBERT: *(From outside)* I'm not sure if…
GEORGE: *(From outside)* She said to go in.
ROBERT: *(From outside)* But what if she's… What if she's not in a fit state of dress?
GEORGE: *(From outside)* Well, it'll only be like a Saturday night in Manchester.
MARY: I said enter!

GEORGE enters the room, carrying a small basket of fruit, but ROBERT is lingering and fiddling with his tie pin, so MARY only sees GEORGE at first.

MARY: Ooh, lovely. Some fruit. Pop it over in the corner there. *(She looks up to see him properly)* Oh. Hello. We've not met before, have we?

GEORGE shakes his head, flummoxed. He has never seen such a glamorous woman before, nor one wearing so much make up. He can't take his eyes off her.

MARY: Well… Thank you, my sweet. I'll see if I've got a coin for you. p

MARY takes a glittering bag from the side of the dressing table.

GEORGE: (*His speech returns*). They're not for you. They're for my grandma. She'd murder me if I didn't bring her oranges back.

MARY: (*Turns to face him fully now and lowers her voice, reassuringly*) Well, now, my little fellow. So, why have you brought them here? (*She notices ROBERT hovering in the doorway*) Oh! Come in, come in, sir.

GEORGE: You can have a grape, though. Just one, mind.

ROBERT: I'm so sorry to intrude, Madam; the gentleman in the foyer didn't say that you would be in your … your dressing mode.

MARY: Oh, give over. (*Her voice suddenly drops from a more refined accent and into broader Scouse*) I'm more than decent for a respectable gentleman. Now, who's this little darling here? And I do like that fez! My son has one just like it!

GEORGE: I'm George. Pleased to meet you.

GEORGE *gives a formal bow. MARY claps her hands together.*

MARY: Lovely – and I'm pleased to meet you, too.

GEORGE: Are you the actress?

ROBERT: George… (*He trails off and looks at the painting on the wall*)

MARY: Oh bless! Yes, I am, George. My name is Mary Lyon and I'm … would you like to introduce me to your companion here? You're obviously good at introductions. And he's not as chatty as you are.

GEORGE: This is Grandad. Or the Honourable Robert Stanley, Esquire, Justice of the Peace and mayor of Stalybridge. Plus, grocer, innkeeper and tea-trader!

ROBERT: Now, now, George; that's 'retired' – 'retired' occupations and titles of mine. You know that full well. And it's not pertinent to…

GEORGE: Alright… this is Grandad Robert Stanley, vice-chairman of the Liverpool Moslem Institute.

MARY: Oh! How very…

MARY *rises to greet him and shakes his hand firmly.*

MARY*:* How lovely to meet you at last! I've heard so much about you!

219

ROBERT: Have you?

MARY: Oh yes! Abdie mentions you such a lot. And you too, George; he's mentioned you too.

GEORGE: Has he?

MARY: Oh, yes. He told me, Robert, about your loss. I was so sorry to hear about the death of your son.

ROBERT: Ah. Thank you.

MARY: Such a tragedy, leaving four children and… oh, dear little George. You lost your father, didn't you?

GEORGE nods and bites his lip, embarrassed.

MARY: So, I must express my condolences to you, too. (*She extends a hand to him and he takes it. But then she pulls him into her rather large bosom and crushes him in a huge hug. George looks startled, but quite happy*)

ROBERT: Thank you for saying that. Most kind.

MARY: It makes me want to weep – just the thought of… Oh, George. Your mama – how is your dear mama?

GEORGE is *still rather dumbfounded and feeling his face where Mary's cheek has rubbed up against his.*

GEORGE: She's as … as good as can be expected. I think. Don't you want to embrace Grandad, too? I'd expect he'd like that.

ROBERT is dumbfounded and is about to say something but then MARY bursts out laughing.

MARY: Oh, I'm sure your grandad has his own lovely wife to hug. But you! You're quite the little man, aren't you? I expect your own mother is very proud of you.

GEORGE: (*Not hearing her*) You smell lovely. Like … violets.

MARY: (*Tinkles a laugh*) Oh, you little love. Why don't you sit on the chaise longue there… Oh. (*She notices ROBERT trying to avert his gaze from the painting*) I can cover that up if you like? I know that in Islam you're not meant to…

ROBERT: (*Waving his hand*) Not at all! I'm a British chap, after all, and used to these sorts of things being all over the place.

GEORGE: He's from Stalybridge. You see a lot of women with not enough clothes on there. Although they're not usually so beautiful.

MARY bursts out laughing.

MARY: So, my painting; it doesn't bother you then, my young chap?

GEORGE: Why should it? There should be more paintings like that! We should have them on the walls in our classroom. Although then I don't think I'd be able to concentrate.

MARY: *(Chuckles)* The very idea. Now. What can I do for you two gentlemen? Are you planning to take some tea? Stay on for the performance?

ROBERT: Oh no, Miss Lyon. We've a train to be catching fairly soon.

GEORGE: But Grandad! Wouldn't it be just wonderful to watch Miss Lyons do her performance?

ROBERT: *(Flustered)* I'm sure it would, but we promised your grandma to be back in time for tea. She's making something special.

GEORGE: *(Suspicious)* It's a Wednesday. She never makes anything other than potato pie on a Wednesday. And it's certainly nowt special.

MARY: Oh dear. Poor you.

GEORGE: And on some Wednesdays we don't even have a pie crust on it! How can it be a pie without no pie crust on it? I ask you!

MARY: Well, I'm sure she has her reasons. I imagine your grandma works very hard looking after everyone. A woman's work is never done.

GEORGE: She says it's because of her arthritis – that she can't do the pastry on the days her hands are bad. And she won't let my Auntie Mary-Jane or my Auntie Sarah – who live with us - do it. Grandad says he once broke a tooth on the pastry that Auntie Sarah tried to make.

MARY laughs and pinches GEORGE's cheek.

MARY: Oh, he's a one!
ROBERT: No, I'm afraid it's true.

MARY: So, you live with your grandparents then, George?

GEORGE: Yes. My brothers are with Mam in Chorlton. It's only down the road from us. And my sister Marguerite – she's gone to live with Auntie Alice. Mother wasn't coping with us all very well, after our dad…

MARY: Well, you have a good and loving family, George! To look after you like that.

GEORGE: I suppose so. But Auntie Mary-Jane can be a bit of a pain, can't she, Grandad?

ROBERT: Perhaps that's not how we should describe her.

GEORGE: She's a suffragist. And always rattling on about her female issues.

ROBERT: *(To MARY)* She's very … single-minded.

GEORGE: But I prefer it to living with my brothers. They just skriked all the time and ate too much. So, there was never anything left for me and our Marguerite.

MARY: Well, perhaps you could entice your aunties over here? They could come and see one of the famous performances at The Empire!

GEORGE: Well … they're both very old and not married. So, I would have to work hard on them to bring them over to Liverpool for a bit of a lark.

MARY: Worth a try!

GEORGE: *(Pauses)* Hmmm. I wonder if the Sheikh would marry one of them and have them as another wife of his? Auntie Sarah is really very pretty still, even though she's old now – she's got big brown eyes like a cow and…

ROBERT: George!

MARY: *(Laughing)* Oh – but Abdie can't cope with two wives, never mind three! We run him ragged between us, we really do.

GEORGE: You'd have to be barmy to want two, if you ask me.

MARY: Oh, George – you really are a little comedian. We could do with a young fella like you here on the stage.

ROBERT: Perish the thought! He's bad enough when he's not on the stage.

MARY: But it's so refreshing to meet a boy who isn't living in constant fear of his elders.

GEORGE: That's true! I'm not feared of 'em!

MARY: (*Laughing*) Because I've never held any truck with the old-fashioned so-called virtue of 'being seen and not heard'; have you, Mr Stanley?

ROBERT: To be quite honest, when I am around George for more than a few hours I do wish that a figure of authority would somehow come and impose such a virtue.

MARY: (Still *laughing*) Oh, you're a terror too!

ROBERT: I do try. But anyway, Miss Lyon. This is why we are here. From the Sheikh.

ROBERT *hands her the envelope.* MARY *glances at the envelope and then places it on her dressing table.*

MARY: Oh, dear Abdie. He never forgets. Even though we don't see as much of him as we would like to.

ROBERT: He's a very busy man.

MARY: He certainly is.

ROBERT: In all my years, I can honestly say that I have never met anyone more prolific in his output. But, also, so generous and kind in his manner.

MARY: Coming from you, Mr Stanley – of whom Abdie holds the highest regard for – that is a very pleasing thing to hear.

ROBERT: Nothing but the truth.

MARY: And I shall certainly convey it to him when he comes for supper with the family tomorrow.

ROBERT: Please don't. I would hate for him to think that I am the crawling type. I cannot stand fawners.

GEORGE: Crawlers and fawners make Grandad sick to his stomach. He's always saying that. They're nearly as bad as obsequious people, aren't they, Grandad?

ROBERT: Quite. Now, Miss Lyon – you must excuse us as we have a train to catch. We can't afford to be late as my wife is quite the disciplinarian.

GEORGE: Quite frankly, she's terrifying, is Grandma, if you're late.

MARY: Well, then – I had better not keep you any longer, but … look. Next time, we'll have tea together – yes?

GEORGE: Ooh, yes please!

MARY: And perhaps you will both come again and bring Mrs Stanley? And perhaps bring your aunties, George?
GEORGE: *(Reluctantly)* If I must.
MARY: And I must give you a parting gift for the trouble that you've gone to, in bringing me my envelope.

MARY picks up bags and boxes on her table.

MARY: Now, there isn't very much that's suitable for males in this dressing room but … George. Here you are.

MARY hands him a small pistol.

GEORGE: Oh, blimey!
MARY: And before you get too excited – it isn't a real pistol. Well, not one that fires bullets. It's to light cigars or cigarettes – you see?

MARY demonstrates the lighter by putting a long cigarette in a holder between her lips and lighting it. ROBERT looks horrified. GEORGE looks as though he will faint with happiness.

GEORGE: I think that's even better than a real pistol! As it won't get me into trouble with the law, will it, Grandad?
GRANDAD: That's erm… most … incredibly generous, Miss – Mrs Quilliam.
MARY: Just so long as you don't take up smoking, George; it's not good for the vocal cords. And it makes your eyes ever so red and unattractive.
GEORGE: Don't worry. I won't.
MARY: Now, as for you – you naughty old grandad who doesn't get people presents from Liverpool – I am afraid that I have nothing that I can give you. So, you will have to make do with this…

MARY suddenly steps forward and places a big kiss on ROBERT'S cheek, above his beard, leaving a lipstick mark.
MARY: I wouldn't normally be so forward with one of Abdie's Moslem friends, but you're a native Englishman. And like me, you're of the working classes!

ROBERT looks somewhat stunned at this overt display of affection.

ROBERT: Well… well, that's …

MARY: And of course, our Lord Jesus – the prophet, as the Moslems see him – would frequently kiss people as a greeting and as a sign of affection. All Jewish people did. So, you can either view me as … as a follower of Abrahamic traditions or as a dangerous, Bohemian showgirl. Ha!

GEORGE: Jewish people also washed peoples' feet as a way of greeting them. But you wouldn't want to go near Grandad's feet. Grandma says she needs a proper saw to cut his toenails and …

ROBERT: *(Cuts him off)* George!

MARY: Now. Off you both trot – don't miss your train!

They smile and nod. George gives her a little bow and they leave the room.

OUTSIDE IN THE CORRIDOR

GEORGE: Well! This *has* been a good day. I've come away with a fez, a fan, a free ice-cream, a knife from Abyssinia and a sort-of gun. And I've seen a pretty lady with lots of face-paint! Can I come to Liverpool with you again, Grandad?

ROBERT: Hmm. We'll see.

GEORGE: I think that you've had a good day too. But I bet you wished you had a proper cuddle in her chest, like I did. And do you know what, Grandad? Your face is still as red as a beetroot! But don't worry - just rub that lipstick-thing mouth-print off your face and no-one need ever know. I'm sworn to secrecy.

ROBERT: George…

GEORGE: What?

ROBERT: Put a sock in it.

---ENDS---

14. MRS PANKHURST HAS HER CAKE

CONTEXT:

Emmeline Pankhurst lived just ten minutes' walk from the Stanley's in Manchester. As well as leading the suffragette movement, she was also the registrar for the district from 1897 to 1908.[72] Pankhurst had been a member of the Independent Labour Party, but over time her politics changed; standing as a Conservative candidate.

Whilst we do not know what Robert's views were on the emancipation of women, he was in favour of education for females; three of his daughters were teachers and his granddaughter won a place at grammar school. Given her acts of civil disobedience, however, it is likely that Emmeline and Robert would not have been in agreement on many issues; for example, she had taken the opposite side to Robert during the Bulgarian Crisis of 1876.

Old Corn Exchange, Manchester

We have no firm evidence that any of Robert's daughters were involved in the struggle for emancipation, but the timeline, the close proximity of their homes and the many debates taking place at the nearby Secular Hall and other institutions, make it likely that Emmeline and Robert already knew each other before Emma's death. Documentation shows that Emmeline was responsible for registering the deaths of Robert's son, John, and for Emma Stanley, signing the certificates and handing them back to Robert.

This scene imagines an encounter between Emmeline and Robert, two individuals who in many ways were poles apart when it came to the desire for rapid social change, but who had much in common in terms of personality and drive.

---

[72] 'Suffragette' was first coined by the Daily Mail in 1906 as a derogatory term, but Emmeline happily embraced the name for the WPSU.

EXCHANGE TEA ROOMS, MANCHESTER, MARCH 1902

A RAINY SPRING DAY. **EMMELINE PANKHURST,** AGED 43, OPENS THE EXCHANGE TEA ROOM'S DOORS AND BATTLES WITH TRYING TO SHAKE HER UMBRELLA OUTSIDE. A WAITRESS TRIES TO INTERVENE BUT EMMELINE SMILES AND DECLINES ANY ASSISTANCE, NOR WILL SHE ALLOW THE WOMAN TO TAKE HER COAT FROM HER. SHE IS SMARTLY DRESSED, IN A MINT-GREEN TAILORED SUIT AND A LARGE HAT WITH DARK RED MATERIAL ROSES. SHE PLACES HER UMBRELLA IN THE STAND AND HER COAT AND HAT ON THE PEG. **ROBERT STANLEY**, AGED 79, IS ALREADY WAITING FOR HER AT A TABLE. HE HAS AN ASTRAKHAN COAT AROUND HIS SHOULDERS AND UNDERNEATH IS WEARING THE TRADITIONAL VICTORIAN GENT'S SUIT WITH POCKET-WATCH; NOW SOMEWHAT OUT OF FASHION, BUT GIVEN HIS AGE, THIS IS EASILY FORGIVEN. HIS BEARD IS QUITE LONG BUT VERY NEATLY CULTIVATED.

ROBERT: *(Standing and bowing slightly)* Do take a seat, Mrs Pankhurst.

EMMELINE: Thank you, Mr Stanley. Have you been over at the Corn Exchange?

ROBERT: Yes. Chatting to some old tea-trading friends there. Modern monstrosity, that place is! Bring back the old Corn Exchange, I say![73]

EMMELINE: Well, we must move with the times. I've just been at a meeting at the town hall. I'm shocked that it was only built in 1877. The place is already looking so dated!

ROBERT: Ah, but Mrs Pankhurst – you're a lady who wants the times to move far too fast, I think.

EMMELINE smiles wryly but sits down.

---

[73] The Old Corn Exchange building was demolished in 1897 and was replaced by a newer Corn Exchange building by 1903.

ROBERT: Very pleasant here though. Our tea rooms in Rusholme aren't quite as nice as the ones in the city, are they?

EMMELINE: No. Although the house prices in our stretch are ever-increasing!

ROBERT: We're obviously trend-setters. Now, Mrs Pankhurst; I've taken the liberty of ordering us tea and cake.

EMMELINE: Lovely.

ROBERT: Yes, the waitress – a rather abrupt girl it has to be said - informed me that they've run out of scones.

EMMELINE: Oh, Mr Stanley! You just pronounced it 'sconns'.

ROBERT: I'm sorry?

EMMELINE: As in 'gone'. Mary-Jane told me that her father was a die-hard champion of the Lancashire dialect.

ROBERT: Yes?

EMMELINE: So, I thought you would have preferred to go for the Lancashire pronunciation - 'scone' as in 'bone'.

ROBERT: These days I mix with people of so many accents and dialects from abroad that I can no longer keep track of what I used to think was 'correct pronunciation'.

EMMELINE: Top marks, Mr Stanley! Who is to say that one way is the right way to pronounce something and another way is wrong?

ROBERT: Indeed.

EMMELINE: In fact, a good friend of mine, Mr George Bernard Shaw, a neighbour from Bloomsbury, has told me he is writing a book about this very notion. Pygmalion, he intends to call it. All about an arrogant professor trying to teach a poor street girl how to speak 'correctly'. He's basing it on the concept of Madame Butterfly.

ROBERT: I'm familiar with Mr Shaw. He's the nephew of the late Lord Stanley of Alderley.

EMMELINE: Oh, goodness, yes. Lord Stanley - another one of your Moslem converts, wasn't he? Were you two related?

ROBERT: Heh – we used to joke about that. Lord Stanley used to introduce me as his 'Brother in Islam – as well as in name.' But so far, we've not been able to establish a bloodline connection.

EMMELINE: Shame.

ROBERT: And if it is ever proven, our Stanley branch were obviously the poor relatives.

EMMELINE: You know, George Bernard Shaw was none too fond of his uncle; said that Lord Stanley was a frightful bore.

ROBERT: Well, that was very unfair of him. He was a somewhat scatty old soul. But gentle. And full of wonderful stories about his travels and his beliefs.

EMMELINE: Ah, it was probably the beliefs that made George take against him. He always came over all peevish if you dared to talk religion.

ROBERT: (*Tutting*) Sadly, far too many people do these days. So, Mrs Pankhurst, what have you done with your daughters?

EMMELINE: Well, Christabel is over at Manchester University, you know. Studying the law – and furiously swotting for her final exams.

ROBERT: The law! An excellent vocation.

EMMELINE: Well, it would be if she were allowed to practise it. But as you know, she's unable to. Being a woman.

ROBERT: Ah. Yes. It does seem a bit…

EMMELINE: And Sylvia – she's the artistic one – she's down in Kensington at the Royal College of Art.

ROBERT: How very talented. And the other girl … erm …

EMMELINE: Adela. Everyone always forgets Adela. Goodness knows why, she's the fiery one! She makes Christabel look like a pussy cat.

ROBERT: Really?

EMMELINE: Yes. And she's - well, she's down at the police station.

ROBERT: Oh.

EMMELINE: Yes. Having to sign some silly form after she bit a policeman. She was very much provoked though.

ROBERT: No broken windows this week?

EMMELINE: (*Twinkle in her eye*) No broken windows. We don't always plan for these things, you know.

ROBERT: I'm sure. But Mrs Pankhurst, these acts of … well. They seem to be on the increase.

EMMELINE: I'm sorry to say that the suffragists have rather forced the hand of many of us. Peaceful means just won't make for rapid change.

ROBERT: I think you're going to end up in rather a lot of trouble
…

EMMELINE: I'm sure we can cope.

ROBERT: And I must say that I'm relieved my Mary-Jane hasn't been taken into police custody for any of your demonstrations.

EMMELINE: (*Mischievously*) You must think us a terrible influence on her.

ROBERT: (*Shaking his head firmly*) Hardly. She may be middle-aged and unmarried, but she's always been quite the … independent sort.

EMMELINE: You don't mind that in a woman?

ROBERT: Not at all! Just so long as she's been educated properly. If not through good schooling, then through good reading.

EMMELINE: Well then, perhaps I might be able to persuade *you* to become one of our founding members.

ROBERT: Of what?

EMMELINE: A new organisation – the Women's Social and Political Union.

ROBERT: (*Holds his hands up, smiling*) Ha! I don't think so, Mrs Pankhurst. I don't need any more strings to add to my bow in the membership and committee department.

EMMELINE: Well, I'm joking of course. No men allowed. Another area where we differ from the suffragists.

ROBERT: Hmm. Yes.

EMMELINE: Unfortunately, most chaps seem to like chasing airs and graces and titles and memberships for the sheer sake of it.

ROBERT: Not me. Well, not anymore. These days I prefer to spend time with a different set of acquaintances for whom status-seeking is frowned upon.

EMMELINE: Ah yes, like your friend, Mr Quilliam. A fascinating character... Now, shall I be mother?

A young waitress puts down the teapot and cups. They thank her. She half mutters a 'You're welcome.'

EMMELINE: (*Pouring the tea*) What a strange thing to say, isn't it? 'Shall I be mother?' As though only a woman – and a mother – is capable of pouring the tea.

ROBERT: I'm sure – like many of these sayings - no harm is meant by it.

EMMELINE: Hmm, I disagree. Even in our use of everyday language, women are subconsciously directed towards certain roles.

ROBERT: Do you think?

EMMELINE: Yes. In fact, I'd say that sometimes, the use of everyday colloquialisms can be even more oppressive than the many other legal and societal restrictions on women.

ROBERT: I've never really given it much thought.

EMMELINE: Well, you should do, Mr Stanley.

ROBERT: Still, in relation to the brewing and pouring of tea, I can tell you that no such tradition exists within the Ottoman Empire and in the Middle East.

EMMELINE: No?

ROBERT: No. Indeed, the ritual of tea-making is very much something that the men like to preside over.

EMMELINE: *(Sipping her tea)* And you're the tea expert!

ROBERT: Only a little. Fifty-odd years.

EMMELINE: Goodness.

ROBERT: So, I know a thing or two, I suppose. For example, you should have let your tea cool a bit more, before you took a sip.

EMMELINE? But I like it scalding hot!

ROBERT: No, no! You can't taste the blend properly that way. That's the wrong way to enjoy it.

EMMELINE: But I *enjoy* it hot!

ROBERT: Well, see, it isn't the right way to...

He stops as he sees her grinning at him from over her teacup.

ROBERT: Mrs Pankhurst, you're deliberately trying to rile me!

EMMELINE: *(Bursts out laughing)* I'm sorry for teasing you. Now, tell me; with all your knowledge on the tea industry, you must have done an awful lot of overseas travelling.

ROBERT: Sadly, I haven't.

EMMELINE: But you seem to be so knowledgeable about the world outside of these shores.

ROBERT: The thing is, I never had the finances to travel. And then there were my various business pursuits and my civic duties.

EMMELINE: Ah.

ROBERT: Not to mention my familial duties; we had eleven children. No easy task.

EMMELINE: I'm sure your dear wife managed a great deal of that!

ROBERT: Well, naturally. And my Emma always wanted me home as much as possible. Yes, we all know who wore the trousers, who was the real head of the household!

EMMELINE: Ah, language again! 'Who wore the trousers' and 'head of the household'. These enforced roles, they infiltrate everything that we do - everything that we say.

ROBERT: (*Smiles, shaking his head*) Mrs Pankhurst, your observations are always most thought-provoking. I am quite pleased that I made your acquaintance. Thanks to Mary-Jane.

EMMELINE: Mary-Jane is a treasure and a stalwart. She is a credit to you and to your late wife.

ROBERT: Thank you. Mary-Jane is … well. They do say that the most talented and quick-witted can be a tad bit prickly to live with.

EMMELINE: Yes. Much like the literary sorts - where Richard and I lived in Bloomsbury.

ROBERT: Oh, I can imagine.

EMMELINE: Yes. They can write the most exquisite, spiritually uplifting sonnet, but are frightful horrors on the domestic front! The drink, the gambling, the scores of bedfellows hopping in and out of one another's boudoirs...

ROBERT: Hmm, well, that doesn't sound quite like Mary-Jane...

EMMELINE lets out a filthy laugh.

ROBERT: (*Embarrassed*) Of course, I was referring to the lack of drink and gambling on Mary-Jane's part. I didn't mean to allude to the subject of bedfellows…

ROBERT trails off. EMMELINE has dissolved into fits of laughter and is finally sobered up by the arrival of the bored-looking waitress, this time with plates of cake. The waitress places them on the table and a soldier at a table nearby calls her over. They immediately start flirting with each other.

ROBERT: (*Changing the subject*) Now… Oh-ho – she's brought seed cake! I specifically asked for Victoria sponge.

EMMELINE: Not to worry.

ROBERT: Dear, dear. These young waitresses, they're far too busy making eyes at soldier-boys instead of listening to their paying customers.

EMMELINE: Well, let's not send the cake back. I shall act like a man.

ROBERT: How so?

EMMELINE: I shall be quite content to have my cake and to eat it.

ROBERT: We should really…

EMMELINE: No - I much prefer seed cake. Victoria sponge always reminds me of the late Queen herself, too rich and too stodgy.

ROBERT: Mrs Pankhurst! Are you an anti-royalist?

EMMELINE: Oh, no. I'm quite the traditionalist. In fact, I'm increasingly moving towards the Conservative Party these days. A far cry from my Independent Labour days.

ROBERT: Good to hear.

EMMELINE: But, yes, I was not a huge fan of Victoria.

ROBERT: Perhaps because she was not a supporter of female suffrage?

EMMELINE: (*Waving her hand*) Hmph. Well, that goes without saying. And I was appalled that she never addressed her own limitations of statute.

ROBERT: (*Brushing cake crumbs from his beard*) How so?

EMMELINE: The heirship entitlements. She should have challenged the ruling that first-born women can become the heir, over their younger brothers.

ROBERT: I can't imagine that one ever being changed!

EMMELINE: Mr Stanley, I believe that within this very century, all of this will change.

ROBERT: No.

EMMELINE: Yes. And sadly, no thanks to Victoria.

ROBERT: I'll believe it when I see it! But, somehow, I don't think either of us will be around.

EMMELINE: Probably not. (*She takes a large bite of cake*)

ROBERT: If anything, things seem to be going backwards in this country.

EMMELINE: How so?

ROBERT: Look at the Balkans. Look at what this government has been doing to the Ottoman Empire, driving them towards the arms of Germany. Treating the Russian danger with the most casual regard!

EMMELINE: Hardly a surprise, when half our royals are Russian and German these days. *(Looks at her empty plate)*

ROBERT: Hmm. You have a point. *(Gesturing at his cake)* Yes, yes, do take some of mine; go on. Have your cake and eat it, like you say.

EMMELINE:*(She forks a piece of his cake)* I had no time for breakfast today; up making placards before I could get to the day-job!

Silence for a few seconds as EMMELINE finishes off the cake.

ROBERT: You're a busy lady, Mrs Pankhurst. You deserve your tea and cake; my cake, too. *(He smiles)*

EMMELINE: *(Wiping her mouth with a napkin)* Ha, well. I must thank you, Mr Stanley. For this lovely invitation to take tea together.

ROBERT: Still, if it had been one of my blends, it would have been a far superior pot of tea.

EMMELINE: No doubt.

ROBERT: But… It's the least I could do, after you were so kind to me those few weeks ago.

EMMELINE: Only doing my job, Mr Stanley.

ROBERT: Come, now. Most registrars would not put an entire afternoon to one side, to listen to an old man's ramblings. After he had lost his wife.

EMMELINE: Don't be silly. Christabel took over for me. She's perfectly capable of signing bits of paper.

ROBERT: Well, I very much appreciated a listening ear.

EMMELINE: And I appreciated Mrs Stanley. From the few little chats that we enjoyed; it was evident that she was a wonderful woman.

ROBERT: She was.

EMMELINE: Your Mary-Jane always sang her praises.

ROBERT: She was a rare breed. A man could not have wished for a better companion.

EMMELINE: It is horrible to lose your life partner. Nine years now since I lost my Richard… *(She tries to distract herself from melancholy by sipping her tea, but then pulls her face)* Tepid! You probably prefer it like that!

Robert chuckles sadly.

EMMELINE: I sometimes wonder which is worse. Husband or … I lost my … my dear little boy, Frank, too. He was four.

ROBERT: I had to bury a little one. He was just one. And then, my youngest son, John. The same year that you lost your husband.

EMMELINE: Yes. That was when I first met Mary-Jane – and you and Mrs Stanley.

ROBERT: Indeed. Our John was 35. It is no age.

EMMELINE: A hard year for both of us.

ROBERT: Yes.

EMMELINE: But so many households in Manchester suffer this.

ROBERT: You have a difficult job.

EMMELINE: Ah. I have to close my mind off to my own sadness when I'm registering deaths. I'd be weeping all over the certificates. It would be a selfish thing to do.

ROBERT: Yes. People would complain about the smudged ink.

They both smile wanly.

EMMELINE: When I lost my boy, I was … unreachable. I locked all his playthings and even his photographs away.

ROBERT: When we lost our little lad, Emma was the opposite. Just carried on as normal. Still, I suppose she had another seven or eight to see to at the time.

EMMELINE: People are so different in their grief.

ROBERT: And yet when our John passed away – a grown man, with his own family - Emma just stared out the window for a whole month. I was … I was quite worried that she'd gone off her head at one point. You'd think that…

EMMELINE: …Because her son was grown, she would be less affected?

ROBERT: Well, I wouldn't say that exactly. It's just that, well, I carried on going to the mosque. It was good for me.

EMMELINE: Yes?

ROBERT: You see, in Islam we have a certain approach to death. We make special prayers and we then turn from our own grief to focus on the needs of others. And we trust that Allah will bear us through it all.

EMMELINE: When was it, that you turned to Islam, Mr Stanley? And … don't you have to recite a verse out loud?

ROBERT: Yes. It was April 1898, when I said Shahada.

EMMELINE: Could you say it for me now? In Arabic?

ROBERT: Of course!

ROBERT *clears his throat and holds both hands palm upwards. Then he says the Shahada in Arabic.*

ROBERT: Lā ʾilāha ʾillā llāh muḥammadun rasūlu llāh.

ROBERT *finishes and notices that the waitress and the soldier have stopped flirting and are now staring at him, as are the people at several other tables.*

EMMELINE: (*Loudly, defensively*) Honestly - you'd think that people had never heard a foreign language before!

ROBERT: It's probably the context. In a tea-room – like this …

EMMELINE: So, Mr Stanley; what does all of that mean?

ROBERT: It means, 'There is no god but God, and Muhammed is the messenger of God'.

EMMELINE: I like the Arabic language. Sounds very earthy.

ROBERT: (*Whispers to her*) Do you think that I just offended anyone?

EMMELINE: (*Whispers back*) If you did, then they jolly well deserved it!

ROBERT: (*Still quietly*) Hmm, it's important to be considerate of other peoples' feelings. That's one of the reasons that Abdullah – the Sheikh – doesn't wander around in Turkish robes.

EMMELINE: Oh yes?

ROBERT: Yes. He prefers to be suited and booted in his usual lawyer's clothes. There's no point in trying to be different just for the sake of it.

EMMELINE: Sensible enough. How old is Mr Quilliam?

EMMELINE *gestures to the waitress to bring more tea. The waitress mutters under her breath and then rolls her eyes at the soldier. She stomps off.*

ROBERT: Why, he is... (*Thinks for a second*) He is 46.

EMMELINE: Are his parents alive?

ROBERT: No. Why do you ask?

EMMELINE: Do you think that ... perhaps ... perhaps you are some sort of father figure to him?

ROBERT: Oh, I doubt that. He knows far more about Islam then I do. He is incredibly well educated. Immeasurably intelligent.

EMMELINE: I think you sell yourself short, Mr Stanley. I would imagine that you are rather important to him.

ROBERT: Well...

EMMELINE: Perhaps that was why your wife's grief was so much more visible. After your John's death.

ROBERT: I'm not sure that I follow.

EMMELINE: Please don't take this the wrong way, Mr Stanley. But ... for your family – and for your wife in particular - it must have been ... difficult.

ROBERT: In what way?

EMMELINE: To see her husband's affiliations and affections change. Turning to Islam, gaining a new Moslem 'family'...

ROBERT: Well, well! I have ... never really thought about that sort of thing.

EMMELINE: I'm sorry, I don't mean to... it's just that, surely it must have been difficult for them?

ROBERT: Oh, there were a few words at the time. But ... I just did the logical thing and battled on.

EMMELINE: I'm sure. But perhaps your Emma reacted the way she did after losing her adult son because she felt ... rather alone in her grief.

ROBERT: But she most certainly wasn't!

EMMELINE: It's just that when you said how … uncharacteristically overwrought she was…

ROBERT: Hmmm. (*Distracted*)

EMMELINE: It made me wonder whether … she felt overwhelmed with loss. Perhaps felt … she was also losing her husband. To the faith of Islam, I mean.

ROBERT: But she hadn't lost me! If anything, she saw more of me than ever in our last few years together. (*He begins to shake his head determinedly*)

EMMELINE: Oh, please, I'm just trying to explain to you how a woman's head – how a mother and a wife's head – might work.

ROBERT: (*Smiling sadly*) There you go again. With your women.

The waitress comes back with the tea and this time bangs the teapot and cups on the table, not bothering to collect the used ones.

EMMELINE: (*Pours the tea*) I just thought, perhaps she felt that *you* had recently gained a … sort of a … son in Mr Quilliam. Whereas she…

ROBERT: (*His eyes filling, he turns his head to one side and blinks*) Yes. I see what you mean. (*He blows out a breath*) I really am a silly old man not to have thought of any of this.

EMMELINE: Oh, but you shouldn't feel bad about it, Mr Stanley! Really, you shouldn't! Did Emma try and prevent you from becoming a Moslem?

ROBERT: No. Never. She made the odd joke. But she was never scornful about it. She saw what it meant to me.

EMMELINE: And what about the rest of your family?

ROBERT: Not quite as … supportive.

EMMELINE: And did Emma try and prevent you from going to Liverpool?

ROBERT: Not at all! She said it put me in a good temper. That I moaned less about the horse muck and the noise of the trams.

EMMELINE: Ha! (*Sips her tea*) Perfect temperature. Do try it scalding, Mr Stanley.

ROBERT: (*Pretends to scowl at her*) And, come to think of it, (*he smiles, recollecting*) she said it was the first time in her life that I regularly bought her a bunch of flowers. Or a bag of humbugs on the way home.

EMMELINE: Well, there you have it, then. You have no reason to feel sad about things. She probably just felt very confused about losing your John. And the new choices in *your* life.

ROBERT: Perhaps. But I wish that I'd noticed this more. At the time.

EMMELINE: *(Sighs)* Well. We can't change the past. Only take lessons from it.

ROBERT: Very true, Mrs Pankhurst. The Prophet Muhammed – peace be upon him – said that we should go to all lengths and even cross continents to seek learning. *'Seek learning in China,'* he said!

EMMELINE: I like the sound of that.

ROBERT: And you've made me think. Perhaps my own children feel that they have lost their father - or a piece of their father - to Islam.

EMMELINE: Yes?

ROBERT: Yes. Maybe this is why some of them have been so rude and dismissive about Moslems.

EMMELINE: But also, our schools don't teach people very well. About other cultures and beliefs.

ROBERT: True. And my children were born and bred in Stalybridge. Very different to Manchester.

EMMELINE: I'm sure.

ROBERT: Stalybridge isn't like it was when I was a boy. Back then, the place was famous for self-educated men who were experts on art, music, botany, mechanics! No, now the folk there are less cosmopolitan in outlook.

EMMELINE: Hmm. But these places – over your side of Manchester. They all became mill towns.

ROBERT: Indeed. And Stalybridge was the first true Cotton Town. People have turned their noses up at the gift of learning there.

EMMELINE: Most likely they didn't have the time as the mills grew. Locked like slaves into the factory system.

ROBERT: There's never any excuse for ignorance. Why - even though they *now* have a very fine library there, not enough folk in Stalybridge choose to educate themselves these days.

EMMELINE: Speaking of self-improvement; the next time that your Mr Quilliam comes to Manchester to give a lecture, you must inform me of the venue and date.

ROBERT: Oh, yes?

EMMELINE: Yes. I look forward to hearing his wise advice on how us women would all fare better if we were partnered up with a man and his several other wives.

ROBERT: Mrs Pankhurst *(points his finger at her)* I will not be telling you any of his lecture dates if you are going to turn up and heckle him with a group of your female revolutionaries.

EMMELINE: *(Laughs into her teacup)* I wouldn't dream of it. I hear he has some quite … carefully thought out logic behind it all. And it would be most enlightening to meet the famous man himself.

ROBERT: Hmm, well. I think that your own family are rivalling the Sheikh in the fame stakes these days.

EMMELINE: The Pankhursts? More like notorious! To the Establishment, at any rate. Certainly, they like to send fellows to spy on us.[74]

ROBERT: Really?

EMMELINE: Yes.

ROBERT: I suppose I shouldn't be too surprised by that. I have been having the same problem myself.

EMMELINE: You, too?

ROBERT: *(Lowering his voice, looking around)* It's happening more and more.

EMMELINE: To the folk who have converted?

ROBERT: Yes. The Sheikh is used to it, of course. As are Brothers Djem and Nawaz - two of the other converts from 'round these parts. Now, I'm not sure if the likes of Lord Stanley ever had to put up with it, but … the women are experiencing it as well.

EMMELINE: *(In low tones)* The women?

ROBERT: Yes. The first woman to convert in Liverpool, Sister Fatima - Elizabeth Cates – was under some sort of surveillance too.

EMMELINE: Goodness.

---

[74] The Pankhursts and all other leading social and political reformers of the time – including Quilliam and the other Muslim converts – were under British surveillance. In particular, the Muslims and their overseas affiliation with – and closeness to – the Ottoman Empire rendered them to be 'people of interest' to the British Establishment. See *His Own Man*.

ROBERT: Yes. Sadly, she's no longer with us. She died. Far too young.

EMMELINE: Poor dear.

ROBERT: And being a young white woman, she was quite a target for attacks by local lads. Had horse muck rubbed in her face on a couple of occasions by some nasty varmints.

EMMELINE: Horrible! And I had no idea … no idea at all that such things happened to you Moslems, until I met Mrs Stanley. Outside the Infirmary that time.

ROBERT: Hmm. The day that they'd thrown rocks at me. (*Smiles*) And you came over with flowers, afterwards.

EMMELINE: Despicable creatures. But clearly, none of this is stopping you from worshipping.

ROBERT: Oh, no. And neither do these sinister shadows that follow us around the country, jotting down our every move and mannerism.

EMMELINE: Ah yes, I've seen how those little notebooks come out. If Christabel is with me, she actually goes over to them. Asks them if they are writing poetry and, if so, might they like to share it with her!

They both laugh.

ROBERT: Heh – I did something similar the other week. I was sitting on a bench outside the Exchange. And there was a fellow on a seat opposite. He'd been tailing me.

EMMELINE: Yes?

ROBERT: So, I got up, walked twenty paces and then looked back. Sure enough, the chap was following me, but I saw that he'd left his umbrella at his bench. So, I turned 'round sharpish, trotted back to his bench and picked his umbrella up.

EMMELINE: Oh, goodness. What did he do?

ROBERT: He was very flummoxed, when he saw me holding it out to him. And so, I said, *"First rule of spy school. Never let your suspect hand you your umbrella back. Good day."*

EMMELINE: (*Chuckles*) Excellent! I hope you're remembering to write all of these things down for your memoirs.

ROBERT: Ha! I don't think so.

EMMELINE: Why not?

ROBERT: Well, who would be foolish enough to want to read about an old man, who changed his religion and who ended up having tea with a female enemy of the state?

EMMELINE: Mr Stanley, I feel sure that one day there will be a sufficient number of fools out there who regard you as a captivating read.

ROBERT: Well, if that ever happens, Mrs Pankhurst, then this country will certainly have come to rack and ruin.

EMMELINE: Ha!

ROBERT: Yes, it will be filled to the brim with illiterates and half-wits. More tea?

EMMELINE: Don't mind if I do. Even if we are drinking it lukewarm.

ROBERT pours the tea.

--- ENDS ---

15. GUNPOWDER TEA … AND PLOT?

MARY-JANE STANLEY'S MONOLOGUE

CONTEXT:

Emma Stanley died in 1902, some four years after Robert converted to Islam. She was 76 years old and had been married to him for 55 years. Emmeline Pankhurst signed the death certificate in Robert's presence.

Emma was buried in St Paul's graveyard, Stalybridge. Robert continued to live in Manchester with two of his daughters and travelled to Liverpool often. Within a year of his conversion, Robert had become a close friend of Abdullah Quilliam, who had appointed him vice-chairman of the Liverpool Muslim Institute (LMI). Quilliam visited Robert's home in Manchester, where they would have tea together before Quilliam went on to deliver one of his lectures. Robert was often listed as a VIP at the mosque's events, particularly those that celebrated the visits of royalty and foreign dignitaries, and

Six of Robert's children (L to R) Thomas, Mary-Jane, Sarah, Emma, William, Alice

Robert's civic credentials were used to impress others.

However, at this time, trouble in the Balkans, Armenia and Afghanistan between Christian nationalist factions and Muslims was growing. The Turks were routed from North Africa and their economy began to fail. By 1907, Quilliam needed to demonstrate to non-Muslims that British Islam was not a religion of 'traitors', that it was a logical faith that had convinced civically minded, respectable men. He decided to feature 'Brother Robert Reschid Stanley – A Distinguished British Mussulman' in his April 1907 edition of The Crescent.

But one year later, everything had changed. Quilliam had been struck off as a lawyer after being accused of malpractice in a divorce case (he had been trying to assist a woman in proving her husband's adultery). Quilliam fled to Constantinople and some believe that other forces may have been at play; Quilliam and the other converts were increasingly coming under British intelligence surveillance because of their friendship with the Turks, a nation that was edging closer to an alliance with Germany.

Perhaps because of this, by 1911, Robert had left Manchester and was back in Stalybridge, living at the home of his youngest daughter, Alice. He died in September and was buried in the same Christian grave as his wife, Emma.

Whilst we do not know what his last months were like, whether he had any sort of janazah or Muslim prayers said over his grave, we do know that Quilliam was back in the country at the time of Robert's death. Quilliam was now living in Preston, under the nom de plume of Henri de Leon – a name that he took to his own grave in 1932.

This scene imagines how Mary-Jane may have felt during the last few years of her father's life. It considers why the family may have decided to keep quiet about Robert's conversion to Islam – or at least to play it down. It suggests why it might have taken nearly another century before Robert's family were able to find out about what this remarkable man did.

MANCHESTER, MARCH 1908

MARY-JANE IS 53 YEARS OLD. SHE IS SMARTLY DRESSED, IN A DARK DRESS THAT DISPLAYS THE PURPLE, GREEN AND WHITE SUFFRAGETTE PIN. SHE IS POURING HERSELF A CUP OF TEA IN THE FRONT ROOM OF THE STANLEY FAMILY'S MANCHESTER TERRACED HOME. UPPER WORKING-CLASS, SHE HAS A

STALYBRIDGE ACCENT BUT WITH WHAT SHE FEELS IS
A REFINED TWIST. A CLOCK CHIMES THREE O'CLOCK.

Emmeline Pankhurst has a bit of a new fan. My dad! Something of a
surprise to the both of us – to me and to our Sarah, I mean.
Apparently, Dad and Emmeline have met for tea on a number of
occasions over the last few years. Well! They'd kept that one quiet,
hadn't they?
Because he'd certainly been no fan of hers when we first moved
here, nine years ago now. Yes. It irked him considerably every time I
went 'round the corner to one of the meetings at the Pankhurst's
house. Bunch of 'rabble-rousers' he'd call us. Mum used to say, *"Oh
leave our Mary-Jane alone, Robert. She's fifty now. She's entitled to her
obsessions, just like you are."* Heh. Nicely, put, Mother. But … but now
he tells us that he'd warmed to Mrs Pankhurst a few years back,
when he'd first got talking to her at the registrar's office. We'd been
there, getting Mum's death registered. Emmeline needed to make
ends meet after her husband died and ended up becoming the
registrar. Christabel helps out a bit there, too.
Anyway, I'd been a little bit disconcerted that day because he'd
decided to wear his fez there. I thought it might be asking for
trouble, what with how things have been with the Ottoman Empire
and those shenanigans going on over there. But Mrs Pankhurst
didn't bat an eyelid when he shuffled in with it perched on his
noggin. Still, she's probably far more used than most to your
eccentrics and to your bohemians.

That was five years ago now. He only brought the subject up the
other day because we'd bumped into Emmeline at the train station.
We'd spotted her, giving some money to a beggar. Smelt dreadful,
he did. Got a whiff of him as we stepped off the train. Anyway, we
had a quick chat and as we walked away, Dad said, *"I changed my mind
about that woman, you know. An admirable lady."*

She sips her tea.

I said nothing. I was that shocked. He never admits that he's been
wrong about anything. So, he carried on, *"Mind as sharp as a razor.*

245

Although I would never have thought that a leader of the suffragette movement would be quite so flirtatious." Flirtatious! Mrs Pankhurst! I tried not to laugh. At first, I'd thought it was because she'd said to him at the train station that his fez suited him very well. Men of his generation always think that any woman who pays them a compliment is attempting coquettish behaviour, don't they? But then he said, no. Said that he'd had tea with Mrs Pankhurst on a number of occasions and, although they disagreed on many things, they'd often put the world to rights. And that she could be a bit of a tease – even with an old man like him!

Well, I said, you'd never mentioned your little tea parties to me! And why should I, he said. It was of no particular consequence. And then he winked and said – well, we were only trying to throw all of the spies into confusion, the two us meeting together so that the anti-Ottoman agents and the anti-suffragette agents think that we're planning some sort of sinister Moslem and sisterhood overthrow of the state.

Pause.

I can never tell whether he's joking or not sometimes.

Pause.

Sarah's not keen on her, though. Emmeline. Or Christabel. Or any of them. But then Sarah's the sort to always need a man in her life. As soon as her husband died, she was back from Accrington, moving in with us. Dad's always said that Sarah's the 'proper' daughter and I'm more like he hoped his sons would turn out to be. Apart from our John – now gone, bless him – he's always seemed disappointed in them. He's had five boys altogether and I can't say that any of them have been great successes in life. He's a hard act to follow, though.

But, our Sarah – oh, I can't be doing with her attitude towards men. She fawns all over them. And she's got this thing about any woman who might display what she says are 'male characteristics'. She says things to me like, *"You're brutal, you are Mary-Jane. You're worse than any of the boys that I've ever taught."* Well, she forgets that I've been a teacher for decades too. But I see things a bit differently than she does. And she's never even tried to understand why boys in our society end up as brutish as they do. Why they try and cut each other's ears off in the playground and the like.

A noise from outside; a brass band. She goes to the window, looks out and promptly closes the curtains.

Whit walks are early this year. They never look as cheery, though, as they always did back in Stalybridge. Miserable lot here. Mum always said that she'd like a brass band at her funeral. Never happened though.

Pause.

Looking back, I suppose we should have discussed with Mum and Dad what their plans were for burial and all of that. But after Dad decided to change his 'direction of spiritual travel', shall we say, we never really did get down to it. So, when Mum went and the doctor had asked me whether we'd be having a burial in Southern Cemetery here in Manchester, I said no. That she'll be going back to Stalybridge because we'd got a perfectly good family grave there and it'd be a shameful waste of money to do anything else other than that. Well, Sarah had a good go at me when he'd gone. Said that I shouldn't have mentioned the word "money" so soon. *"Mum's only just passed on, for goodness sake,"* she said. So, I said, *"'Passed on'? You make it sound like she's just left the army! The only honest word is 'died', Sarah! Dead!"*
Well, she dissolved of course. Dad whisked her out of the room. So, then our Bob, younger than me but with him being a man he forgets this, spoke to me very sharply. Said that we should all be looking to father's needs and that at this time, he shouldn't have to go about mopping up other people's tears. It's ridiculous, the way Bob has always referred to Dad as 'Father'. Bob's only a corporation gas man. Ideas above his station.

Pause.

Well, afterwards, when I was in the kitchen making yet another set of sandwiches for everyone, I heard our Alice pipe up. They were obviously all talking about me. *"I don't see it that way at all, Bob,"* she was saying. *"Mary-Jane just speaks a slightly different language to most folk."* She's got a good head on her shoulders, does Alice. Shame that she's never been able to have the children that she's always wanted. All these women wanting their men and their babies! Not like me. Oh, no.

Pause.

What is it with their babies? I mean, the men are as bad. Take Dad, for instance. Self-taught, widely read, councillor, magistrate, rose to become mayor and all of that. A great logical thinker, but when it comes to reproductive matters, he clearly had a blind spot. Probably thought that large families were testament to manly achievements or something. I mean – I step out with the Pankhursts and the other ladies of a Thursday. We go to the homes of the poorest women in Manchester and teach them that a large family is archaic, not a cost-effective way to run a household. So, if a group of downtrodden women in the slums of Manchester can understand this, I can't understand why a highly intelligent man like Robert Stanley couldn't grasp it.

She drinks her tea.

Sometimes I lie awake at night, calculating the sort of education my parents could have afforded for their children if they had let sense rule and had had three of us instead of eleven.

Pause.

I can't really blame Mum for the size of our family, though. Until a woman has control over her own body, it's impossible to prevent children from popping up left, right and centre. Mrs Pankhurst suggested, at one meeting, that every young woman should be provided with a big stick on the eve of her wedding in order to keep her new husband at bay with. Everybody laughed, but I suspect that she wasn't really joking.

Our Sarah's another one who hoped for a big family but ended up being disappointed. She married that widower, Mr Whittaker, up in Accrington, then took on his children, and then they had another one together. But as soon as he popped his clogs, she was back here with us! Well, the children were all old enough to fend for themselves, so, she said it was her duty now to look after our parents in their old age. I said – well, I've been managing perfectly well with that one on my own, thank you very much.

But of course, not one of her boys ever gets in touch. Not so much as a postcard! It's disgusting. Well, she's only got herself to blame for that. Boys. Because I'm a firm believer that no matter how selfish the natural male spirit can be, it can be cajoled towards having a little bit of care for a mother as they age. But only if a mother has put her foot down, and not spoiled them in childhood. Or they'll not give a fig for her in later life.

She had another motivation for moving to Manchester, though, did our Sarah. She might be forty-six now but she's still the prettiest in our family. She thought that Manchester provided more of a chance to 'bag a man'. And let's face it, her chances in Accrington would have been limited. They're all a bit inbred up there. Like Glossop. And Marsden. These end-of-the-line places.

And she doesn't like going out on her own, but she won't come to the Pankhursts with me. *"It's not for me,"* she says, and then, *"I'm not one for placards and leaflets."* And the last time, she came out with, *"The difference between you and me, Mary-Jane, is that – as a species – I'm very fond of men."* Well! Even Dad was surprised at that barbed little comment; he was drinking his tea at the time and it went down the wrong way. Well, I wasn't going to let that one go, so I replied, *"We had noticed that, Sarah. But unfortunately, your womanly charms seem to have waned somewhat in recent months."*

A little bit *pointed* of me perhaps, but she *has* been letting herself go. There's a difference between being fashionably slim and looking like a scrag-end. Lack of males about to try for, I suppose. She blames the Boer War for that. Ridiculous. The British army barely had any casualties compared to the Boers. And most of the Boers killed were those poor women and children by men in 'our' army.

She grimaces.

Pause.

But on the subject of death again, it strikes me that things would be far better if we all talked about it a bit more. No one in our family knew what Mum wanted. Nor do we know what our Dad wants. Although, well … I do … but only as the result of a conversation I was not meant to be privy to.

She pours more tea. Adds milk.

I'd just got back from work and I was hanging my coat up. They mustn't have heard me come in and their voices were raised. They weren't arguing, exactly; well – not like the Partingtons next door to us in Stalybridge used to. They went at it like hammer and tongs, those two. They owned the cheese shop. She hit him on the head with the tin bath once; well, we could only presume it was the bath, because we heard this almighty clatter and moments later the front door banged. Then another almighty crash and her voice shrieking, *"And you can take the bloody bath with you as well – you need it, you dirty sod!"* Mother looked out of the window and said, *"I'd stay put where you are if I were you, Mary-Jane. Mr Partington's on their front doorstep with only a bowler hat to cover his shame."*
But anyway, this little 'discussion' that they were having – it seemed to be about making their wills. Dad was saying that they wouldn't be using their usual solicitors. He was saying they'd be using Mr Quilliam instead. Mum goes, *"Well he might be a Sheikh, but what does he know about wills?"* Dad replied, *"Abdullah is a fully qualified lawyer - a professional. Often deals with criminal law, too. Plus, he does work for free, for the poor."* Mum goes, *"Well, I can't see why we need him! We only want our wills doing! We've not murdered anyone this week!"*
It went on a bit. So, I hovered outside still, and then Dad starts saying he's sorry, he knows she doesn't like talking about things like death. So, that's why he's written it all down for her to read. What he'd like. And then it goes quiet. She's obviously reading something. So, then she goes; *"Well – to start with, I've no idea what 'janazah'*

means," and he says, "It's the Moslem funeral ceremony." "Hmph," she says. "'Janazah'. Sounds more like a carnival." And then it's quiet for another minute and she goes, "What's all this about women not being able to see your body? Why would women want to see you without your togs on anyway when you're dead?" And he says; "No – it doesn't mean with your clothes off. It's just that in Islam modesty is important. Women shouldn't see you in your least dignified state. When you're dead." "But you'll be dead," she says. "And … I'm your wife! What am I supposed to do? Run out of the room the minute you take your last breath? Chuck a tablecloth over you?" "But it's a Moslem funeral rite," he says. "Well, I'm not a Moslem," she says. Stalemate for a bit and then he says, "Well … I'm sure that there could be some sort of compromise, where you're concerned. But I'd like our daughters, at least, to respect what Moslems do." And now she's going into the kitchen and I hear her calling back, "Well, our Annie's in Australia and I can't imagine any of the other four would particularly want to see you when you've kicked the bucket."

And then she's back in the living room. Sounding a bit less put out. She's saying, "Well, so long as I can have a proper Christian burial in Stalybridge; we've paid for the plot. And our two boys are already there." He's quiet for a minute and then he says, "Of course, but I'd like to do a Moslem prayer over you," and then he starts chuckling and he goes, "So at least you'll be hedging your bets." She gives it back to him, "Oh, I'll have none of your Arabic chanting over me! And for goodness sake, don't tell our Mary-Jane any of this. She'll be dragging random women in from the streets to view your body just to upset your Moslem men."

They both burst out laughing. And whilst I was relieved at them sounding a bit happier about their rather … macabre arrangements … I felt a little put-out that it was at my expense. I'd never insult someone's religion! Well. Not intentionally at any rate.

She drains her cup.

GO TO BLACK

Come up on Mary-Jane, standing at the front room window. Morning. Arms folded, looking out. Clock chimes 9 o' Clock.

Well, we had Mr Quilliam himself round here last week for tea. What an honour. I suggested Dad might like to take him out for a meal to Sam's Chop House on Deansgate, but he said no, it won't be halal in places like that and, anyway, it was very important in Islam to offer hospitality and welcome in the bosom of one's family. I wanted to say, well, that's all very nice, but you won't be the one running around cleaning the house from top to bottom and then spending forever in the kitchen. But I kept my gob shut. Because I suddenly remembered Mum saying, *"I don't begrudge him his little tea parties, Mary-Jane. He's never been a drinker or a gambler. Never a womaniser. And you can't say that for many men in this day and age."*

She wanders over to a side-table. Picks up a packet of tea and looks at it.

Nine years since our John died. Dad missed him a great deal, as his tea partner, too. But since I've retired from teaching, Dad's been taking me down to the Corn Exchange. He's wanting me to get a bit more involved in the tea business. He even said, *"You're better than any chap I've known when it comes to those taste buds of yours, Mary-Jane!"* I realise that it will sound most unlady-like to some, but after smearing ink on my tongue and impressing blotting paper upon it, it turns out that I have more pronounced taste buds than 95 per cent of the population! Fancy that. And he's entrusted me with some of the finest leaves from all over the world.
So, I got to choose which blend we'd be drinking when Mr Quilliam – or the 'Sheikh of the British Isle's' to give him his correct title - came for tea.

Reads the label out on the packet.

'Gunpowder tea - for men with fire in their belly.' No… I felt that the Sheikh didn't need any more encouragement. So, ignored this one and chose a jasmine-based one instead.

Pause.

As for Quilliam himself, I felt that at times he was trying too hard to be manly, perhaps. For example, he tore up here in his new motor car.[75] Instantly, two dozen little boys were outside, gawping at their shiny new mechanical god. And no sooner had he walked through the door, he's firing facts at us on its capability of speed and mileage capacity and what have you. Didn't drive it himself, though. Had brought a chap called Brother Jamil with him to do the driving. Quilliam wasn't wearing his traditional Turkish robes, either. Says he only wears them at ceremonial occasions. That was a bit of a relief, because there are some rather thuggish characters lurking about on the street sometimes and they wouldn't take kindly to a man wearing a frock. Nor did he bring the pet monkey which he's a bit famous for keeping. I expressed disappointment at this, but apparently it gets frightfully car sick and monkey-vomit is quite ruinous to leather upholstery.

She picks up a dusting cloth from the window ledge and goes to the mantlepiece. Picks up a bust of Charles Dickens and starts wiping it.

Well, then we had over 30 minutes on the technicalities of army manoeuvres in Armenia and the various strategies now required in order to protect the Caliph's boundaries. I was quite bored by the time we had finished the sandwiches, so I thought it might be more pertinent to ask after Mrs Quilliam. Instantly, Sarah got one of those 'looks' on her face. Afterwards she said to me, *"Didn't you know that he's got two wives and children with both of them?"* and I said, *"Why on earth would I know that sort of thing? None of these men ever show any interest in our lives, why would I want to know about theirs?"* So, she goes, *"Well, you asked about Mrs Quilliam!"*[76] Leading me to point out that Mrs Quilliam, well 'the Mrs Quilliams', are women, and therefore should be asked of a bit more, as opposed to being overlooked.

Pause.

---

[75] Quilliam was one of the first in the country to purchase a motor car. The excitement of his drives to Manchester – where he had tea with Brother Reschid - were related in great detail in *The Crescent*.

[76] Very little has been written about Quilliam's three wives; they have been sadly overlooked – partly because of the sheer charisma of Quilliam's personality, partly because women's lives were not well documented during this era, and perhaps also because people have presumed that they would have been the sorts to have been somewhat easily-led and influenced, because they agreed to be in a polygamous relationship with Quilliam.

Anyway, my query led Mr Quilliam onto what turned out to be his favourite subject: polygamy. I'd heard this was a practise of some of the Moslems. Apparently, the first Mrs *Hannah* Quilliam – from a *'highly respectable family'* - produced four children, all with English and Moslem names. And the second Mrs *Mary* Quilliam – a 'chorus girl at the Liverpool Empire' – those were his own words - had been in a 'married' relationship, if you like, with… well. Since about the same time. Hmmm. Children, too. He said he'd married Miss Lyon in a Moslem ceremony – the nikah or something he called it – but she had remained a committed Christian and had recently stated a preference for formalising their marriage under English law, which he was now thinking of obliging her with. I remarked that this would be a very generous thing for him to do. He obviously detected my tone, as he then went on to inform me that, as a lawyer, he specialised in marital law and was out to protect the rights of women which the British legal system rode roughshod over – but not in Islam, of course. Oh no. And that, surely, I must agree with him, what with me being a chum of Mrs Pankhurst and all (a nod at my suffragette pin, there).

She pats the suffragette pin on her chest.

Now, apparently, Moslem men are permitted to take another wife in order to manage their inclinations towards lustful desires. Quilliam states that this then dispenses with a man's need to take a mistress so that, subsequently, women are treated with more respect and have more monetary rights. He went on and on, saying that the Prophet Muhammed felt that this practise should only take place where a man was wealthy enough to take on an additional family and, in addition, that the first wife – or wives – should always agree to a chap taking on another one. He said that, often, it's a kindly way for a man to help a poor widow out. Muhammad himself did this, apparently. Yes. Easy for you, I thought. You've got enough money to support two women. I can't imagine your average Moslem fella gives two hoots about whether he can support more than one female. He'd be far too interested in fulfilling the physical transactions that he'd feel entitled to.

She puts Charles Dickens back and picks up a china maid to wipe.

Well, then he says that polygamy also helps to prevent unwanted orphans. And it's true, you've got to give them credit for setting up their 'Medina Orphanage' in Liverpool, as they've called the place. But I put it to him that rather than hitch a woman to a man who neither wanted nor needed her that surely it would make more sense to invest in scientific research so that improved receptacles could be created to prevent pregnancies in the first place? But then I noticed Dad's face - it looked like his eyes were going to pop out of his head. So, I stopped short of mentioning Mrs Pankhurst's idea of a presenting women with a big stick on their wedding night.

Mr Quilliam wrapped up his case for the defence by explaining that if I would like to come and meet both Mrs Quilliams - and see their very happy living arrangements - I would not fail to be convinced. That both had certainly had the best of him over the years, as opposed to the day-to-day drudgery of having a husband at home day in and day out. He invited both Sarah and I to visit them in Liverpool. Sarah seemed eager. Mind you, she doesn't get out much, these days.

Pause.

Before he left for his lecture on Constantinople, he said, *"Brother Reschid, Miss Mary-Jane is a most refreshing woman; so spirited and opinionated!"* And Dad replied, *"Well, I've tried to beat it out of her, Abdullah, but there's some women that never learn."*

Sarah decided to go with them to the lecture. She was all smiles. Proper bloom in her cheek again.

It's strange. She's never shown much interest in the Ottoman Empire before. But I suppose the 'accompanied by magic lantern slides' was the clincher.

She left me on my own to clean and tidy up.

She puts the china maid down and walks back to the window, duster in hand.

So, whilst I don't agree with him on the polygamy thing, I do have to say that Quilliam was nothing like the trouble-causer that some of the newspapers paint him to be, preying upon Christian innocents, threatening the very fabric of the British Empire and all of that. And actually, I do think that he and his converts have had some dreadful things said about them: traitors, anti-Establishment, all that rot.

After they'd all left, I started thinking a bit more about Mum and when Dad had first started spending time over in Liverpool. Did she know about Mr Quilliam and his lifestyle? She never said anything. I felt awful, thinking about that; I started thinking - had she been sitting there, fretting that Dad might take on another wife, keep her parked over in Liverpool...? Not that our dad would be so foolish as to do such a thing at his age. Though many would, given half the chance.

GO TO BLACK.

Come up on Mary-Jane in the front room. An afternoon in March 1908. She is sitting at the table with a little set of scales, measuring and blending tea. The clock chimes 3 o' clock.

Dad was attacked last week, again.[77] Stone-throwing outside the mosque, like last time. Nothing serious, he said. Just silly Liverpool youths. I was furious. I said, you're 80 now, you need to stop all your trips over there! But what can you do? Like Mrs Pankhurst said, some folk live for thinking that they can change the world. If they think they're having no impact, they'll just give up.
Sarah encourages him. Sometimes goes over there with him. No idea what she does there whilst he's at the mosque.

She pours measured tea into a pack. Seals it. Starts measuring more out.

Pause.

---

[77] We have no evidence that Robert ever suffered an anti-Muslim physical attack, but the converts in Liverpool frequently encountered both verbal and physical abuse. At the time when Mary-Jane's monologue is set, there would have been grave concerns about the loyalty of the Muslim community in relation to the British Empire. See *His Own Man*.

There're spies everywhere now, he says. He's convinced some particular fella with a grey raincoat is tailing him. I think that it's because of that little article that Quilliam wrote about Dad in *The Crescent*. It was meant to be a celebration of him: 'A Distinguished British Mussulman'. Him having been a mayor, a magistrate, advised the caliph, etcetera. Good publicity for the Moslems in Britain, Mr Quilliam thought. Brother Reschid Stanley, the grand old duke of British Islam, etcetera. But if you ask me, it's attracted the wrong sort of attention.

Pours tea into another pack. Seals it. Stops measuring and stares into the distance.

Dad says he's seen the chap hanging around outside here. At first, I thought that it was his age; they often get like that when they get elderly. But no. He says it's been happening to lots of the other converts. All to do with the fact that they're felt to be too loyal to the caliph, and because Turkey seems to be getting friendlier with Germany. Well, if there's any truth in them being under suspicion, it's absolutely ridiculous. You can't get anyone more patriotic than Dad. He was always writing to Queen Victoria. Probably still does, even though she's been dead for six years.

Letter again today for Sarah. Same Liverpool post-mark.

GO TO BLACK.

Come up on Mary-Jane. It is May 1908. The room is bare, containing only packing boxes and open trunks. She is wrapping the Charles Dickens bust in newspaper. It is early evening. The clock chimes 6 o'clock.

It's all gone to pot. It's…

Pause.

Quilliam's fled to Constantinople. Struck off The Rolls - can't practise as a lawyer anymore. The papers are saying that he set a trap to try and catch some chap in the midst of committing adultery.

This is 'malpractice', apparently. But it seems to me, though, that Quilliam had only been trying to help some poor woman get a divorce from her pig of a husband.

She places the bust in one of the boxes.

Dad says that it was all a set-up. And all the Moslems are saying ... talk of Russian agents and of the British government hounding the Sheikh out of the country.
The mosque in Liverpool has closed. The converts all seem to be moving away. Quilliam's son has taken over but he doesn't seem to attract the same sort of loyalty from the followers. Dad said that there's always been something about him that unsettles him somewhat and that some sort of funeral fund has gone missing, too. No one's sure what's happened with that.[78]

She picks up the china maid and starts wrapping it.

Not sure if I should ask Dad whether he paid into it or not. It's a delicate subject, death. But ... oh, I don't know which one of them is the more heartbroken. Dad or Sarah. But still, at her age! It's not like she hasn't already had a fair crack of the whip at the marriage game.

GO TO BLACK.

Come up on Mary-Jane. It is now September 1911 and her hair is completely grey. She is in a plainly decorated room – a lodging house in Scarborough, heralded by the cry of seagulls and the faint sound of the waves. She is wearing black and is standing at the window. Packets of tea are placed on the bed, alongside a newspaper. A church clock strikes 2 o'clock.

I came up to Scarborough the week after Dad's funeral. I've decided to carry on with his tea trade. Travelling about, selling his blends.

---

[78] Quilliam's son, Robert 'Bilal' Quilliam, did not prove to be the sort of leader that his father was. A solicitor, he proved to be a strong proponent of the trade union movement but was struck off as a solicitor for debts that he owed, and then imprisoned for two years. The issue of what happened to the funeral funds from this period has never been resolved.

Nice little boarding house, this one turned out to be. And I've found a few places interested in tea from the Levant.[79]

Pause.

It happened at our Alice's. Dad had wanted to go back to Stalybridge. You want to be near your real home, I think, in your last days. Anyway, Alice is a good nurse, more patience than I have. She couldn't fit me and Sarah in too, so we lodged near to Thompson Cross.
I'd thought of contacting the mosque. I could have telegrammed them, I suppose, but after what I'd read about Quilliam's son, he just didn't sound as...

Pause.

We did get a letter from Quilliam; well, Dad did. I didn't let Sarah see it. Back from Constantinople now and living in Preston. He's decided to assume a new identity – 'Henri de Leon' is now his name. A bit bizarre, to say the least.[80] Anyway. He wanted to visit. But ... we had no time to contact him. These things often happen so fast.

She nods towards the bed.

Newspaper today saying Asquith is 'deeply concerned' about Germany now. Turkey too, no doubt.

She goes to the bed and picks up a packet of tea. Walks back to the window with it in her hands.

The night before it happened, I was sitting next to Dad's bed, at our Alice's. I glanced out the window and suddenly noticed a man outside. Lit up by the gas light, scribbling something in a notebook.

---

[79] Syria, but sometimes used to refer to the broader eastern Mediterranean region.
[80] There is some disagreement amongst scholars as to whether Henri de Leon was a real-life friend of Quilliam's and that the Sheikh assumed de Leon's identity after he died, or whether Henri de Leon was simply an 'alter ego' that Quilliam invented for personal i.e. marital reasons. Quilliam's third wife, Edith, was said to be the widow of a Henri de Leon and that following his death, she married Quilliam. Academics continue to investigate the complex matter of Quilliam's identity and marriages.

Then he knocked at the neighbour's house, opposite. Man, in a grey raincoat, it was.

Pause.

I'd known it were coming. He'd been quiet a long time. His colour changed – started going grey. His eyes fixed towards the window. Well. He'd always liked looking out the window before … before things had gotten worse with him. The direction of the train station, Alice had said. That's what he likes to look for, she said. The trains. It was just me on my own with him. Clock ticking. Dad breathing. A little sigh. He moved his hand.

She squeezes the packet of tea.

I said, *"Dad? Do you want something?"* He gave a little nod. *"Some water?"* I asked. No response. His hand trembled and then moved, like he was trying to reach towards the side-table. *"Your book … your Qur'an?"* I said. Another little nod. I picked it up – dratted heavy thing it is. Of course, I didn't know what to read to him, so I just opened it and started reading out from it; just randomly. It was something to do with there being no compulsion to follow the faith. Well, I don't know. Couldn't concentrate properly.
Anyway, that's when he started saying something. In Arabic. So, I just nodded. Smiled at him. Pretended that I knew what he was saying.
And then he looked over at me. And he had such … such love … in his eyes. For me. And then. Then … he went.

She swallows. Breathes deeply. Blinks hard.

I closed the book and then … I closed his eyes. When I put the book back on the shelf, something dropped out of it. An envelope – his handwriting. 'In the event of my death,' it said. So, I opened it. And then I read it. And then I thought … I thought … Best not.

And then I went over to the fire.

She tosses the tea back onto the bed.

We had the burial at St Pauls. Nice day. No rain. And afterwards, the wake at The Traveller's Call. *"You're the matriarch now,"* said Alice when we were having sandwiches. I said, *"Well, what about our Annie?"* She goes, *"Well, she's in Australia. Anyway. Suits you more, being the matriarch."* So, I said, *"I've never liked that term – 'matriarch'. It's a word that men have created to make women feel that being stuck in the home and bringing up children is something to be proud of. To stop them from realising that they can do just as important jobs as men or that they can go into politics."* And then I heard our Bob saying to someone, *"Here she goes. Let's go and have another pint, quick."*

She puts her hand on the window and looks out.

Then Alice says, *"Do you think Dad would have minded? Him being … here. A Christian burial?"* I just cut her right off. I said *"Of course he wouldn't mind. He never said anything to the contrary, did he? And anyway, the men spend half of their lives bossing us about, but it's always left to us women to sort the death side of things out."*
"See?" says Alice. *"Spoken like a true matriarch."*

GO TO BLACK.

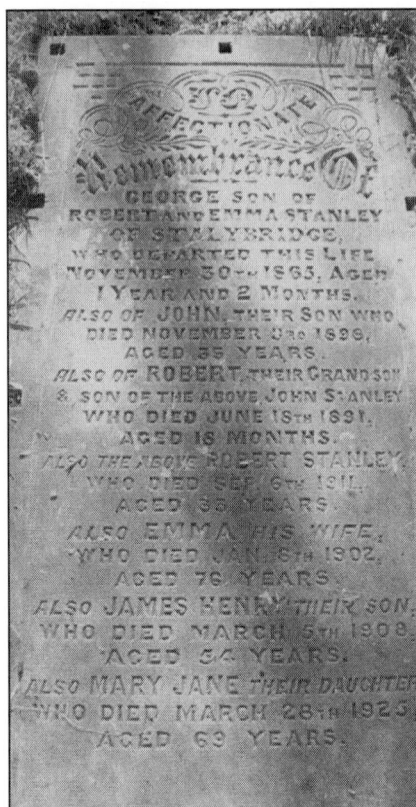

Robert and Emma's family grave at St Paul's, Stalybridge. It was destroyed only weeks after our family located it - to make way for a car park

BIBLIOGRAPHY

Al-Djazairi, S. *A Short History of Islam*, IIH, 2006.

Al-Djazairi, S. *The Myth of Muslim Barbarism*, Bayt al-Hikma, 2007.

Ansaria, H. *The Infidel Within: Muslims in Britain since 1800,* 2004.

Arnstein, W.L. The Murphy Riots: A Victorian Dilemma, in *Victorian Studies* (1975) 1991.

Bagley, J. *A History of Lancashire*, Phillimore, 1976.

Basu, S. *Victoria and Abdul,* The History Press, 2010. See also screenplay by Lee Hall, 2017.

Birt, Y. The Quilliams, Popular Conservatism and the New Trade Unionism in Liverpool, *Islamic Review Special Edition*, 2019.

Chamberlain, J. *Speeches of the Right Hon Joseph Chamberlain,* 1918.

Chapman, S. *The Cotton Industry in the Industrial Revolution*, 1979.

Clark, P. *Marmaduke Pickthall: British Muslim,* Beacon, 2016.

Denby, P. *Two Into One Will Go – A History of the Parish of St George, Stalybridge,* Trinity Press, 1990.

Dennis, R. *English Industrial Cities of the 19th Century*, CUP, 1988.

Diamond, M. *Victorian Sensation: Or the Spectacular, the Shocking and Scandalous in Nineteenth Century Britain*, Anthem Press, 2003.

Dinwiddy, J. *Radicalism and Reform in Britain, 1780-1850*, Continuum, 1992.

Disraeli, B. *Sybil: or The Two Nations,* OWC, 2017.

Edsall, N. *The Anti-Poor Law Movement,* MUP, 1971.

Engels, F. *Condition of the English Working Classes in 1844*, CIPP, 2017.

Epstein and Thompson (ed), *The Chartist Experience: Studies in Working Class Radicalism and Culture, 1830-60*, Palgrave, 1982.

Epton, N. *Milord and Milady*, Oldbourne, 1962.

Forrest, D. *Tea for the British,* Chatto, 1973.

Foster, J. *Class Struggle and the Industrial Revolution*, Methuen, 1974.

Gammage, R. *History of the Chartist Movement, 1837-1854*, Forgotten Books, 2012.

Geaves, R. *Islam in Victorian Britain – the Life and Times of Abdullah Quilliam*, Kube, 2010.

Geaves and Gilham (ed), *Abdullah Quilliam and Islam in the West*, Hurst and Co., 2017.

Gilham, J. *Loyal Enemies: British Converts to Islam, 1850–1950*, 2014.

Green, E. *Prophet John Wroe: Virgins, Scandals and Visions*, The History Press, 2005.

Haidt, J. *The Righteous Mind: Why Good People are Divided by Religion and Politics,* Vintage, 2012.

Harrop, S. *Victorian Ashton*, TLAC, 1987.

Hill, S. *Bygone Stalybridge*, Rigg, 1987.

Holyoake, G. *The Life of Joseph Rayner Stephens*, Weidenfield, 1981.

Hopkins, E. *A Social History of the English Working Classes 1815-1945,* Arnold, 1979.

Locke, (ed) *Looking Back at Stalybridge*, see Harrop's 'Why was Stalybridge First?' TMBC, 1989.

Locke, (ed) *Looking Back at Ashton,* TMBC, 1997.

Longden, B. *The Life of Robert Stanley*, 2012.

Longden, C. *Popular Radicalism in Ashton, Stalybridge and Hyde, 1828-1842*, Dissertation, 1994.

Longmate, N. *The Hungry Mills,* Maurice T Smith, 1978.

Mitford, M. *The Stanleys of Alderley,* Hamilton, 1968.

Nevell, M. *Tameside 1700–1930*, TMBC, 1993.

Nevell, M. *People who made Tameside*, TMBC, 1994.

Probert, Rebecca (ed) *Catherine Exley's Diary,* Brandram, 2014.

Pugh, M. *The Pankhursts,* Vintage, 2008.

Rogers, J. *Mr Wroe's Virgins,* Faber and Faber, 1991.

Rose, J. *The Intellectual Life of the British Working Classes*, Yale, 2001.

Said, E. *Culture and Imperialism,* Vintage, 1994.

Seddon, S. in *Early Muslim Communities in Manchester 1830-1950*, unpublished manuscript.

Squires, P. *Anti-Social Policy*, Wheatsheaf, 1990.

Thompson, D. *Chartists,* Breviary, 2013.

Thompson, D. *Outsiders: Class, Gender and Nation,* Verso, 1993.

Tobin, P. *Southcottians in England,* UoM, Thesis, 1978.

Urquhart, D. *Russia and Turkey*, Ridgway, 1835.

Waller, P. *City and Nation*, OUP, 1983.

Ward, J. *Popular Movements 1830–1850,* Macmillan, 1990.

Wild, J. *Black Gold*, Harper, 2005.

Williams, G, *Ruling Britannia. A Political History of Britain 1688–1988,* Longman, 1992.

Wroe, J. *Divine Communications*, Christian Israelite Press, 1822.

Wroe, J. *Revelations on the Scriptures*, Christian Israelite Press, 1849.

Manuscripts and Papers

Ashton Town Council Minutes, 1849.

Ashton, Stalybridge and Dukinfield District Waterworks Committee, 1872–1878.

Declaration of Councillor Interests, Stalybridge TC, 1871–1876.

Overseers of the Poor Accounts book, Ashton, 1853.

Parliamentary Papers, Select Committee on Parliamentary and Municipal Elections, 1869.

Stalybridge Town Council Minutes 1863–1876.

Stalybridge Town Council Sub-Committee Minutes 1863–1876.

Report of the Committee on the Conditions of the Working Classes in Dukinfield, Ashton and Hyde, MSS, MCRL, Oct 1836.

Tameside Archives – newspaper cuttings of Ashton-under-Lyne pubs 1877–1897.

Printed Sources

Ashton Reporter (1855–1906).

Islamic World (1895–1908).

Manchester Courier (various, 1824–1911).

Manchester Guardian (ditto).

Manchester Times (ditto).

Sheffield Courier (1831, 1876).

The Crescent (1895–1908).

The Stalybridge Reporter (1872–1911).

The Voice of the People (1831).

Trade Directories (various, 1848–1911).

Wheeler's Manchester Chronicle (1830-1848).

Recommended Reading

The companion book to this publication, *His Own Man – A Victorian 'Hidden' Muslim,* provides a wealth of information on all the issues addressed in this book.

For those interested in finding out more about British Muslim convert communities, I recommend any publications or books by Birt, Geaves, Gilham and Seddon. Many of the more locally focussed books in this bibliography will appeal to those mostly living in the North of England and further reading can be found at the various local studies libraries in the region. For those interested in family history, see the relevant appendix in *His Own Man* for further information.

Robert's first shop on Melbourne St, Stalybridge - his great x 2 grandson, Brian and great x 4 grandson, Gregory are standing outside

BRINGING FAMILY HISTORY TO LIFE

If reading this book has inspired you to try and build a better picture of your own ancestral background then the good news is that researching family history has never been easier. There is some bad news, however; genealogy can be utterly addictive.

Now that we have the internet, it has never been easier and faster to examine your ancestral roots. The discipline of family history has been rapidly embraced by the, predominantly older, white working classes of Britain, as records become easier to access and people retire at an earlier age. However, there has been far less take-up of family history interest amongst non-white groups and younger sections of the community. So, it would be excellent to see more of these amateur-expert groups passing on their knowledge and support to these other sections of the community. In particular, people who hail from immigrant backgrounds may need more help than others; many are often filled with trepidation at the thought of investigating what can often feel like highly complicated trails to navigate.

Thanks to the sheer wealth of information online that now exists, a beginner embarking on their family history research can feel completely overwhelmed. So, my first piece of advice for a newcomer to family history is not to attempt to 'go it alone.' Practically every local authority in Britain has its own local history studies and archives section and this is where you will nearly always find a group of devoted genealogy enthusiasts, eager and willing to share their experience with you. Face-to-face contact is very important when delving into your family history and gaining the support of volunteers through physical meetings will be more helpful to you than just relying on email.

The kindness and generosity of the family historians in the locations that I am the most familiar with (Tameside and Kirklees) has been staggering. Many of these people work alongside local history studies and archives sections and offer hour-long (or more) slots a week where they will sit with you and help in your research. So, if you happen to live in an area which offers such an incredible opportunity, grab it with both hands and get your hours booked in with them!

One of the aims of these two books about Robert Stanley is to encourage people from different backgrounds and communities to work with each other through the pursuit of family history. This book is not the place to begin to tell you how to conduct family history, but I thought it might be useful to provide a few tips for those readers who are curious about this wonderfully enriching pastime:

o **Family Tree** – If you already have possession of a family tree (no matter how scruffily produced) then this is your first port of call. If you don't have one, then ask around; you might be pleasantly surprised and find that a lot of the groundwork has been done already and that 'just the gaps' need to be filled.

o **Interviewing** – Learn from my own family's mistake with Robert: *when they're gone, they're gone.* There are plenty of books and online resources on the best way to interview other family members, but don't forget that it might also be useful to interview close family friends (who often know a side to a person that a family is not aware of). The younger generation, too, can be brilliant at mining information from the older generation (my daughter is an expert on ferreting out information from her grandparents that I never seemed to gain access to!)

o **Visit your Local Studies/History Archives** - The local authority-run ones are free, but they sometimes charge a small amount for printouts, photocopies etc. Some local areas run family history/genealogy centres that are not part of the local council and they may need to charge you a few pounds for going along and getting advice. I would recommend that you visit both if you are fortunate to have them in your area; building up a bank of helpful, friendly volunteer experts is crucial and the more people that know about what you are trying to research, the better.

o **Read Books** – There are too many books on genealogy and starting your family history to mention, but before you go anywhere near a computer, and before you begin to chat to your local experts, buy a simple book (the 'Dummy's Guides/Idiot's Guides' are good enough but - ironically - can provide more detail than you will want to know in the beginning). Better still, borrow a book on the subject from your local library.

o **Get Help with Creating your Family Tree** – There are many different approaches to creating and developing a family tree. You can buy all sorts of software to help you to do this but get advice from one of the experts before you part with your credit card number.

o **Online Research Portals** – There are literally hundreds of free and not-so-free databases that you will want to head for once you have fleshed out your family tree and you want to pursue more B/M/D (birth, marriages, deaths) information. Perhaps the one website that every family historian in the world owes a great debt to is the free www.familysearch.org which was set up by the Church of the Latter Day Saints. This website is really staggering in terms of the volume of information that it contains and for the service that it has given to family historians. However, as well as needing to access BMD information, you will probably find that you also need items such as immigration records, newspapers, legal cases, wills and probate etc. and this does not come free of charge. There are many 'pay for' services online but most people plump for the excellent www.ancestry.co.uk or www.findmypast.co.uk where you can pay as you go or subscribe annually. Both also offer a 'free day' most years for those who want to try them out. But most local history archives will also give library members free access to them through their own computers. Phone ahead and find out exactly what your library has on offer, because booking a space on their computers normally needs to be done several days in advance.

o **Family/Local History Groups** – You don't necessarily have to join one of these groups, but by simply being aware of their events and talks you might stumble across some fascinating and useful links for your own research. Get on their email/newsletter list as soon as you can.

○ **Creating a Work of 'Faction'** – Not everyone finds it easy to compile a non-fiction account of their ancestors' lives. Even though I had written two non-fiction books before writing my first two novels, I would still say that the 'flow' of fiction – and especially of dialogue – is more enjoyable for me, that it comes more naturally. And this is an approach that certainly brings a story to life for those who cannot bear to read, or to listen to the 'dry facts'. So, if you prefer to write fiction, you might want to try something similar to what I have attempted in 'Imagining Robert'; turn your family history into an entertaining story that can combine the truth, as well as including a dash of colourful imagination. But don't forget to consider the issues of litigation and the greater law of 'do as you would be done by.'

And finally – NEVER tell yourself that *your* family, *your* story, is too 'boring' to research or to put into print. Every single one of us have aspects of our lives that are truly fascinating.

If you would like to learn more about how to produce creative fiction, using your family history – get in touch and request a workshop in your local area.

Some of Robert's direct descendants today; enjoying Christmas together

Good luck with your hunting!

QUESTIONS FOR READERS

1. Robert was from a poor background, but he had a hand-up from his wealthy uncle. With this in mind, should we still think of him as being working class?
2. The Christian Israelites were, in many ways, closer to the Jewish faith than to Christianity. Do you think that this had a bearing at all on Robert's perception of God/Allah?
3. Prophet John Wroe: was he a charlatan or the victim of 'fake news'?
4. What would you say were the main drivers of Robert's desire to see justice carried out?
5. Do you think that Robert believed that 'all (men) are equal'?
6. Did Robert chase local power and prestige for the sake of it or because it was the 'right thing to do'?
7. We don't have any evidence of what the women in Robert's life thought about him; but fiction can be a powerful way of thinking more about this. Do you think that *'Imagining Robert'* reflected how Emma Stanley and the other women in Robert's life might have felt about his conversion?
8. Do you think that Robert wanted to move from the pub because he was growing closer to Islam?
9. Would you say that Robert's relationship with Quilliam was intellectual, spiritual or more fraternal?
10. Do you think that Quilliam's fleeing the country in 1908 was for a more sinister reason than the legal scandal? Do you think that it was a contributing factor to Robert's death in 1911?
11. Although we have no evidence that Robert was friends with the Pankhursts, he certainly met Emmeline. Would Robert's views about the role of women in society have changed as he aged? If so, was this because he became a Muslim or for another reason?
12. Why would Robert's family have chosen to have him buried in a Christian graveyard, rather than in a Muslim plot in Liverpool or Manchester?

13. Do you think that Robert's family deliberately covered up his conversion?
14. The keeping of the fez, the tie pin and the copy of *The Crescent* for over 100 years by a Stanley relative with no accompanying explanation: was this mere coincidence or was something else at play?

ABOUT THE AUTHOR

Christina Longden

Christina grew up in the Tameside area of Greater Manchester and was first-generation university educated. She studied History at the University of Birmingham and went on to complete an MSc in Social Housing at the University of Salford. She worked in social housing across the North West and became a consultant to Whitehall on social policy. She moved to Namibia, Africa, in 2003 where she lived with the Kalahari Bushmen, producing two books about them and giving birth to her first child there.

On returning to the UK, Christina settled in the Colne/Holme Valley area and wrote two Northern comedy dramas: *'Mind Games and Ministers'* and *'Cuckoo in the Chocolate'*. Christina manages the Lorna Young Foundation, an international charity that supports poor farmers in developing countries. Her family are one of the three founding families of Dark Woods Coffee - one of the UK's most respected high end and ethical roasteries.

Christina is the great x3 granddaughter of Robert 'Reschid' Stanley, the 'Hidden Victorian Muslim Convert' and sister to Steven, who is a teacher, activist and also a Muslim. She is married with two children and is passionate about supporting more people in discovering public libraries and reading, along with working to broker better relationships and understanding between Muslims and non-Muslims. Christina is founder of Past Truisms CIC, a social enterprise that works to overcome barriers between communities, using the arts as a medium to bring people together.

Books – Links to Christina's books (paperback and eBooks) can be accessed via the websites above.

Speaking engagements - Chris carries out speaking engagements about her writing, books and her family's remarkable background. She runs workshops on how to use family and personal histories to create 'faction' stories and productions. She is also a 'Library Champion' and holds workshops for parents and teachers who want to persuade children and young people to fall in love with reading and writing.

www.robertreschidstanley.wordpress.com

www.funnylass.com

On behalf of Robert's descendants, thank you so much for reading this book.

Brian Longden playing his ancestor in Arakan's trailer about Robert Stanley.

If you enjoyed being entertained by this book and if you want to find out more about the fascinating life of Robert and the incredible historical events that he lived through, why not read the historical biography about him?

Christina Longden, Robert's great x3 granddaughter has compiled a thoroughly researched account of Robert's life and times. *His Own Man: a Victorian 'Hidden' Muslim*, can be read in tandem with *Imagining Robert* and will add even more historical and personal detail for the reader.

HIS OWN MAN

A Victorian 'Hidden' Muslim
The Life and Times of Robert 'Reschid' Stanley

by Christina Longden, 2019.